Hiking Michigan's Upper Peninsula

Hiking Michigan's Upper Peninsula

A Guide to the Area's Greatest Hikes

Second Edition

Eric Hansen
Revised by Rebecca Pelky

FALCONGUIDES

GUILFORD, CONNECTICUT
HELENA, MONTANA

To my parents, Homer Richard Hansen and Dorothy Shaffer Hansen, who taught me to navigate the wilds of the backwoods at a very young age

FALCONGUIDES®

An imprint of Rowman & Littlefield
Falcon, FalconGuides, and Outfit Your Mind are registered trademarks of Rowman & Littlefield.

Distributed by NATIONAL BOOK NETWORK

Copyright © 2016 by Rowman & Littlefield

Maps by XNR Productions Inc. © Rowman & Littlefield
Photos by Rebecca Pelky

British Library Cataloguing-in-Publication Information Available

Library of Congress Cataloging-in-Publication Data Available
ISBN 978-1-4930-0991-6 (paperback)
ISBN 978-1-4930-1511-5 (e-book)

∞™ The paper used in this publication meets the minimum requirements of American National Standard for Information Sciences—Permanence of Paper for Printed Library Materials, ANSI / NISO Z39.48-1992.

Contents

Eric Hansen's Acknowledgments x

Rebecca Pelky's Acknowledgments xi

Introduction 1

    Hiking the Upper Peninsula 1

    North Country Trail 2

    Weather 3

    Seasons 3

    Being Prepared 4

    Wildlife 6

    Impact on the Land 7

    How to Use This Guide 8

    How to Use the Maps 9

Map Legend 10

Ironwood/Ontonagon Area Hikes

  1 Black River Waterfalls 12

  2 Escarpment 16

  3 Lake Superior Shoreline 19

  4 Lake Superior/Big Carp River Loop 23

  5 Little Carp River Cascades 28

  6 Mirror Lake Loop 32

  7 Norwich Bluff 36

  8 Norwich Bluff to Victoria 40

  9 Presque Isle River Waterfalls Loop 44

10 Shining Cloud Falls 48

11 Trap Hills Loop 51

12 Trap Hills Traverse 55

13 Union River Cascades Loop 61

Iron River/Watersmeet Area Hikes

14 Bond Falls 65

15 Clark Lake Loop 68

16 Deer Island Lake 71

17 O-Kun-de-Kun Falls 75

Houghton/Copper Harbor Area Hikes

18 Bare Bluff 80

19 Canyon Falls 83

20 Craig Lake 86

21 Estivant Pines Loop 90

22 Horseshoe Harbor 93

Overview

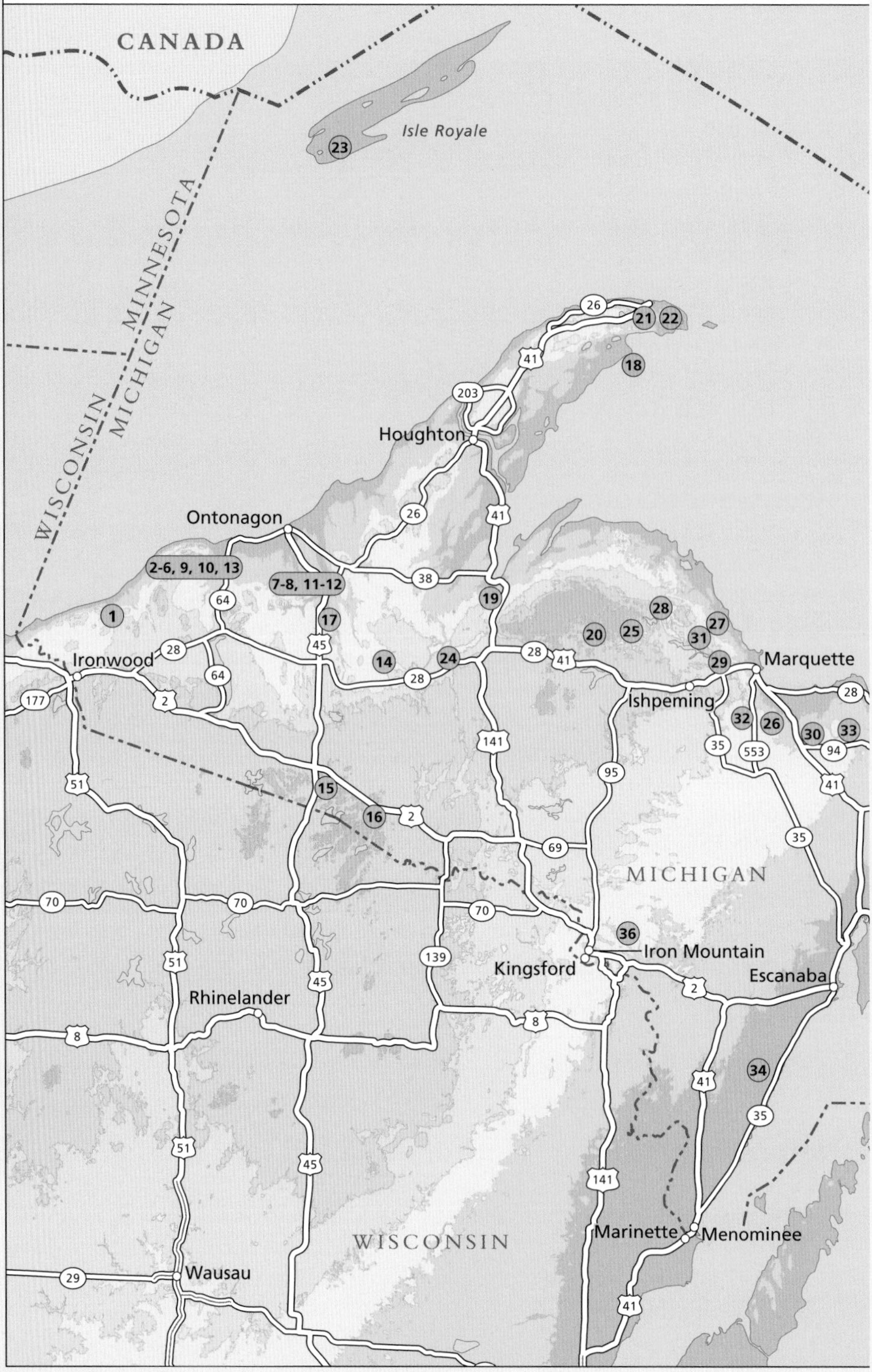
CANADA
Isle Royale
MINNESOTA
MICHIGAN
WISCONSIN
MICHIGAN
Houghton
Ontonagon
Ironwood
Marquette
Ishpeming
MICHIGAN
Iron Mountain
Kingsford
Escanaba
Rhinelander
WISCONSIN
Marinette
Menominee
Wausau
1
2-6, 9, 10, 13
7-8, 11-12
14
15
16
17
18
19
20
21
22
23
24
25
26
27
28
29
30
31
32
33
34
36

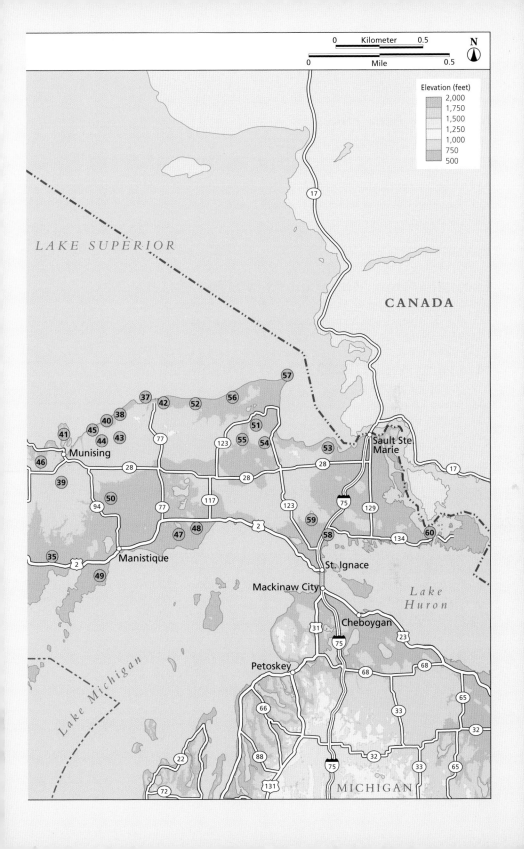

23 Isle Royale 96
24 Tibbets Falls/Oren Krumm Shelter 100
25 White Deer Lake 103

Marquette Area Hikes
26 Blueberry Ridge 108
27 Echo Lake 111
28 Falls of the Yellow Dog 114
29 Hogback Mountain 118
30 Laughing Whitefish Falls 122
31 Little Garlic River 126
32 Morgan Creek/Carp River Falls 129
33 Whitefish Lake Preserve 133

Escanaba/Iron Mountain Area Hikes
34 Cedar River Loop 138
35 Bay de Noc–Grand Island National Recreation Trail 141
36 Piers Gorge 144

Munising Area Hikes
37 Au Sable Point/Log Slide 148
38 Beaver Lake Loop 151
39 Bruno's Run Loop 154
40 Chapel Loop 158
41 Grand Island Loop 162
42 Grand Sable Dunes Loop 166
43 Miners Falls 170
44 Twin Waterfalls 173
45 Pictured Rocks 176
46 Rock River Falls 180

Manistique Area Hikes
47 Birch Point 184
48 Point Patterson/Cataract River 188
49 Portage Bay 191
50 Seney National Wildlife Refuge 194

Newberry/Paradise Area Hikes
51 Giant Pines Loop 198
52 Mouth of the Blind Sucker River 202
53 Naomikong Point 206
54 Tahquamenon Falls 209
55 Tahquamenon West/North Country Trail 213

56 Two Hearted River...217
57 Whitefish Point..221

St. Ignace Area Hikes

58 Horseshoe Bay...226
59 Maple Hill..230
60 Marble Head..233

Appendix A: Hike Finder..236
Appendix B: Contact Information and Additional Resources...........................240

About the Author..243
About the Reviser...244

Eric Hansen's Acknowledgments

This book would not have been possible without the help of many people. I would like to thank the numerous hikers who found time to return my questionnaires and inform me of their favorite routes. Many of those folks are active in the Michigan Nature Association, the Milwaukee Nordic Ski Club, the North Country Trail Association, Northwoods Wilderness Recovery, the Sierra Club, The Nature Conservancy, the Upper Peninsula Environmental Coalition, or the Wisconsin Let's Go Hiking Club.

Doug Welker and Marjory Johnston generously shared their immense knowledge of trails and routes in the Upper Peninsula. Charlie Eshbach and Jeff Knoop tutored me on the Tip of the Keweenaw. Denise Herron steered me to the Little Garlic River and other gems. Mikel Classen tipped me on the picturesque coast near the Blind Sucker River. Jessie Hadley, of Woods and Waters Ecotours, offered keen insight into the quiet corners of the eastern U.P.

Bob Sprague, park interpreter at Porcupine Mountains Wilderness State Park, was a vital sounding board for my hike selections there. Bob Wild, park interpreter at Tahquamenon State Park, passed on his considerable knowledge of that notable ecosystem.

Jon Dorn, managing editor of *Backpacker* magazine, assigned a Trap Hills article that sparked this book project. Kristin Hostetter, of that same publication, sharpened my writing skills during her tenure as equipment editor. Thanks also to other editors there—Annette McGivney, Dennis Lewon, Gina DeMillo, and Kris Wagner for savvy advice, and a string of assignments that dovetailed well with this book project. Jim Gorman, during his time at *Backpacker*, drilled me on the fundamentals of landscape writing.

Dave Foreman and Howie Wolke provided inspiration with their visionary volume, *The Big Outside*, an inventory of North American wilderness. John Hart, author of the practical and poetic guidebook, *Hiking the Great Basin*, set a standard I will always aspire to.

Thanks to all the tireless activists of the Trap Hills Conservation Alliance. Dave and Judy Allen, Doug Cornett, Jon Saari, and Scott Bouma offered valuable advice and timely support.

I'm grateful to poet Harvey Taylor for spiritual sustenance over the years. My aunt, Marjorie Swann Edwin, a fearless campaigner for human rights and the planet, supplied a steady stream of encouragement.

I also owe thanks to copy editor Katie Sharp, project editor Jan Cronan, and the rest of the staff at Globe Pequot for their knowledgeable assistance.

Special thanks to my spouse, Anne Steinberg, for frontline editing that kept me on track and a faith in this project that smoothed the rough spots.

Rebecca Pelky's Acknowledgments

Thanks to James McCommons for introducing me to this project and to Abigail Alft for introducing me to Bond Falls. Also thank you to all of my NMU friends and colleagues who hiked with me and helped me stay on track (literally and figuratively). And, of course, more appreciation than I can express for Tyler and Mike, who I think sincerely believe that I can do anything, even when I don't believe it myself. Finally, very special thank you to my mother, who hates me hiking alone, but always supports me nonetheless.

Introduction

Hiking the Upper Peninsula

Wild and off the beaten track, the Upper Peninsula has a long history as the backwoods retreat of the Upper Midwest—a 300-mile-long swath of secluded forests; sparkling, pristine water; remote shorelines; and eye-catching vistas. Better yet is the sheer mystery of the place. Here, less than a day's drive from several major metropolitan areas, civilization sits just a little closer to the primitive. The U.P. has a well-deserved reputation for rewarding adventurers who invest the time to explore its hidden bays and high reaches.

The excursions in this book represent the best hikes in the Upper Peninsula according to only two people. While we think every one of these hikes is beautiful for various reasons, they are also meant to be a starting point for further exploration. In other words, don't take our word for it. Let the places in this book lead you on to your own adventures. Everyone has different reasons for being in the woods, whether that be wildlife watching, exploring historic sites, geology, or just plain old peace and quiet. These sixty hikes represent only a small fraction of the breathtaking spaces and trails to be explored in the Upper Peninsula. For example, we've offered several beautiful hikes in the Porcupine Mountains Wilderness State Park, Pictured Rocks National Lakeshore, and Isle Royale National Park. However, each of these areas incorporates extensive trail networks that you can use to extend the explorations that begin with this book.

That being said, I obviously have my favorite spots and I would love to share them. It would be difficult to choose between the many waterfalls scattered like glittering stardust throughout the U.P. Each one has its own distinct personality. Some, like the mighty Tahquamenon and Black River Falls, are larger than life and thunderous, while others, like Memorial Falls, trickle shyly through shaded sandstone canyons. Still others, like Bond Falls and O-Kun-de-Kun Falls, feel like settings for fairy tales. Find the ones that suit you best and spend time with the places that become, in some way, a part of your personality. If you enjoy history with your hike, like I sometimes do, Union Mine, with its insight into early mining efforts in the Upper Peninsula, is a must see. The Trap Hills from Norwich Road to Victoria also sport some interesting prehistoric sites, as well as a landscape which itself seems to speak from another age.

While most of the U.P. is considered prime real estate for wildlife viewing, there are a few spots that are especially known for specific species. Isle Royale National Park and Craig Lake are two primary spots for moose. Craig Lake was one of the original drop sites for the moose reintroduction project in the mid-1980s. Seney National Wildlife Refuge and Whitefish Point are also significant, especially in spring and fall, when migrating birds use them as rest stops and flight corridors to and from Canada.

Lake of the Cloads in the Porcupine Mountains

For high vistas, some of my favorite spots include Horseshoe Harbor for its sheer sense of isolation and age, Marble Head at sunrise, and, of course, the sweeping view of Lake Superior from the colorful ridges along the Pictured Rocks shoreline.

But like I said, don't take my word for it. Instead, find the trails that speak to *your* nature. My goal has been to offer something for everyone, at any skill level, with any of the varied interests that we bring to the woods with us. I hope I've succeeded, and that this book helps you find places that take your breath away, that inspire you, that fill your soul with all those intangible things that we take with us when we leave.

North Country Trail

In the 1960s a 60-mile-long footpath was built in the Chequamegon National Forest in Northwest Wisconsin and named the North Country Trail (NCT). At the time there were no great ambitions for it to be more than a trail through Wisconsin's Northwoods. The name, however, caused a stir. In the years that followed, the idea of a trail stretching across a wide tier of northern states spread, and a movement to build the NCT was born.

As of 2014 the North Country National Scenic Trail features more than 4,600 certified, off-road miles of trail. Those trail segments are along a route that crosses seven states and stretches from northern New York to North Dakota.

Some of the most scenic stretches of that long national pathway are in the U.P. The list of notable NCT segments that made the cut for this book is extensive and includes the thunderous whitewater of the Black River Waterfalls and sweeping vistas of the Trap Hills in the west. In the central U.P., NCT hikes along the quiet shores of Craig Lake and the charming Little Garlic River are well worth a visit. Farther east the NCT offers spectacular views of Lake Superior in the Pictured Rocks and Mouth of the Blind Sucker River trail segments. The stretch along the Tahquamenon River, including the famous waterfalls, is a "can't miss." A little north of the Straits of Mackinac, the Maple Hill stretch is a subtle forest beauty.

Trail maps and up-to-date reports on new trail additions are on the North Country Trail Association's (NCTA) website (see Appendix B). Hikers can also find information there on local chapters and insight on how they can help maintain the trail.

Weather

Weather in the U.P. is a source of local pride, often seen as a test of character. At its fiercest it will challenge you with ninety-degree heat and below-zero windchills. Fortunately there is a lot of fine hiking weather between those extremes. In addition to the obvious seasonal variation, there is sometimes a wide difference between the weather on the north and south shores of the U.P. At times, strong onshore winds create these differences. The Great Lakes often have a moderating effect on temperatures along their shores, resisting heat and cold that may be dominant just a few miles inland.

For hikers more than a casual distance from their vehicle, it pays to know the forecast and be prepared for worst-case scenarios, such as cold rain showers accompanied by strong winds. Several hikes in this book follow Great Lakes shorelines. Be aware that coastal routes are glorious in good conditions but merciless in their exposure to high winds when the weather gets rowdy.

While weather changes can affect hiking in the day to day, there are other considerations that can change conditions in the long term. Weather patterns are shifting as environments adjust to long-term climate changes. This means that seasons and storms can be unpredictable. There may still be ice and snow on the trails into June, migrations and fall colors might not follow expected historical patterns, and water levels on rivers and inland lakes could be higher than normal for each season. The levels of the Great Lakes vary from year to year as well. Some lakeshore hikes described as having deep beaches may be under water as more precipitation and longer winters have recently led to increased water levels on Lake Superior especially.

Seasons

Spring hiking, with its woodland wildflowers, colorful birds, and open sight lines through the leafless forest, can be the best of the year. It is a time when marsh walks along dike routes, such as the Seney National Wildlife Refuge, can lead to extravagant bird migration scenes. Bug presence is minimal, and weather is often temperate and ideal for walking. The weather can be volatile, however; keep track of forecasts and bring appropriate clothing. Right after snowmelt, trails are frequently wet or muddy. A walk along a sandy beach may be appealing then. Also remember that there may be fine hiking along Lake Michigan beaches while the Lake Superior snowbelt is still thick with snow.

Summer, with its long hours of daylight, lends itself to lengthy hikes, with time to linger at distant destinations. Hot temperatures are a comfort factor directly related to how much of a hike is in the deep shade of the forest canopy. Shady forest trails tend to be reasonably comfortable throughout the summer. One way to escape summer heat is to walk near the Great Lakes shorelines and enjoy cooler lake-effect temperatures. Bugs are numerous in early summer and slowly decline as the season progresses. Thunderstorms can soak hikers and expose them to dangerous lightning.

Fall is a favorite season for many hikers. It is hard to disagree with the merits of a forest ablaze with color. Shorter daylight hours dictate an earlier return from hikes. Full rain gear is a good idea for the cooler temperatures and lingering rain showers of fall. Bug season ends, and hikes that would be miserable in June are prime in late September. Hunters are out and about, however, so wearing some blaze orange is prudent.

Winter snow cover on hiking trails is a sure thing in the U.P., which may halt the hiking season, but for snowshoe and ski enthusiasts it is a pleasant opportunity to travel the trails in another manner. There are a few extraordinary winter hikes to ice caves, either on the frozen surface of the lakes (to Grand Island, for example), or on trails packed down by frequent use (try the Eben Ice Caves near Chatham).

Being Prepared

Two truths are the basis of a savvy clothing strategy. First, layer your clothing and you will have options. Temperature, wind, shade, and precipitation can change during a hike. If you have clothing choices, you will be able to add or subtract a layer and be more comfortable when those changes occur. You will be able to walk without becoming overheated, cold, or wet. Second, synthetic thread does not absorb water as cotton thread does. Essentially this means that any moisture in the fabric dries quicker because it is between the threads, not within them. This fundamental advantage of synthetic clothing keeps the hiker drier, with less chance of becoming chilled. In cool temperatures or high winds, that advantage can become a critical safety factor.

The season and length of your hike determine what clothing is essential. A cap and sunblock could be the bottom line for a short warm-weather hike, but consider a long-sleeved shirt and pants for protection from the sun, bugs, and briars.

Rain gear quality should reflect the relative threat of becoming chilled and hypothermic. On a short, warm-weather hike, that threat may be low, but in cooler temperatures, and on longer outings, take along full rain gear as well as a sweater and warm hat.

Often overlooked, but charming and secluded, unnamed falls on the Little Carp River

Hiking boots are a basic part of your clothing system. Boots that feature a water-proof/breathable liner will keep your feet toasty in a chilly autumn rain and ease the going when trails are wet.

During summer, consider adding mosquito netting to your clothing line-up. Insects can cause discomfort and distract you from your reasons for hiking in the first place. Ticks are also prevalent, and deer ticks carry Lyme disease. Tall socks, long pants, and sleeves with tight cuffs can reduce access to skin. Still, all U.P. woodsmen and -women know that the after-hike tick check is an integral part of any trip into the backwoods. Water is imperative for any hike. Bring more than you think you'll need, in case you're in the woods longer than expected, especially on hot sunny days.

Being prepared has its equipment aspects, but in the end it is mental. We set out on hikes with a set of assumptions in place. We are confident that our physical capabilities and gear can deal with the conditions and terrain we expect to find. In a way we are using a mathematical formula that goes like this: confidence + conditioning + gear + conditions that are reasonable and as expected = successful outing. Trouble arises when one of the factors in this formula changes and the formula no longer computes. That change could be a severe heel blister, twisted ankle, sudden lightning storm, or cold rain squall. At that point conditions may exceed our capacity to deal with them. Even a fanny pack has room for a small amount of gear that can make a big difference when problems arise. At a minimum take a compass, energy bar, water, knife,

Summer on the Presque Isle River, when water levels often run low

aspirin, bandages, antibacterial ointment, matches, and space blanket emergency bag. Tightly folded garbage bags take up less room than your wallet and can pinch-hit as an emergency shelter or rain gear.

Wildlife

It is important to remember that time in the backwoods is shared with a variety of animal species. For the most part, these animals pose no threat to even a solo hiker, and will move away when they hear you approaching. However, there are a few precautions to keep in mind. Bears are often the first animal that comes to mind when people worry about dangerous encounters. While it is true that black bears can be aggressive, incidents of bear-related injuries are extremely uncommon, and mostly occur when a person attempts to approach a bear. If you encounter a bear on the trail, don't run, but back cautiously away. Almost always, a bear will run away when it notes your presence. If not, they can usually be scared away by loud noise or pepper spray.

Moose can actually be more dangerous, especially in spring and fall when they are protecting young or mating. If you encounter a moose, place a large solid object, like a sturdy tree, between yourself and the moose. They are not agile enough to dart around objects to charge you. Also keep an eye on their ears. Just like a horse, if a moose is upset, its ears will be laid back along its head.

There is a healthy population of wolves in the Upper Peninsula, but human-wolf encounters are infrequent, and attacks on hikers are unheard of. If you're lucky enough to hear or see a wolf, enjoy the experience. As with any other wildlife species, do not approach wolves.

It is also notable that trail cams have recently recorded cougars in isolated areas of the Upper Peninsula. However, there have been no reports of interactions between humans and cougars.

Impact on the Land

Zero impact is to hiking and camping what catch-and-release is to fishing. It all boils down to one concept: With a little forethought, we will still be able to enjoy the outing we are taking today in 5 years—or 50.

If you pack it in, pack it out. Leave nothing but footprints. Human sanitation is especially important in the backwoods, away from toilets. Dig a 6-inch-deep hole, well away from any stream or water, relieve yourself, and cover the hole with dirt. Pack out your used toilet paper in a plastic storage bag.

You, and others like you, can make the critical difference in whether the places we enjoy today are worth visiting in the years to come. Your knowledge of savvy methods to respond to threats to the U.P.'s wild lands is a key part of the strategy to protect them. Citizen watchdogs are the eyes and ears that blow the whistle on polluters and other illegal activity.

You are not alone. You can plug into a broad network of like-minded folks. A good place to start is with the following organizations: Save the Wild U.P., the Superior Watershed Partnership and Land Trust, the Sierra Club, and the Upper Peninsula Environmental Coalition (see Appendix B for contact information). You can also do a great service for yourself, other hikers, and the community at large by keeping abreast of conservation issues that impact the U.P. Information is power. For example, zebra mussel populations are taking over all of the Great Lakes except Superior. On some Lake Michigan shoreline hikes, you may find yourself crunching over beaches buried in deep piles of zebra mussel shells. Also, wolf hunting has recently been reinstituted in the U.P., and there is some concern that the population is not yet strong enough to maintain itself with the added population stress of yearly hunts.

Finally, and perhaps most disturbing, sulfide mining (a type of mining associated with notable pollution) continues to be a concern in the Upper Peninsula. At least two proposals for sulfide mines seem to be imminent. One of those mines would be on the Yellow Dog Plains in western Marquette County. The other would be near the Menominee River. Sulfide ores exposed to air and water create sulfuric acid and pollute water systems. This type of pollution can't be easily fixed, and, once polluted, the ecosystem remains poisoned for thousands of years.

Field research for this guide included over 1,000 miles of hiking and rehiking every foot of trail described. The purpose of this book is to organize that pool of knowledge in a way that allows you to locate outings suitable to your tastes and abilities. You can make an initial screening of the hike chapters by checking the Hike Finder in Appendix A. The hike locator map offers a quick scan of which hikes are in a given area. Further, each section begins with a description of nearby towns, and will help you find more information on trails and stock up on gear and supplies. All hikes in a specific section include directions from a (relatively) nearby town. Hike chapters begin with a summary of the facts needed to evaluate that hike. The "Type of hike" section puts each hike into one of four categories:

Loop hike. A loop hike begins and ends at the same point without walking the same stretch of trail more than once. At times finishing the loop may require a small amount of road walking to return to the starting point.

Lollipop hike. A lollipop hike is a loop with a stem, or occasionally two stems. If the loop segment of the lollipop is very small in proportion to the stem, it falls into the category of out-and-back hikes.

One-way shuttle hike. A one-way shuttle hike involves walking from one point to another, typically using a second vehicle or a bicycle for the return trip.

Out-and-back hike. An out-and-back hike is one where you hike to a location and retrace your steps to return to your point of origin.

The total mileage for each hike appears under the heading "Distance." Keep in mind that most mileage figures, whether from official sources or my notes, are an estimate.

Each hike has an overall **Difficulty** rating:

Easy. These are well-marked trails, and the length is less than 6 miles. There is reasonably good footing and no obstacles worth mentioning.

Moderate. These hikes are on marked or obvious trails, old woods roads, or lanes. They are less than 10 miles long, and footing may be rougher in places than easy hikes. Moderate hikes may include, for example, narrow but good trails along the sides of steep inclines.

Difficult. This rating reflects either a hike length of more than 10 miles or conditions or navigation that require considerable skills and/or perseverance. Difficult hikes may be on unmarked trails or old woods roads or involve considerable off-trail travel. The footing may be rough and there may be steep climbs.

An asterisk after the overall difficulty rating indicates a route or trail that requires some attention to follow. Some scanning may be necessary to spot the next blaze, and the trail itself may be faint or show no wear marks at all on the ground.

"Best months" lists the time during which the hike is normally free of snow and reasonable to walk. Early or late season snowstorms can change that. Keep in mind that after the snow melts, standing water can still make some areas impassable without wading or off-trail navigation around temporary ponds.

Any map listed from a land agency or trail organization shows the featured hike or a large portion of it. These maps are often basic but perfectly adequate for easy hikes and some moderate ones. USGS topographical maps are useful for some moderate and difficult hikes. Unfortunately it is not unusual for these maps to predate the existence of the hiking trail in question. Topographical maps that show the area, but not all of the trail mentioned have *(inc.)*, for incomplete, after them. Having both the land agency map and the topographical map is a good idea. The North Country Trail Association also has worthwhile maps.

A "Fees and permits" section lists necessary items such as state park vehicle stickers or backpacking permits.

Each hike summary also includes a brief description, "Finding the trailhead," which describes how to locate the start of the hike from a nearby town. Finally there are headings that list nearby "Camping," as well as a "Trail contact" if you need more information. GPS coordinates for each trailhead have also been added to the new edition.

Other important aspects of each hike are listed under the "Special considerations" heading.

How to Use the Maps

The maps in this book are designed to provide quick and easy reference for each hike. Please refer to the Map Legend on the following page for a list of symbols used throughout the book. Each map visualizes a starting location, a highlighted trail, and arrows to indicate the direction of travel as detailed in the text section of the hike. Landmarks and physical characteristics of the landscape are noted as navigational references or points of interest. Further, the maps use elevation tints, called hypsometry, to portray relief. Each gray tone represents a range of equal elevations, as shown in the scale key with the map. These maps will give you a good idea of elevation gain and loss. The darker tones are lower elevations and the lighter grays are higher elevations. The lighter the tone, the higher the elevation. Narrow bands of different gray tones spaced closely together indicate steep terrain, whereas wider bands indicate areas of more gradual slope.

Map Legend

═══〈43〉═══	Interstate Highway	▬	Bench
══〈141〉══	US Highway	≋	Boat Launch
══〈139〉══	State Highway	⏑	Bridge
══[H-58]══	County Road	⌂	Building/Shelter
═══════	Local Road	▲	Campground
======	Unimproved Road	∩	Cave
▬▬▬▬▬	Featured Trail	†	Cemetery
- - - - - -	Trail (verified)	—	Dam
– – – – – –	Trail (unverified)	⌶	Gate
· · · · · · · ·	Cross–Country Route	🗼	Lighthouse
⊢−⊢−⊢−⊢	Railroad	🅿	Parking
▮▮▮▮▮▮	Boardwalk	▲	Peak/Summit
⌒⌒⌒⌒	Bluff/Cliff	🛆	Picnic Area
▪—▪▪—▪▪—▪	International Border	▪	Point of Interest
– – – – –	State Border	🛈	Ranger Station
〜〜〜	Small River or Creek	🔭	Scenic View/Viewpoint
〜 〜 〜	Intermittent Stream	○	Town/City
⟛	Marsh/Swamp	◇	Trail Junction/Mileage Marker
⬭	Body of Water	①	Trailhead
▬▬▬▬	National Forest/Park	❓	Visitor/Information Center
– – – – –	National Wilderness Area	≋	Waterfall
──────	State/County Park		
──────	National Lakeshore		

Ironwood/Ontonagon Area Hikes

S et in the farthest corner of the western Upper Peninsula, this area encompasses some of the region's most rugged and alluring landscapes. The Porcupine Mountains, the Trap Hills, and the Black River Waterfalls each have extraordinary features to recommend them. From high rock ridges facing endless Lake Superior shoreline, to some of the most impressive waterfalls in the U.P., to ancient and secluded landscapes on long stretches of North Country Trail, hikers could easily spend a full 2 weeks exploring just this relatively small area.

Ironwood, Michigan, population 5,500, lies to the southwest of the Porcupine Mountains (also known as the Porkies) and Trap Hills, while Ontonagon, a small town to the north of only about 1,500 people, is known locally as the gateway to the Porcupine Mountains.

Ontonagon features a charming downtown along the banks of the Ontonagon River, just before it joins Lake Superior. The US Forest Service has an outpost here on US 45, and there's a visitor center on the site of the Ontonagon County Historical Museum at the corner of River and Spar Streets.

Ironwood is a larger town with a few more amenities. If you need to stock up on gear or supplies before heading into the Porkies or the Trap Hills, stop by Steep Creek Outfitters, a great locally owned business, which also serves locally sourced food items.

Dunham's Sports
1440 East Cloverland Dr.
Ironwood, MI 49938
(906) 530-6700

Ontonagon County Chamber of
Commerce
PO Box 266
Ontonagon, MI 49953
(906) 884-4735
www.ontonagonmi.org/home.html

Porcupine Mountains Ontonagon
Area Convention and Visitors Bureau
PO Box 1
Ontonagon, MI 49953
(906) 884-2047

Steep Creek Outfitters
930 East Cloverland Dr.
Ironwood, MI 49938
(906) 364-7336

1 Black River Waterfalls

Highlights: A spectacular parade of five waterfalls

Location: 15 miles north of Bessemer

Type of hike: Out-and-back, in 2 stems

Distance: 8.3 miles

Difficulty: Difficult

Fees and permits: None

Best months: May through October

Camping: Ottawa National Forest's Black River Harbor Campground, a quarter-mile west of the trailhead, has 40 campsites.

Map: USGS Black River Harbor (inc.) quad

Trail contact: Ottawa National Forest, (906) 932-1330, www.fs.usda.gov/ottawa

Finding the trailhead: From Bessemer drive 15 miles north on Black River Road (Gogebic CR 513) and turn right (east) into the Black River Harbor Recreation Area. The trail begins at a paved walkway through the park and picnic area. GPS: 46.664624, -90.046636

Special considerations: Parts of these trails are eroded and rough and have an abundance of exposed roots. Use caution on wet rocks near the river and waterfalls.

The Hike

Waterfall fans have many incredible choices in the western U.P., but it's difficult to top the drama of the Presque Isle and Black Rivers making thunderous descents to Lake Superior. Like a peerless set of twins, both rivers sport a parade of waterfalls that stand tall in any short list of U.P. whitewater shows. Better yet, both sets of cascades are compact, creating outstanding hikes.

This hike tours the westernmost of those two streams—the Black River—as it tumbles through a delightful gorge to Lake Superior. First the route skirts the river's mouth at Black River Harbor and ascends its east side to the perfect vantage point for Rainbow Falls. After offering that memorable view, the trail returns to the river's west side, passing four waterfalls before arriving at Conglomerate Falls. From that cascade the route returns to the river mouth.

Begin your tour by walking northeast from the trailhead's information board, following an asphalt path to the Black River Bridge (Mile 0.1). Cross the sturdy suspension bridge to the river's east bank and follow the North Country Trail (NCT) up steps to the top of the bluff, where the broad dirt trail curves south. Consider a short side-trip here. In the middle of that curve on the NCT, a narrow footpath runs north 120 paces to a bench—a pleasant spot to soak in views of Lake Superior and the Porcupine Mountains to the east.

To resume this hike, walk south, following the NCT through fine hemlock groves as it descends to a perfect vantage point to view Rainbow Falls (Mile 0.9). This spectacular 40-foot drop begins with a water slide down a rock ramp and accelerates into two thumping ledge drops.

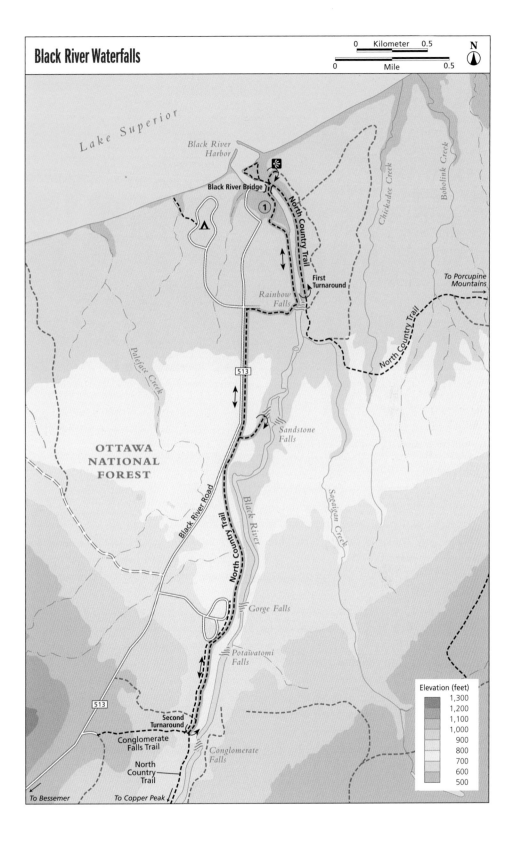

Potawatomi Falls during a dry spell, showing the conglomerate riverbed. The Black River races to Lake Superior in a set of five thumping waterfalls.

Next retrace your steps north to the Black River Bridge (Mile 1.7), cross and walk south past the trailhead. An NCT sign marks the spot where the trail ascends into the woods, heading south to the west side of Rainbow Falls, where nearly 200 steps descend to a viewpoint overlooking the top of the falls (Mile 2.2).

Reverse your path, ascend the stairs, and follow the broad trail southwest to the Rainbow Falls Trailhead parking area. There, go straight, walking west 110 paces, following NCT blazes to CR 513 (Mile 2.5). Turn left (south) and hike 0.8 mile on the shoulder of CR 513, to a Forest Service sign marking the trailhead for Sandstone Falls (Mile 3.3).

There, turn left (east), walk sixty paces on pavement, then northeast on a broad dirt Sandstone Falls Trail. Descend almost 140 steps to a viewpoint at Sandstone Falls's two-step plunge (Mile 3.6). The river drops 5 feet off a broad sandstone ledge, pauses, and then tumbles an additional 20 feet.

From here return to the Sandstone Falls Trailhead (Mile 3.9) and walk to the southwest corner of the parking area. There the NCT runs south, first near CR 513, then turning southeast. Soon it approaches the rim of the river gorge, and steps descend to a viewpoint for Gorge Falls (Mile 4.5). Upstream, a dark, forbidding chute of bedrock and conglomerate leads to a pinch point. The current narrows to an 8-foot-wide flume and tumbles 20 feet to the gorge below.

After viewing Gorge Falls, return to the rim and walk south along the broad dirt path. In short order the rim path passes two more sets of stairs descending to viewpoints, then arrives at stairs descending to Potawatomi Falls (Mile 4.6). Potawatomi Falls is a knockout, a sparkling and complex bridal veil cascading 40 feet. Even during dry spells, Potawatomi puts on a good show, and the geology of conglomerate rock that usually lies hidden beneath whitewater is fascinating in its own right.

Return to the rim and follow the NCT south along the top of the bluff. At times a tad rough and eroded, roots exposed, the trail arrives at Conglomerate Falls (Mile 5.3). Here the river splits around a rock dome, taking a stepped plunge into the gorge, a 30-foot descent. During my visit, large trees littered the center dome, mute testimony to the river's power.

Conglomerate Falls marks the southern turnaround point for the hike. To return to the trailhead, follow the NCT north, downhill to the Black River Harbor parking area.

Miles and Directions

0.0 Trailhead.

0.1 Black River Bridge.

0.9 Rainbow Falls (east side); first turnaround point.

1.7 Black River Bridge.

2.2 Rainbow Falls (west side).

2.5 Trail joins CR 513 (walk on shoulder).

3.3 Sandstone Falls Trailhead.

3.6 Sandstone Falls.

3.9 Sandstone Falls Trailhead.

4.5 Gorge Falls.

4.6 Potawatomi Falls.

5.3 Conglomerate Falls; second turnaround point.

6.0 Potawatomi Falls.

6.1 Gorge Falls.

6.7 Sandstone Falls Trailhead.

7.5 Trail leaves CR 513.

7.8 Rainbow Falls (west side).

8.3 Trailhead.

2 Escarpment

Highlights: A ridge walk offering a parade of sweeping views

Location: Porcupine Mountains Wilderness State Park (PMWSP)

Type of hike: Out-and-back

Distance: 6.4 miles

Difficulty: Moderate

Fees and permits: Michigan DNR Recreation Passport

Best months: May through October

Camping: PMWSP's Union Bay Campground, with 100 campsites, is 2.5 miles east of the trailhead. There is one backcountry campsite, with a bear pole, along the trail, at approximately Mile 1.1. Check PMWSP regulations before using backcountry sites.

Maps: USGS Carp River, Government Peak quads; PMWSP by Nequaket Natural History Associates (available at the visitor center)

Trail contact: PMWSP, (906) 885-5275

Finding the trailhead: From the intersection of M-107 and South Boundary Road in PMWSP, drive 3.5 miles west on M-107 to the Government Peak Trailhead. GPS: 46.818104, -89.694534

Special considerations: The Escarpment Trail follows an exposed ridgeline. Although glorious in fine weather, it can be unpleasant in high winds or thunderstorms.

The Hike

For many Porkies' veterans, the Escarpment is at the top of any "don't miss" list of outings. Open meadows on this ridge offer long sight lines and memorable views of the area's landmarks. Far to the west, past Lafayette Peak's craggy south face, Lake Superior sparkles on clear days. To the southeast the Trap Hills dimple the horizon. Hundreds of feet below the Escarpment's rocky heights, Lake of the Clouds feeds the headwaters of the Big Carp River.

Begin your Escarpment hike by walking southwest on the broad, stony Government Peak Trail as it ascends into the woods above the trailhead. About 200 paces later, at Mile 0.1, bear right (southwest) on the Escarpment Trail as the Government Peak Trail goes left (southeast).

The Escarpment Trail soon settles into a steady ascent, reaching the first view at about Mile 0.6. An opening in the woods, a mixture of meadow and bedrock, offers long sight lines to the southeast, where the Trap Hills dot the horizon. Here a pattern develops. Five more minutes of uphill hiking brings you to another viewpoint. It's similar in orientation to the first, but the increased elevation adds a new sight to the eastern view: the deep blue of Lake Superior.

Another five minutes of walking, with the trail still rising, brings striking new vistas to the west. Below the Escarpment's long ridgeline, mile-long Lake of the Clouds appears; beyond the ridge Lake Superior shows. Here, at Mile 1.2 of the hike, Cuyahoga Peak's wooded apex is a little north of the trail.

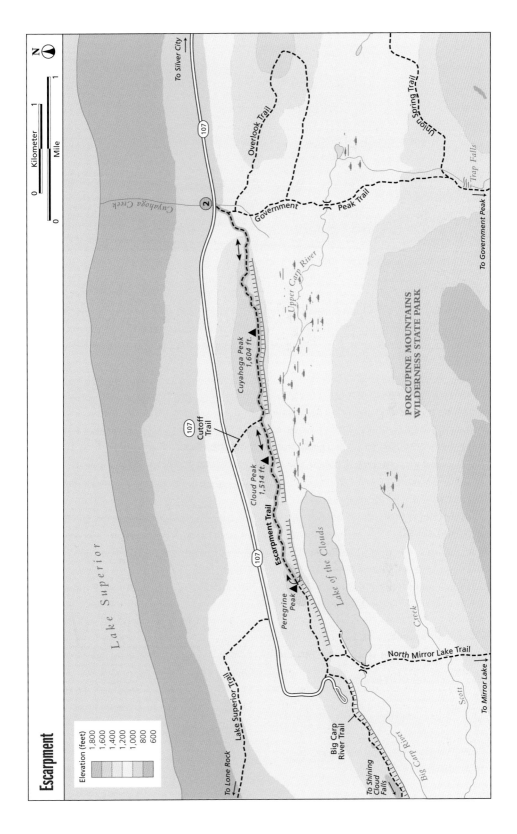

Escarpment

Elevation (feet)
- 1,800
- 1,600
- 1,400
- 1,200
- 1,000
- 800
- 600

Lake Superior

Cuyahoga Creek

To Silver City

Overlook Trail

107

2

Government

Peak Trail

Union Spring Trail

Trap Falls

To Government Peak

Upper Carp River

Cuyahoga Peak
1,604 ft.

107
Cutoff
Trail

Cloud Peak
1,514 ft.

Escarpment Trail

Peregrine Peak

Lake of the Clouds

107

Lake Superior Trail

To Lone Rock

Big Carp River Trail

To Shining
Cloud
Falls

North Mirror Lake Trail

Scott Creek

Big Carp River

To Mirror Lake

PORCUPINE MOUNTAINS
WILDERNESS STATE PARK

N

0   Kilometer   1

0   Mile   1

Views from the Escarpment Trail stretch past Lake of the Clouds to Lafayette Peak and beyond.

As you continue walking west, the plateau-like ridge becomes more open and the views broader, stretching east, south, and west. There is an airy feeling to this stretch, a delightful sense of height, long sight lines, and a pristine landscape as far as the eye can see.

The path descends into a wooded saddle in the ridgeline, reaching a junction with the M-107 Cutoff Trail at Mile 2.0. Go straight (west) on the Escarpment Trail, as the M-107 Cutoff Trail leads off to the right (north).

Ascending from the saddle, the trail reaches Cloud Peak at Mile 2.3. A tad lower than Cuyahoga Peak, Cloud Peak still offers memorable views. I spotted Copper Peak 15 miles to the southwest. A half-mile off and 500 vertical feet below me, the rhythmic wing beats of a great blue heron caught my attention as the bird cruised along the Lake of the Clouds shoreline.

After Cloud Peak, the trail dips and rolls as it runs west before rising to another high point at Mile 3.2, a crest sometimes known as Peregrine Peak. Hikers visiting in June may spot the peak's namesake falcons, a species famous for their 100-mile-an-hour, stun gun–like dives to knock out prey. Whether or not falcons are nearby, this is another memorable viewpoint and a fine place to linger. It also makes a suitable turnaround spot for the hike. Retrace your steps eastward to return to the trailhead.

Miles and Directions

- **0.0** Government Peak Trailhead.
- **0.1** Escarpment Trail junction.
- **1.2** Cuyahoga Peak.
- **2.0** M-107 Cutoff Trail.
- **2.3** Cloud Peak.
- **3.2** Peregrine Peak; turnaround point.
- **6.4** Government Peak Trailhead.

3 Lake Superior Shoreline

Highlights: A wild Lake Superior shoreline; broad views; and intricate, tilted bedrock strata
Location: Porcupine Mountains Wilderness State Park (PMWSP)
Type of hike: One-way shuttle
Distance: 9.0 miles
Difficulty: Difficult*
Fees and permits: Michigan DNR Recreation Passport
Best months: May through October

Camping: Backcountry camping is permitted along the hike within the PMWSP regulations. Union Bay Campground, with 100 campsites, is 5.5 miles east of the trailhead.
Maps: USGS quads Carp River; Government Peak quads; PMWSP map by Nequaket Natural History Associates (available at the visitor center)
Trail contact: PMWSP, (906) 885-5275

Finding the trailhead: From the intersection of M-107 and South Boundary Road in PMWSP, drive west 6.4 miles to the Lake Superior Trailhead. GPS: 46.811270, -89.754622
Special considerations: The start and finish of the hike are 3 miles apart along M-107. Six miles of this hike are off-trail. Although the navigation is relatively simple, this hike requires some confidence. If you think that the quality of this outing would justify some precise footwork on the rocky shoreline, I would encourage you to sample it. Alternatively, if you have an intense dislike of rough trails, it is doubtful you would enjoy the shoreline portion of this hike. For some the tilted bedrock strata of the shoreline may be reminiscent of routes in the canyons of the Southwest. Also consider that this is a shoreline route. It can be glorious in fine weather and dreadfully exposed when high winds and squalls hit.

Remote shorelines are important wildlife habitat. As you are hiking be sure to give wildlife lots of room, especially during the spring and early summer nesting season.

Biting flies may be a factor along the shoreline in late June or early July. Check conditions at the PMWSP visitor center.

The Hike

Having a vast stretch of Lake Superior shoreline to yourself has a way of growing on you. The appeal deepens when you realize that much of that shoreline features a tilted bedrock stratum, a playful obstacle course for nimble hikers, and a haven for miniature wildflower gardens tucked into rocky nooks and crannies.

Better yet, the hike begins with 3 miles of downhill trail that offer high views of Lake Superior, and finishes with a memorable off-trail walk through cathedral groves of hemlocks.

Begin your hike at the Lake Superior Trailhead on M-107, walking north. Initially the trail is broad, and a virgin hemlock forest marks the first few minutes. The trail soon enters an area where the trees are stunted because a fire seared the soil and killed the nutrients.

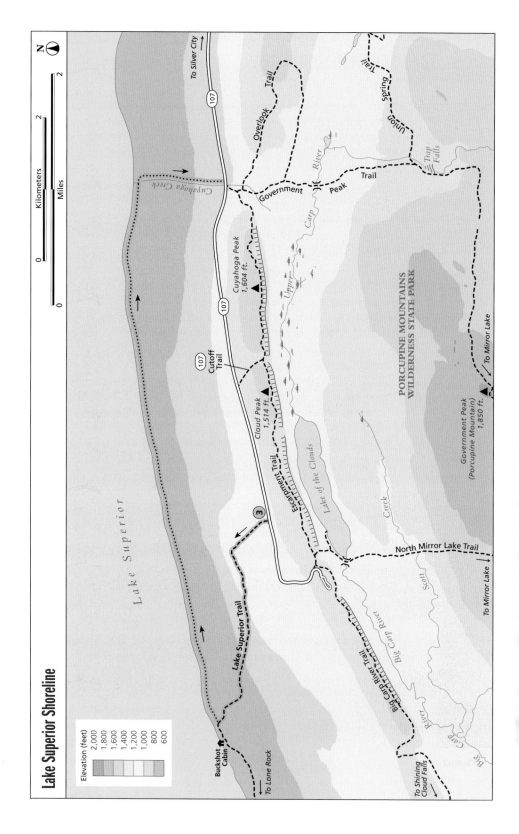

Lake Superior Shoreline

Elevation (feet)
2,000
1,800
1,600
1,400
1,200
1,000
800
600

N

0   2   Kilometers
0   2   Miles

Lake Superior

To Lone Rock

Buckshot Cabin

Lake Superior Trail

Cuyahoga Creek

To Silver City

107

107

107

Overlook Trail

Cutoff Trail

Cloud Peak 1,514 ft.

Cuyahoga Peak 1,604 ft.

Government Peak Trail

Upper Carp River

Union Spring Trail

Trap Falls

3

Escarpment Trail

Lake of the Clouds

North Mirror Lake Trail

To Mirror Lake

Big Carp River Trail

Big Carp River

Scott Creek

To Shining Cloud Falls

Big Carp River

To Mirror Lake

Government Peak (Porcupine Mountain) 1,850 ft.

PORCUPINE MOUNTAINS WILDERNESS STATE PARK

The trail descends and occasionally rises slightly to shallow ridges that mark ancient shorelines. Exploring the rock glades that dot these rises can yield rich rewards: secluded ledges with Lake Superior views. At Mile 1.3 a conglomerate spine of rock, a "whaleback," parallels the trail for 150 paces, offering more views and an alternative route for agile hikers.

At Mile 3.0 the trail reaches the spur for the Buckshot Cabin. Backtrack past the long boardwalk you just crossed to a small boardwalk bridge over a minor drainage. Follow the east side of that drainage north, off-trail, about 200 yards to the Lake Superior shore, which is marked by reefs of slanted bedrock.

This is a good time for a reality and weather check. With good conditions hike east, the beginning of the 5-mile shoreline segment of this hike. The bedrock quickly ends and for about 1 mile the shore consists of hamburger-shaped cobble, footing that is tolerable but also a bit tedious.

Persevere through the cobble stretch and the shoreline begins a bedrock rhythm I found most enjoyable. This is hiking similar to moderate whitewater paddling—minor route-finding challenges are almost constant but hardly threatening. It's a world full of small wonders—lakeside rock featuring smooth wave-washed radii, springs, and

Sunset over the tilted bedrock of Lake Superior's coast east of Buckshot Landing

seeps nourishing green patches; frogs in "tide pools"; mossy crevices; and tiny colonies of wildflowers. These are tough wildflowers, able to withstand the full force of Lake Superior gales.

Beyond the intricate shoreline scene, the big wonder—the largest freshwater lake on Earth—seems to stretch forever. Bald eagles patrolled the coast, veering offshore as they spotted me.

After 4 miles of shoreline hiking, a wide bay begins. A mile later, at the middle of that broad indentation in the coast, Cuyahoga Creek meets the lake. A mere dribble in late summer, it crosses the bedrock in a series of pools. Just east of the creek's flowing water, take a slightly worn path that leads off the rocks into the forest. The path and a forested flat quickly end at a steep, but short slope. The route is simple. Ascend and stay just east of Cuyahoga Creek, as close to the rim of its ravine as is practical and hike 1 mile south, off-trail through the open forest to where the creek crosses M-107, just east of the Government Peak Trailhead. There are a few minor brushy areas, but in general the forest is open, old, and elegant, and the travel pleasant. Here and there traces of a deer path line the rim of the ravine, easing your way. However, much of the hike features impressive hemlock elders and it was tempting to stay with them rather than walk out to the road and the end of the hike.

Options: Combine this hike with the Escarpment Trail (Hike 2) and you have an outstanding 13.6-mile loop, which ends with a 1-mile road walk. From the Government Peak Trailhead follow that trail south 0.1 mile then turn right (west) onto the Escarpment Trail. Follow that trail west 3.6 miles, past sweeping views, to the Lake of the Clouds Trailhead. From there hike the broad grassy shoulder of M-107 east and north 1 mile to the Lake Superior Trailhead.

Alternatively consider a shorter hike to Lake Superior. The 6-mile round-trip hike to the shoreline east of Buckshot Cabin features both high views of Lake Superior from rock ledges and a perfect break spot on the shore. Depart from the Lake Superior Trailhead on M-107.

Miles and Directions

- **0.0** Lake Superior Trailhead on M-107.
- **1.3** "Whaleback" conglomerate rock parallels trail.
- **3.0** Buckshot Cabin spur.
- **3.1** Lake Superior shoreline.
- **8.0** Mouth of Cuyahoga Creek.
- **9.0** M-107 at Cuyahoga Creek (Government Peak Trailhead).

4 Lake Superior/Big Carp River Loop

Highlights: A classic loop featuring Lake Superior shoreline, Big Carp River cascades, Shining Cloud Falls, old-growth forest, and broad views from the escarpment

Location: Porcupine Mountains Wilderness State Park (PMWSP)

Type of hike: Loop

Distance: 20.5 miles

Difficulty: Difficult

Fees and permits: Michigan DNR Recreation Passport

Best months: May through October

Camping: Backcountry camping along the trail is available within PMWSP guidelines. Four of the park's backcountry cabins—Buckshot, Big Carp 6, Lake Superior 4, and Big Carp 4—line the hike's route. Union Bay Campground, with 100 campsites, is 5.5 miles east of the trailhead.

Maps: USGS Carp River (inc.) quad; PMWSP map by Nequaket Natural History Associates (available at the visitor center)

Trail contact: PMWSP, (906) 885-5275

Finding the trailhead: From the intersection of M-107 and South Boundary Road in PMWSP, drive west 6.4 miles to the Lake Superior Trailhead. Park on the wide gravel shoulder on either side of M-107. GPS: 46.811270, -89.754622

Special considerations: Parts of the Lake Superior Trail can be muddy in wet periods. Waterproof boots and trekking poles are handy for puddle hopping. Between Shining Cloud Falls and the junction with the Correction Line Trail, the Big Carp River Trail fords its namesake stream. The last mile of the hike follows the grassy shoulder of M-107.

Biting flies may be a factor along the shoreline in late June or early July. Check conditions at the PMWSP visitor center.

The Hike

This hike has it all. Every scenic attraction that draws hikers to the Porkies is here. Rock balconies in the first few miles offer broad Lake Superior views, before the trail descends to parallel the lake's wave-washed shore. After a 6-mile-long sojourn near the big lake, the route turns inland, ascending alongside the cascading Big Carp River to Shining Cloud Falls. After the 10-mile mark, old-growth forest brackets the rest of the hike's path as the trail winds its way up the Big Carp River Valley, passing below the cliffs of Miscowawbic Peak. For a grand finale the hike switchbacks up to the Escarpment and offers a parade of far-reaching views from that ridge's heights.

Begin your hike by walking north, on the broad Lake Superior Trail, from the trailhead on M-107. For a few minutes the trail passes through a forest of old-growth hemlock, but that soon changes to much younger growth, an area where fire seared the soil after logging occurred 100 years ago.

Every now and then the trail interrupts its descent, pausing on rises that mark ancient shorelines. Typically these shallow ridges feature rock glades; a little poking around on these slabs often yields your own private viewpoint. A conglomerate spine

Lake Superior/Big Carp River Loop

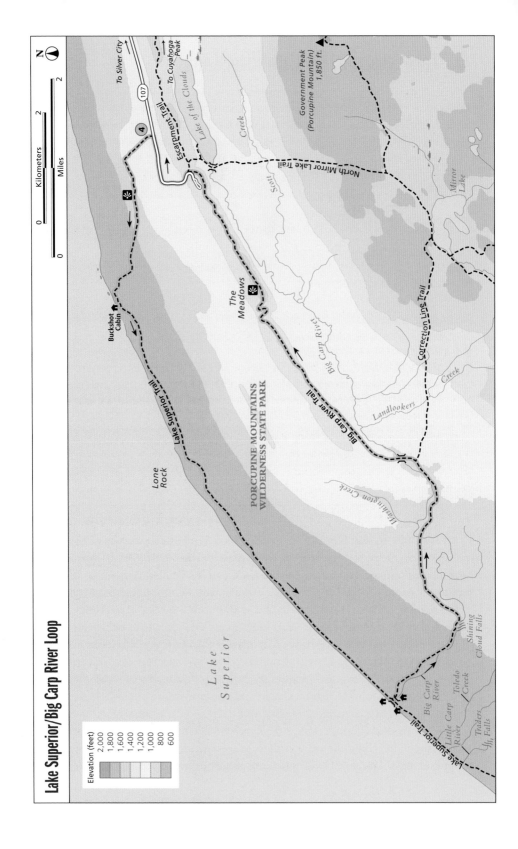

Elevation (feet)
2,000
1,800
1,600
1,400
1,200
1,000
800
600

N

0   Kilometers   2

0   Miles   2

To Silver City

To Cuyahoga Peak

107

4

Escarpment Trail

Lake of the Clouds

Scott Creek

North Mirror Lake Trail

Government Peak
(Porcupine Mountain)
1,850 ft.

Mirror Lake

Buckshot Cabin

Lake Superior Trail

Lone Rock

The Meadows

Big Carp River Trail

Big Carp River

Landlookers Creek

Correction Line Trail

PORCUPINE MOUNTAINS
WILDERNESS STATE PARK

Washington Creek

Lake Superior

Shining Cloud Falls

Big Carp River

Little Carp River

Toledo Creek

Traders Falls

Lake Superior Trail

of rock parallels the trail for 150 paces at Mile 1.3, offering more views and an alternative route for nimble hikers.

At Mile 3.0 the trail reaches the spur for the Buckshot Cabin. Respect the privacy of the cabin folks, but consider visiting a memorable break spot nearby on the slanted reefs of bedrock along the Lake Superior shore. To reach it backtrack past the long boardwalk you just crossed to a small boardwalk bridge over a minor drainage. Follow the east side of that drainage north, off-trail, about 200 yards to the shoreline. Then retrace your steps to the Lake Superior Trail and continue hiking westward. For the next several miles, the path skirts the shore, typically a little inland. You will hear waves but not always see them.

Periodically, short spur trails run to the shore, often at campsites. Aptly named, Lone Rock rises a quarter-mile offshore, near one of these spur paths, at Mile 5.5. About a mile later the trail begins a 1-mile-long segment that is actually on the shore, or just barely inland. A rise to a low ridge, a dip to the shore, and another rise brings the trail to the bluff above the mouth of the Big Carp River.

Bear left (south) on the Big Carp River Trail at Mile 9.0 as the Lake Superior Trail continues right (west). The Big Carp River trail runs south and east, first on a bluff above the river's dancing cascades, then at river level.

About a mile from the lake, the trail ascends another bluff and soon arrives at a cliff-top view of Shining Cloud Falls, 50 feet below, at Mile 10.4. Shining Cloud is a bi-level falls. First the flow drops 10 feet to a ledge, then it splits evenly and tumbles another 12 feet to a pool below. In its second drop the left side cascades down a rock ramp, while the right side is more of a vertical free fall.

Safely descending to the bottom of the falls takes some judgment and balance. First continue east on the trail until you are above the top of the falls. The first routes that appear below you are dangerous. A little farther on you will notice steep, switch-backing dirt paths descending to the top of the falls. When the river is at moderate flow levels, a rock ramp there is dry and leads to the bottom of the falls. Whether that rock ramp is a safe move on any given day is a judgment you will have to make when you are there.

Continue hiking eastward on the Big Carp River Trail, arriving at a ford of its namesake stream at Mile 13.0. At typical summertime river levels, this is an easy wade, not even knee deep. Bear left (north) on the Big Carp River Trail at Mile 14.0 as the Correction Line Trail goes right (east).

About a quarter-mile north of that junction, the Big Carp River Trail crosses its namesake stream again, this time on a sturdy bridge. The trail soon begins a nearly 2-mile-long run beneath the slopes of Lafayette and Miscowawbic Peaks. After traveling through memorable hemlock cathedrals, the trail passes beneath Miscowawbic Peak's cliffs, ascends to a saddle, and continues to the top of the Escarpment. There notable views stretch to the east, past Lake of the Clouds to Cuyahoga Peak, while a blue swath of Lake Superior shows to the west, past Lafayette Peak's rounded summit. Copper Peak's ski jump, 20-some miles off, pierces the southwest horizon. Beginning

Grand finale on the Big Carp River Trail—sweeping views along the Escarpment

at Mile 17.7, and for the next half-mile or so, the views are near constant. This is an open stretch of trail locals call "The Meadows."

Viewpoints continue but become more intermittent as you hike east and arrive at the trailhead, the parking lot for the Lake of the Clouds Overlook at Mile 19.5. Walk east through the large parking lot and continue east and north on M-107. The shoulder is wide and grassy, allowing safe passage to the hike's end, the Lake Superior Trailhead at Mile 20.5.

Options: A 6-mile out-and-back hike to the shoreline east of the Buckshot Cabin features both high views of Lake Superior from rock ledges and a perfect break spot on the shore. Depart from the Lake Superior Trailhead on M-107.

Another short alternative, at the end of the hike's loop, offers sweeping views and quiet ambience. That outing is a 4-mile round-trip on the Big Carp River Trail to "The Meadows." From the intersection of M-107 and South Boundary Road, drive 7.5 miles west on M-107 to the Big Carp River Trailhead. Then hike 2 miles southwest on that trail.

Miles and Directions

0.0   Lake Superior Trailhead on M-107.

1.3   "Whaleback" conglomerate rock parallels trail.

3.0   Buckshot Cabin spur.

5.5   Lone Rock.

9.0   Mouth of the Big Carp River.

10.4   Shining Cloud Falls.

13.0   Ford of Big Carp River.

14.0   Junction with Correction Line Trail.

17.7   The Meadows.

19.5   Big Carp River Trailhead, end of M-107.

20.5   Lake Superior Trailhead on M-107.

5 Little Carp River Cascades

Highlights: The waterfalls and cascades of the Little Carp River and old-growth forest
Location: Porcupine Mountains Wilderness State Park (PMWSP)
Type of hike: One-way shuttle
Distance: 9.6 miles
Difficulty: Moderate
Fees and permits: Michigan DNR Recreation Passport
Best months: May through October. River crossings will be more difficult in periods of high water.

Camping: Backcountry camping is available along the trail, within PMWSP regulations. The park's Presque Isle Campground has 50 campsites and is 5 miles west of the Pinkerton Trailhead.
Maps: USGS Tiebel Creek, Carp River quad; PMWSP map by Nequaket Natural History Associates (available at the visitor center)
Trail contact: PMWSP, (906) 885-5275

Finding the trailhead: From the intersection of M-107 and South Boundary Road, in PMWSP, drive south and west 19.7 miles to the Pinkerton Trailhead. GPS: 46.725159, -89.899254
Special considerations: The Little Carp River Trail fords its namesake stream twice. I found these crossings an easy rock hop during a low-water period in August. At other times they would be a wade. During high-water episodes, they might be dangerous or impossible.

The Hike

This is a poetic route. Elegant old-growth forest begins a few minutes from the trailhead and stays with you until the end of the outing. Three miles down the trail, the sights and sounds of the cascading Little Carp River join in, a near constant companion for the rest of the hike. Lake Superior's shore is also nearby and accessible as a short side-trip.

Begin your hike by walking north on the broad Pinkerton Trail as it drops ever so gradually to the bridge over Pinkerton Creek at Mile 1.0. A bench overlooks the stream, a shady scene of low bedrock ledges and gentle riffles in midsummer.

About a mile later, after threading through memorable hemlock groves, the path reaches another bench. This one is on a bluff high above the swirling cascades of the Little Carp River. The trail swings northward and reaches a junction with the Lake Superior Trail at Mile 2.6. Turn right (east) following the Lake Superior Trail across the bridge over the Little Carp River. You'll reach the junction with the Little Carp River Trail at Mile 2.7.

For a worthy side-trip, turn left (northwest) and walk 0.2 mile on the Lake Superior Trail to the cobble and bedrock shoreline of Lake Superior, the Earth's largest freshwater lake. When you are ready, retrace your steps to the junction of the Lake Superior and Little Carp Trails.

Little Carp River Cascades

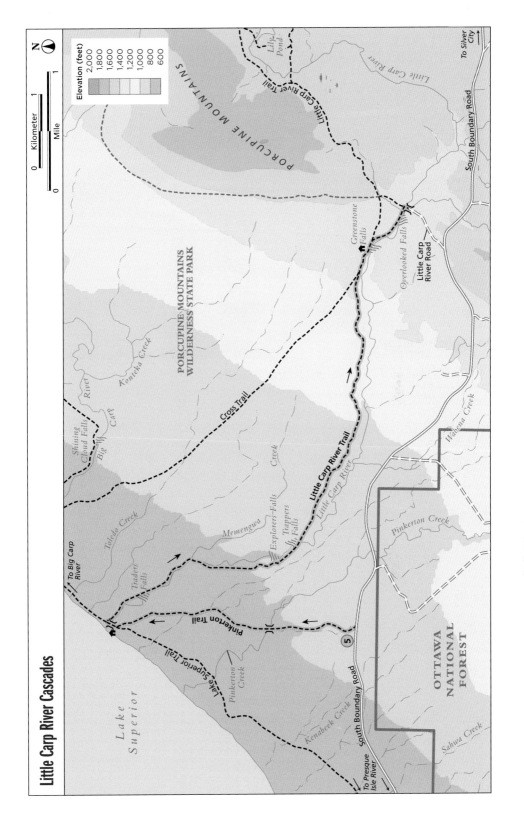

Greenstone Falls, part of the Little Carp River's striking whitewater parade

From this junction turn right (east) and hike upstream on the Little Carp River Trail. After a quick ascent and descent of a bluff, the trail settles down to follow the rushing river and crosses it at Mile 4.1. Now on the west side of the river, the trail winds through a floodplain forest; an overflow channel is nearby. About a mile after the crossing, a scene of subtle beauty unfolds as a series of swirling cascades drops through mossy bedrock formations.

As mesmerizing as the cascades are, the next scene is even more memorable. The river runs down a huge waterslide, roughly 70 feet long and 20 feet high, known as Trappers Falls. Due to the pebbly nature of the conglomerate bedrock, the water shoots up in a zillion small ripples as it races down the slope. When I was there the cascade was backlit, and it was a brilliant, pulsating spectacle.

Just above Trappers Falls the trail crosses the river. About a mile later, the path ascends a low bluff, offering glimpses of cascades 50 yards down slope with picturesque virgin timber framing the view. Watch for some outstanding specimens of white pine trees in this stretch, near a backcountry campsite.

Continue hiking eastward on the Little Carp River Trail as it ascends a low bluff and meets the junction with the Cross Trail at Mile 8.5. Bear right (south); the Cross Trail goes left (north). Soon after the junction the path descends back to the river and a bench by a campsite.

A stretch of charming cascades leads past the Greenstone Falls cabin. At Mile 8.9 the trail arrives at Greenstone Falls, a 6-foot drop that is well worth a break. From there hike east, reaching the well-marked junction of the spur trail that leads to the Little Carp River Road at Mile 9.2.

Turn right (south) on the Little Carp River Road spur trail. Just before the spur trail reaches the road, a series of cascades, including Overlooked Falls, warrants a visit. At Mile 9.6 the spur trail reaches the Little Carp River Road, the end of the hike.

Options: A 6.5-mile round-trip hike to the mouth of the Little Carp River from the Pinkerton Trailhead has considerable appeal. This shorter outing features the forest scenes along the Pinkerton Trail, the charming cascades of the Little Carp River, and the Lake Superior shore.

Another compelling alternative is a 1.4-mile out-and-back hike from the Little Carp River Trailhead to Greenstone Falls. This stretch of river, including the 7-foot drop at Overlooked Falls, is a gem.

Miles and Directions

0.0 Pinkerton Trailhead.

1.0 Pinkerton Creek.

2.6 Lake Superior Trail junction.

2.7 Little Carp River Trail junction.

4.1 Little Carp River Trail crosses river.

5.5 Trappers Falls; Little Carp River Trail crosses river.

8.5 Cross Trail junction.

8.9 Greenstone Falls.

9.2 Spur trail to Little Carp River Road.

9.6 Little Carp River Road.

6 Mirror Lake Loop

Highlights: A loop through the wild core of the Porcupine Mountains, virgin forest, wilderness lakes, clear-running streams, and spectacular views

Location: Porcupine Mountains Wilderness State Park (PMWSP)

Type of hike: Loop

Distance: 12.4 miles

Difficulty: Difficult

Fees and permits: Michigan DNR Recreation Passport

Best months: May through October

Camping: PMWSP's Union Bay Campground, with 100 campsites, is 7 miles east of the trailhead. Backpack camping, within PMWSP regulations, is permitted along the trail.

Maps: USGS Carp River quad (inc.); PMWSP by Nequaket Natural History Associates (available at the visitor center)

Trail contact: PMWSP, (906) 885-5275

Finding the trailhead: From the intersection of M-107 and South Boundary Road in PMWSP, drive 7.5 miles west on M-107 to the North Mirror Lake Trailhead. GPS: 46.803651, -89.765140

The Hike

This hike begins at a famous viewpoint and then wanders through hemlock cathedrals to a wilderness lake. From that serene body of water, aptly named Mirror Lake, hikers are immersed in a memorable route through impressive old-growth forest. For a grand finale, the hike offers a ridge walk, with long sight lines stretching to Lake Superior.

Begin your hike at the far eastern end of the Lake of the Clouds Overlook parking area, at the Escarpment Trailhead. A short paved walkway leads directly from the parking area to the Escarpment Trail just short of the Lake of the Clouds Overlook. Turn left (east), onto the Escarpment Trail and follow this for about 0.3 mile to the intersection with the North Mirror Lake Trail. Go right (south) onto the North Mirror Lake Trail while the Escarpment Trail continues east. Follow the North Mirror Lake Trail as it descends, sometimes steeply, to the bridge over Lake of the Clouds' outlet, the Big Carp River, at Mile 0.7.

The trail then runs steadily south, first climbing slowly, then easing into a steep ascent. That steeper stretch, about a mile south of Lake of the Clouds, parallels a memorable scene: A small stream tumbles down a shady gorge set in a hemlock cathedral. Once past Lake of the Clouds, the rest of the route passes through virgin forest.

Continue hiking south as the path reaches the top of the slope and descends to a trail junction at Mile 3.0. Bear right (west) on the North Mirror Lake Trail as the Government Peak Trail goes left (east). The North Mirror Lake Trail runs southwest, crosses a marsh on a boardwalk, and reaches its namesake at Mile 4.0. The trail then skirts the shoreline, arriving at another junction at Mile 4.3. There, turn right

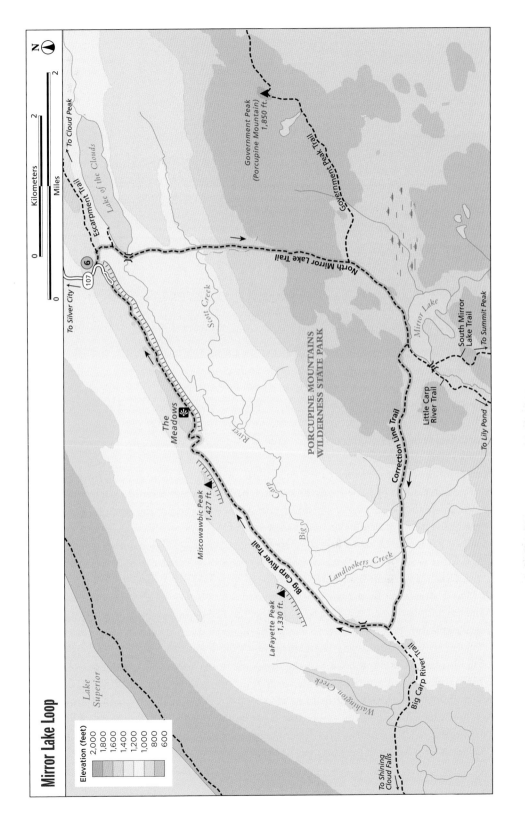

Mirror Lake Loop

Elevation (feet)
- 2,000
- 1,800
- 1,600
- 1,400
- 1,200
- 1,000
- 800
- 600

N

Kilometers
0   2

Miles
0   2

To Silver City

107
6

To Cloud Peak

Escarpment Trail

Lake of the Clouds

Lake Superior

North Mirror Lake Trail

Government Peak Trail

Government Peak
(Porcupine Mountain)
1,850 ft.

Scott Creek

The Meadows

Miscowawbic Peak
1,427 ft.

Big Carp River Trail

LaFayette Peak
1,330 ft.

Big Carp River

Washington Creek

Landlookers Creek

PORCUPINE MOUNTAINS
WILDERNESS STATE PARK

Correction Line Trail

Mirror Lake

South Mirror Lake Trail

To Summit Peak

Little Carp River Trail

To Lily Pond

Big Carp River Trail

To Shining Cloud Falls

The Mirror Lake loop's last miles offer spectacular views along the Escarpment across the Big Carp River valley.

(northwest) onto the Correction Line Trail as the North Mirror Lake Trail goes left (southwest).

Hike northwest as the trail ascends a short, steep slope before passing through a fern garden flanked by a rock wall. This stretch has a well-earned reputation for pleasing forest scenes. Sugar maple, basswood, and yellow birch add to the setting here, but it is a broad swath of hemlock, about a mile west of Mirror Lake, that stands out most clearly. That hemlock stand is old, open forest—elegant and enchanting. This, and other forest scenes in the Porkies, brings a revelation: The whole Northwoods once looked like this. It must have been magnificent.

The Correction Line Trail descends westward, crossing Landlookers Creek at Mile 6.5 and reaching a trail junction at Mile 7.3. There, turn right (north) onto the Big Carp River Trail and follow it across a bridge over its namesake stream.

Soon after that bridge the Big Carp River Trail begins to run along the bottom of the Escarpment's slope. Here too, the hemlock groves are hauntingly delightful. At Mile 9.8 the path offers a unique perspective of the Escarpment's cliffs—a view of Miscowawbic Peak's rock face from its base.

Now ascending, the path swings into a saddle east of Miscowawbic Peak, switchbacks up to the Escarpment, and arrives at a memorable open area known as "The Meadows" at Mile 10.5. For the next half mile, a parade of sweeping views passes to the right of the trail. Long sight lines stretch east to Lake of the Clouds and Cloud Peak beyond, while Lake Superior appears to the southwest, beyond Lafayette Peak's rise. With the hike rapidly winding down, this is a good place to take a break and enjoy the views.

Continue hiking eastward, reaching the Lake of the Clouds overlook and the Big Carp River Trailhead at Mile 12.3. The Big Carp River Trailhead is at the west end of the Lake of the Clouds overlook parking area. Walk 0.1 mile to the east end of the parking area to reach the hike's starting point, the North Mirror Lake Trailhead.

Option: One enticing alternative is to access The Meadows from the Big Carp River Trailhead at the west end of the Lake of the Clouds overlook parking area. Walk west 1.5 miles on the Big Carp River Trail to reach The Meadows. This option offers comparatively easy access to a notable place with outstanding views.

Miles and Directions

0.0 North Mirror Lake Trailhead.

0.3 Escarpment Trail junction.

0.7 Lake of the Clouds.

3.0 Government Peak Trail junction.

4.0 Mirror Lake.

4.3 Correction Line Trail junction.

6.5 Landlookers Creek.

7.3 Big Carp River Trail junction.

7.5 Big Carp River Bridge.

9.8 Miscowawbic Peak cliffs.

10.5 The Meadows.

12.3 Big Carp River Trailhead.

12.4 North Mirror Lake Trailhead.

7 Norwich Bluff

Highlights: Outstanding views from a beautiful escarpment and solitude
Location: Trap Hills, 14 miles south of Ontonagon
Type of hike: Out-and-back
Distance: 6.2 miles
Difficulty: Difficult*
Fees and permits: None, but consider a donation to the North Country Trail Association, www.northcountrytrail.org
Best months: May through October
Camping: Backpack camping along the trail is allowed within zero-impact guidelines. Blue diamond trail markers designate Forest Service land. Vertical blue blazes indicate private land where there is no camping (Whisky Hollow, and east for 3 miles). Bergland Township Park, 21 miles southwest of the trailhead, has 15 campsites.
Maps: USGS Oak Bluff, Matchwood NW quads; North Country Trail Map TMI13, Alberta to Cascade Falls
Trail contact: Ottawa National Forest, (906) 358-4724, www.fs.usda.gov/ottawa; North Country Trail Association website, www.north countrytrail.org/pwf

Finding the trailhead: From Ontonagon, drive 1.4 miles west on M-64 and turn left (south) onto Norwich Road. Drive 12.8 miles south on Norwich Road to the NCT trailhead. GPS: 46.681688, -89.389106
Special considerations: Use caution at the viewpoints; many are atop sheer cliffs. Note that clay and mud may make Victoria Road four-wheel drive only when wet. Don't presume that FR 642 is in a condition that would allow a vehicle to pass.

The Hike

Norwich Bluff offers knock-your-socks-off views—vistas that would make the short list for "best in the U.P." Stand on this bluff's southeast corner and the views to the south, east, and west are unencumbered by screening ridges and seem to stretch forever. Another vista, on the headland's western slope, offers views north to Lake Superior's deep blue waters and the Porcupine Mountains.

Odds are you'll have these views to yourself; soulful solitude seems to come with the territory here. Between the views and the peace and quiet, Norwich Bluff is an intriguing and complex crag and can be habit forming.

This route offers a 6-mile out-and-back tour of the major attractions on the south and west slopes. Those willing to use the trail as an access point for off-trail rambling will find an abundance of interesting side-trips available nearby. Rock ledges offer perfect viewpoints for sunrises and sunsets; shady glens and fern gardens tuck into the corners.

Begin your tour at the NCT trailhead on Norwich Road. Hike southeast and south on the NCT, steadily ascending wooded slopes. At Mile 1.3, the trail reaches the first viewpoint, a broad domelike rock sloping west. Lake Superior is visible to

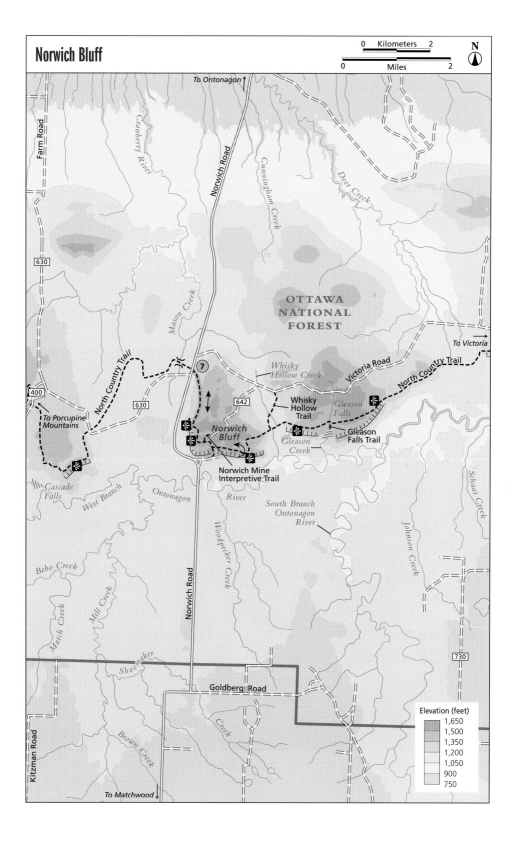

Norwich Bluff

0 Kilometers 2

0 Miles 2

N

Farm Road

Cranberry River

To Ontonagon↑

Norwich Road

Cunningham Creek

Deer Creek

630

OTTAWA NATIONAL FOREST

Mason Creek

North Country Trail

7

Whisky Hollow Creek

Victoria Road

To Victoria→

North Country Trail

400

630

642

Whisky Hollow Trail

Gleason Falls

To Porcupine Mountains

Norwich Bluff

Gleason Creek

Gleason Falls Trail

Norwich Mine Interpretive Trail

Cascade Falls

West Branch

Ontonagon

River

South Branch Ontonagon River

Schaat Creek

Johnson Creek

Bebo Creek

Woodpecker Creek

Mill Creek

Match Creek

Norwich Road

730

Shoemaker

Goldberg Road

Creek

Kitzman Road

Brown Creek

To Matchwood↓

Elevation (feet)
1,650
1,500
1,350
1,200
1,050
900
750

the north, and you can see the easternmost ridges of the Porcupine Mountains to the northwest. To the west the immense gray cliff known as the Hack Site is striking.

Resume hiking east and south, arriving at another viewpoint about a half-mile later. Views are similar to the last lookout, although a little more southerly in orientation. Lake Superior still shows to the north; long sight lines stretch southwest toward the Gogebic Range.

Now swinging eastward the trail traverses the bluff's southern slope, ducking in and out of ravines. At Mile 2.0 it arrives at an intersection with a spur trail (the Norwich Mine Interpretive Trail) that goes north to FR 642. Go straight (east), past the spur trail that goes left (north). The NCT continues eastward, dropping into a hollow where it follows a jeep track southward. Watch for the trail to turn left (east), crossing the drainage as the jeep track continues south.

Ascending steeply from the hollow, about a half-mile later the NCT reaches a stretch that boasts some of Norwich Bluff's most spectacular views. One hundred feet south of the trail, down a piney slope, a broad opening on the cliff tops offers sweeping views. Vistas here fill 180 degrees of the horizon. Far to the right (west) is

Flora and fauna taking advantage of sunny open areas along the trail

the cliffy Hack Site escarpment. Landmarks are harder to come by when you look south and east, but the rolling forestland stretches to the horizon, what seems to be an honest 50 miles. There's an airy feel and a sense of well-being to sitting here. The view from the southern slope appears to be endless forest, with hardly a manufactured item in sight. It's a great break spot and a natural turnaround point for the hike.

Options: Two options are worth considering. First, by walking farther east on the NCT, then taking the Whisky Hollow Trail north to Victoria Road, hikers can construct a 6.5-mile loop. Beginning at the southeastern slope viewpoint (designated Mile 0.0 for this discussion), follow the NCT as it swings north, crosses a hollow, and ascends a ridge. Rock outcrops offer views across Whisky Hollow to the eastern Trap Hills ridgeline.

As the trail descends into Whisky Hollow, watch for the intersection with the Whisky Hollow Trail at Mile 0.7. It is near the bottom of the steep part of the slope. I did not find a junction sign here, but white blazes lead north. Turn left (north) onto the Whisky Hollow Trail, as the NCT goes east. The Whisky Hollow Trail is half faint path, half marked route. Wear marks are thin, but I could always find the next blaze. The path runs north and east, crosses Whisky Hollow Creek, and reaches Victoria Road at Mile 1.6. Turn left (west) and walk Victoria Road (dirt) 1.5 miles to Norwich Road (paved). Turn left (south) and walk 0.3 mile to the NCT trailhead.

A second option is attractive and adds 4.6 miles to the round-trip hike. Instead of turning north on the Whisky Hollow Trail, continue walking east on the NCT 2.3 miles to Gleason Falls. Starting at the southeastern slope viewpoint (Mile 0.0 for this description), pass the junction with the Whisky Hollow Trail (Mile 0.7), walk east on the NCT, and cross Whisky Hollow Creek at Mile 0.9.

Continue hiking east on the NCT, ascending the slope east of Whisky Hollow. About a half mile east of the creek, the trail reaches a series of rock ledges that offer prime views south, as well as southwest to Norwich Bluff. Resume walking east, arriving at the junction with the Gleason Falls Trail at Mile 2.2. Turn right (south) on the Gleason Falls Trail, a narrow footpath along a ledge in Gleason Creek's gorge. The path reaches Gleason Falls, set in a beautiful mossy nook, at Mile 2.3. Return to the NCT Trailhead at Norwich Road to complete this 10.8-mile hike.

Miles and Directions

0.0 NCT Trailhead on Norwich Road.

1.3 Norwich Bluff's western slope viewpoint.

2.0 Junction with Norwich Mine Interpretive Trail.

3.1 Norwich Bluff's southeastern slope viewpoint; turnaround point.

6.2 NCT Trailhead on Norwich Road.

8 Norwich Bluff to Victoria

Highlights: Spectacular views, a remote stretch of the Trap Hills, Gleason Falls and gorge, and solitude
Location: Trap Hills, 14 miles south of Ontonagon
Type of hike: One-way shuttle
Distance: 12.7 miles
Difficulty: Difficult*
Fees and permits: None, but consider a donation to the North Country Trail Association, www .northcountrytrail.org
Best months: May through October
Camping: Backpack camping along the trail is allowed within zero-impact guidelines on Forest Service lands, where blue diamond trail markers are present. Vertical blue blazes indicate private land where there is no camping (Whisky Hollow and 3 miles east, Lookout Mountain area). Bergland Township Park, 21 miles southwest of the trailhead, has 15 campsites.
Maps: USGS Oak Bluff (inc.), Matchwood NW (inc.), Rockland quads (inc.); North Country Trail Map TMI13, Alberta to Cascade Falls
Trail contact: Ottawa National Forest, (906) 358-4724, www.fs.usda.gov/ottawa; North Country Trail Association website, www.north countrytrail.org/pwf

Finding the trailhead: From Ontonagon drive 1.4 miles west on M-64 and turn left (south) on Norwich Road. Drive 12.8 miles south on Norwich Road to the trailhead for the North Country Trail (NCT), which will be on your right (west) just before FR 630 (also on your right). Watch for NCT signs on either side of Norwich Road. GPS: 46.681688, -89.389106

Special considerations: Parts of the NCT have thin wear marks but viable trail marking. Use caution on the viewpoints, many of which are atop sheer cliffs. Hikers may want to budget some time to explore Old Victoria. This historic restored mining village is adjacent to the hike's end. Also note the presence of an NCT trail shelter at Old Victoria, 0.9 mile east of the end of the hike. That shelter's location makes it useful for pre- or post-hike stays. Don't presume that FR 642 is in a condition that would allow a vehicle to pass.

The Hike

This is an outstanding hike, and its list of attractions sounds like a hiker's wish list. Norwich Bluff's sweeping vistas would be on any Trap Hills "can't miss" list; the parade of viewpoints that follows is impressive.

Between the sun-splashed lookouts, a fine forest shades the trail, and clear-running streams tumble off the escarpment. Fern gardens carpet the woodland floor, grouse explode from the shadows, and mossy nooks and crannies invite exploration.

Begin at Norwich Road and hike southeast into the woods on the NCT as it steadily ascends Norwich Bluff's western slope. At Mile 1.3 the path reaches a broad domelike rock sloping west, the first viewpoint. Lake Superior shows to the north, and the broad ridges of the Porcupine Mountains can be seen to the northwest. A large gray rock face known as the Hack Site, a landmark of the western Trap Hills, is

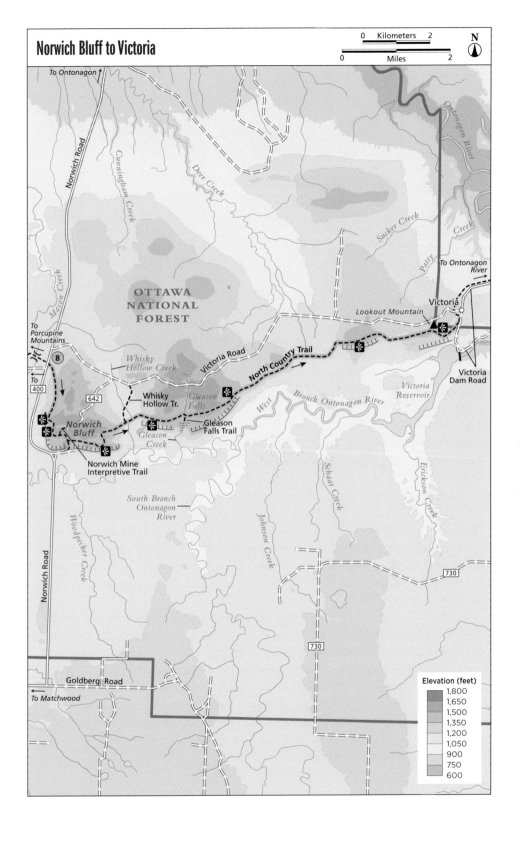

Norwich Bluff to Victoria

To Ontonagon↑

Norwich Road

Cunningham Creek

Deer Creek

Ontonagon River

Sucker Creek

Patty Creek

Mason Creek

OTTAWA
NATIONAL
FOREST

To Porcupine
Mountains

8

To 400

Whisky Hollow Creek

642

Victoria Road

North Country Trail

Lookout Mountain

Victoria

To Ontonagon River

Whisky Hollow Tr.

Gleason Falls

Gleason Falls Trail

Victoria Dam Road

West Branch Ontonagon River

Victoria Reservoir

Norwich Bluff

Gleason Creek

Norwich Mine Interpretive Trail

Woodpecker Creek

South Branch Ontonagon River

Johnson Creek

Schaat Creek

Erickson Creek

730

730

Norwich Road

Goldberg Road

To Matchwood

Elevation (feet)

1,800
1,650
1,500
1,350
1,200
1,050
900
750
600

Although it's always exciting to spot large mammals, there are also many beautiful species of insects, reptiles, and amphibians.

visible off to the west. Hike another half-mile or so south, and another rock dome offers views that are similar but a little more southerly in orientation.

Soon the trail swings east, crossing Norwich Bluff's convoluted southern slope. Go straight (east) at Mile 2.0, past the spur trail that goes left (north) to FR 642. Soon the NCT drops into a hollow and runs south a bit on a jeep road. Watch for the NCT to turn left (east) off that jeep track, climb out of that hollow, and arrive at a corner of the headland that holds spectacular views at Mile 3.1. One hundred feet south of the trail, down a piney slope, a wide opening in the cliff tops offers sweeping views. Unencumbered by screening ridges the views stretch 50 miles or so, with oceans of trees leading to the horizon.

When you are ready resume hiking east on the NCT, which soon swings north and drops to a junction with the Whisky Hollow Trail at Mile 3.8. When I saw this intersection, it was unmarked. Go straight (east) as the Whisky Hollow Trail goes left (north). The NCT then arrives at the hollow's namesake creek at Mile 4.0.

Ascending from Whisky Hollow, the trail reaches a poetic stretch a half-mile later. Spacious ledges on a cliff top offer uncluttered views south and west to Norwich Bluff. As the trail continues to ascend, the vistas continue and improve with height. Peek-a-boo views continue as the trail runs east to Gleason Creek and a junction with the Gleason Falls Trail at Mile 5.5.

Turn right (south) onto the narrow Gleason Falls Trail and follow a ledge on the sidewall of Gleason Creek's steep little gorge to Gleason Falls (Mile 5.6). The 20-foot waterfall has a minimal flow except in wet spells, but the setting, a mossy cleft, is well worthwhile. Retrace your steps to the NCT at Mile 5.7 and turn right (east).

Running steadily eastward the NCT ascends a ridge that reaches an open rock dome, offering a 180-degree view at about Mile 6.7. The trail then descends eastward, crosses several small drainages, and skirts another rock dome on talus slopes at Mile 8.8.

East of the talus slopes, the NCT crosses a mile-long stretch that is relatively flat. The mellow topography ends abruptly when the path takes a steep route to the top of the ridge marked "Point 1,490T" on topographic maps (Mile 10.1). Extensive views and long sight lines open to the south, and the Trap Hills ridgeline leads west.

Now descending, the trail drops into a gap in the ridgeline before ascending to the west end of the ridge that includes the viewpoint known as Lookout Mountain. The NCT reaches that landmark vista at Mile 12.3, a good time and place to savor the views before the hike ends. Below, Victoria Reservoir's blue waters nest in forested green hills. To finish the hike follow the NCT northeast, descending 0.4 mile to Victoria Dam Road at Mile 12.7.

Miles and Directions

0.0 Trailhead at Norwich Road.
1.3 Norwich Bluff's western slope viewpoint.
2.0 Junction with Norwich Mine Interpretive Trail.
3.1 Norwich Bluff's southeastern slope viewpoint.
3.8 Junction with Whisky Hollow Trail.
4.0 Whisky Hollow Creek.
5.5 Junction with Gleason Falls Trail.
5.6 Gleason Falls.
5.7 Junction with Gleason Falls Trail.
6.7 Ridge east of Gleason Creek, viewpoint.
8.8 Talus slopes.
10.1 Summit (1,490 feet), viewpoint looking south.
12.3 Lookout Mountain.
12.7 Victoria Dam Road.

9 Presque Isle River Waterfalls Loop

Highlights: A splendid and famous collection of waterfalls
Location: Porcupine Mountains Wilderness State Park (PMWSP)
Type of hike: Loop
Distance: 2.3 miles
Difficulty: Moderate
Fees and permits: Michigan DNR Recreation Passport

Best months: May through October
Camping: Presque Isle Campground just west of the trailhead has 50 campsites.
Maps: USGS Tiebel Creek quad; PMWSP map by Nequaket Natural History Associates (available at the visitor center)
Trail contact: PMWSP, (906) 885-5275

Finding the trailhead: From the intersection of M-107 and South Boundary Road, in PMWSP, drive south and west 24.1 miles on South Boundary Road. Turn right (north) on Gogebic CR 519 and drive 0.9 mile to the trailhead at the Falls picnic area. Alternatively, from the junction of M-28 and Ontonagon CR 519, just east of Wakefield, drive north 16.5 miles on CR 519 to the trailhead. GPS: 46.707150, -89.974362

Special considerations: During high water the river channel at Mile 0.3 of the hike is impassable and not the dry bedrock described here. Both sides of the river can still be accessed by crossing at South Boundary Road. Parts of these trails are eroded and rough and have an abundance of exposed roots. Use caution on wet rocks near the river and waterfalls. The waterfalls and river currents are dangerous. Boardwalk sections of the trail are there to protect wet areas and ensure hiker safety. Stay on the boardwalk to prevent erosion scars in this picturesque area.

The Hike

Three thundering waterfalls, tucked into a stretch of river just over a half-mile long, put on a memorable show here. A parade of cascades and swirling rapids adds to the setting, while striking old-growth hemlock, virgin white pine, and white cedar line the riverbank. All three falls take their names from Native American spirit warriors.

Begin your tour from the east end of the picnic area parking lot, following a broad trail east fifty paces to a fork. There turn left (northeast), follow the sign that says "Foot Bridge to Island" and walk 170 paces north to the top of a set of wooden stairs.

Descend the stairs to the suspension bridge. Continue descending, going straight (east) as the West River Trail enters on a raised boardwalk from the right (south), halfway down the stairs.

Walk eastward across the bridge (Mile 0.1), pausing to enjoy the unfolding river scene below. Upstream a roaring cascade feeds the swift water below the bridge; downstream, russet river water meets the blue lake. A series of striking potholes mark the bedrock beside the current, half-circles scoured by river gravel churning in powerful eddies.

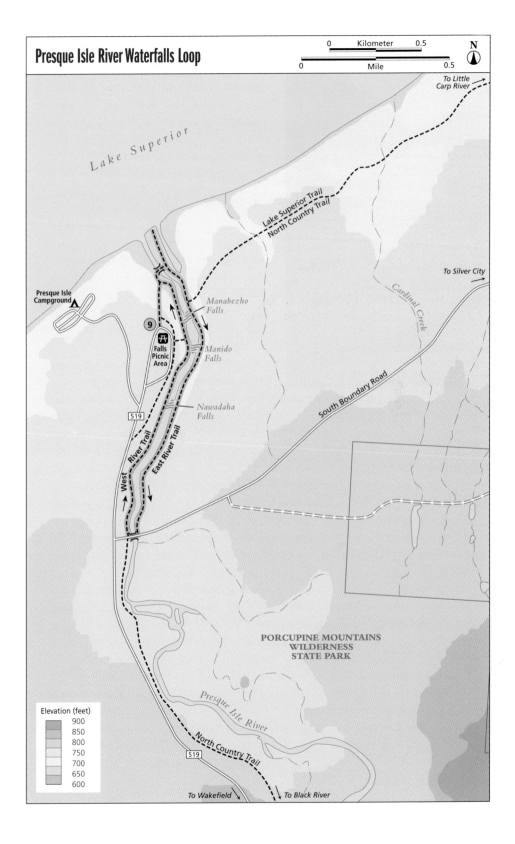

Presque Isle River Waterfalls Loop

Kilometer
0   0.5

Mile
0   0.5

N

Lake Superior

To Little
Carp River

Lake Superior Trail
North Country Trail

To Silver City

Cardinal Creek

Presque Isle
Campground

Manabezho
Falls

9

Falls
Picnic
Area

Manido
Falls

South Boundary Road

519

Nawadaha
Falls

West River Trail

East River Trail

PORCUPINE MOUNTAINS
WILDERNESS
STATE PARK

Presque Isle River

North Country Trail

519

Elevation (feet)
900
850
800
750
700
650
600

To Wakefield   To Black River

Patterned bedrock above Manido Falls, with Nawadaha Falls in the far distance

Once on the island the official East River Trail swings right (south). I'd suggest a short side-trip to explore the island. Walk straight east, less than 100 yards through open forest, and you'll come to a lagoon—the east channel of the river when flows are high. Turn left (north) and follow the lagoon's shore north a short distance to the Lake Superior shoreline (Mile 0.2), a contemplative spot.

When you are ready, retrace your steps, picking up the official trail at the bridge's east end and walk south. At the southern end of the island is scalloped bedrock, the overflow channel's dry waterfall. Just to the west is the rowdy cascade viewed earlier from the suspension bridge.

Hike southeast, crossing the bedrock channel. During high water, this segment is impassable. Do not attempt crossing here when the waterfall is flowing over the bedrock. Continue walking southeastward, following a marked path into the woods, then steeply up a bluff to a trail junction (Mile 0.4). Turn right (south) on the East River Trail, as the Lake Superior Trail goes left (east). Walk south on the wide path, through beautiful old-growth forest, descending the bluff to Manabezho Falls (Mile 0.6).

Manabezho Falls, a booming 22-foot drop, is a knockout. When the river is running low, whitewater leaps over the sharp ledge of bedrock in individual segments across its length. The repeated contrast of dark stone and bright water is dramatic in its own right.

Continue hiking south on the East River Trail (also blazed for the North Country Trail here), reaching Manido Falls at Mile 0.7. Manido Falls, a thumping ledge drop about 8 feet high, spills into a deep pool flanked by broad aprons of bedrock. Although not the tallest or most dramatic of waterfalls, the complex patterns created in the bedrock by constant scouring are fascinating, and definitely worth a visit.

Resume hiking south on the East River Trail, reaching Nawadaha Falls at Mile 0.9. Nawadaha Falls, another 8-foot drop, funnels the river's flow into the near bank, creating a sparkling whitewater show.

From Nawadaha Falls, hike south on the East River Trail, past a steady stream of cascades and swift water to South Boundary Road (Mile 1.3). Turn right (west), crossing the Presque Isle River on the South Boundary Road bridge. Once on the west side of the river, turn right (north) onto the West River Trail.

Hike north on the West River Trail (also marked for the North Country Trail), viewing a mirror image of the sights seen from the West River Trail. A series of steps and walkways lead north past viewpoints at the three waterfalls, then intersect the steps that descend to the suspension bridge that you crossed at the beginning of the hike. There, turn left (west), ascend the stairs, and retrace your earlier steps to the trailhead at the Falls picnic area.

Miles and Directions

0.0 Trailhead at picnic area.

0.1 Suspension bridge.

0.2 Lake Superior shore.

0.4 Lake Superior Trail junction.

0.6 Manabezho Falls.

0.7 Manido Falls.

0.9 Nawadaha Falls.

1.3 South Boundary Road bridge.

1.8 Nawadaha Falls.

2.0 Manido Falls.

2.1 Manabezho Falls.

2.3 Trailhead at picnic area.

10 Shining Cloud Falls

Highlights: Shining Cloud Falls—often mentioned as the best waterfall in the park's interior—plus countless cascades of the Big Carp River, Lake Superior shore, and virgin forest throughout
Location: Porcupine Mountains Wilderness State Park (PMWSP)
Type of hike: Out-and-back
Distance: 10.8 miles
Difficulty: Difficult

Fees and permits: Michigan DNR Recreation Passport
Best months: May through October
Camping: Backcountry camping is available along the trail, within PMWSP regulations. Presque Isle Campground, 5 miles west of the Pinkerton Trailhead, has 50 campsites.
Maps: USGS Tiebel Creek, Carp River quads; PMWSP map by Nequaket Natural History Associates (available at the visitor center)
Trail contact: PMWSP, (906) 885-5275

Finding the trailhead: From the intersection with M-107, drive south and west 19.7 miles on South Boundary Road, in PMWSP, to the Pinkerton Trailhead. GPS: 46.725159, -89.899254
Special considerations: Use reasonable caution on wet rocks near the river and waterfall.

The Hike

Shining Cloud Falls is a bit of a backcountry icon, and rightly so. This waterfall is remote, about as far from a road as you can get in the Porkies, or even for that matter, in the whole U.P. It is not a gimme. It is not one of those waterfalls you can drive up to, or walk a quarter-mile-long manicured path to reach. That said, I think there is much more than sweat equity that elevates the Shining Cloud experience. The waterfall itself is striking, but it is only one part of a remarkable outing, a sojourn with the essence of the Porkies, its wild core.

What follows is a description of one way to hike to Shining Cloud Falls. Besides being the easiest and shortest route, it is arguably the most beautiful. This hike skirts the Lake Superior shore, ascends along the cascades of the Big Carp River, and consistently wanders through virgin forest.

Begin your hike to Shining Cloud Falls by walking north on the broad, shady Pinkerton Trail. Narrow boardwalks bridge a few damp spots. A bridged crossing over the gentle riffles of Pinkerton Creek marks Mile 1.0.

About 1 mile later, after threading through memorable hemlock groves, the path reaches a bench on a bluff high above the swirling cascades of the Little Carp River. Swinging northward, the trail reaches a junction with the Lake Superior Trail at Mile 2.6. Turn right (east), following the Lake Superior Trail across the bridge over the Little Carp River, reaching the junction with the Little Carp River Trail just 0.1 mile later.

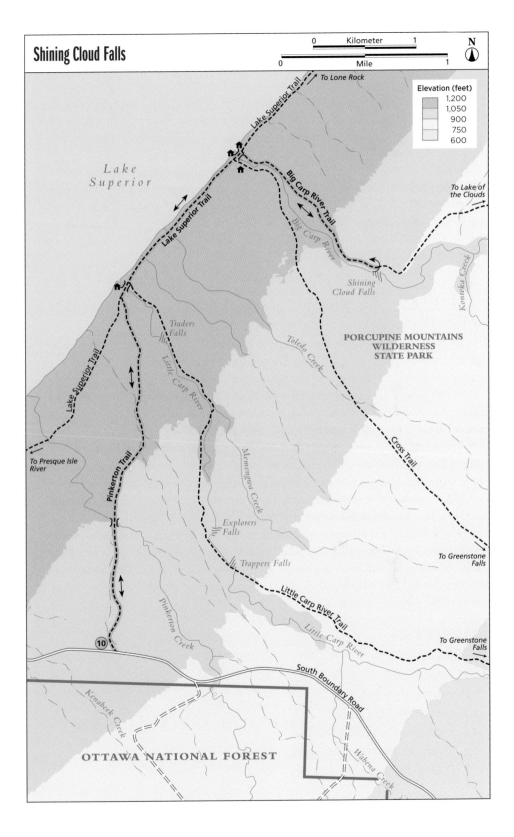

Shining Cloud Falls

Elevation (feet)
- 1,200
- 1,050
- 900
- 750
- 600

To Lone Rock

Lake Superior

Lake Superior Trail

Big Carp River Trail

Big Carp River

To Lake of the Clouds

Shining Cloud Falls

Konteka Creek

Lake Superior Trail

Traders Falls

Little Carp River

Toledo Creek

PORCUPINE MOUNTAINS WILDERNESS STATE PARK

To Presque Isle River

Pinkerton Trail

Memengwa Creek

Cross Trail

Explorers Falls

Trappers Falls

To Greenstone Falls

Little Carp River Trail

Little Carp River

To Greenstone Falls

Pinkerton Creek

10

South Boundary Road

Kenahcek Creek

Wabena Creek

OTTAWA NATIONAL FOREST

Turn left (northwest) on the Lake Superior Trail, as the Little Carp River Trail goes right (south). Follow the Lake Superior Trail northwest 0.2 mile to the mouth of the Little Carp River. Here the trail swings right and begins a run to the northeast. It travels through open woods, typically 100 feet or so inland from Lake Superior, to the mouth of the Big Carp River. An appealing alternative route is a stone's throw north of the trail—the shoreline of our planet's largest freshwater lake (by surface area at least—Lake Baikal in Siberia has the largest volume).

Whether you walk the trail or opt to hike the shoreline, you will reach the mouth of the Big Carp River at Mile 4.0. Just before the bridge a junction marks the departure of the Cross Trail to the right (south). Ignore the Cross Trail and walk northeast across the bridge over the Big Carp River. The trail then swings to the right (east), switchbacks up a bluff, and reaches a junction. Turn right (east) on the Big Carp River Trail as the Lake Superior Trail goes left (north).

About a quarter of a mile later, the trail descends to river level. Robert Sprague and Michael Rafferty, authors of *Porcupine Mountains Companion*, describe a dozen notable cascades and waterfalls in the river's next mile. This stretch of river is liquid poetry, and you should consider budgeting some time to spend here.

One and one-quarter miles from the river's mouth, the path ascends another bluff, and the sound of a large waterfall drifts through the woods. At Mile 5.4 the trail reaches a viewpoint beside a huge standing snag overlooking Shining Cloud Falls and its gorge.

Shining Cloud is a bi-level fall. First the flow drops 10 feet to a ledge, then splits evenly and tumbles another 12 feet to a pool below. In its second drop, the left side cascades down a rock ramp, while the right side is more of a vertical fall.

It is possible to descend to the falls' base safely, but it requires some judgment and balance. First continue east on the trail until you are above the top of the falls. The first routes that appear below you are dangerous. A little farther on you will notice steep switchbacks, dirt paths descending to the top of the falls. When the river is at moderate flow levels, a dry rock ramp leads to the bottom of the falls. Whether that rock ramp is a safe move on any given day is a judgment you will have to make when you are there.

Option: A 6.5-mile round-trip hike to the mouth of the Little Carp River, from the Pinkerton Trailhead, has considerable appeal. That shorter outing features the forest scenes along the Pinkerton Trail, the charming cascades of the Little Carp River, and the Lake Superior shore.

Miles and Directions

0.0 Pinkerton Trailhead.

1.0 Pinkerton Creek.

2.6 Lake Superior Trail junction.

2.7 Little Carp River Trail junction.

4.0 Big Carp River Trail junction.

5.4 Shining Cloud Falls; turnaround point.

10.8 Pinkerton Trailhead.

11 Trap Hills Loop

Highlights: Spectacular views, solitude, and a quiet forest setting in the wild heart of the Trap Hills

Location: 4 miles north of Bergland

Type of hike: Loop

Distance: 6.1 miles

Difficulty: Difficult*

Fees and permits: None, but consider a contribution to the North Country Trail Association, www.northcountrytrail.org

Best months: May through October

Camping: Backpack camping along the trail, within zero-impact guidelines. Bergland Township Park, 4 miles south of the trailhead, has 15 campsites.

Maps: USGS Bergland NE quad (inc.); North Country Trail Map TMI14; Cascade Falls to Ironwood

Trail contact: Ottawa National Forest, (906) 358-4724, www.fs.usda.gov/ottawa; North Country Trail Association website, www.north countrytrail.org/pwf

Finding the trailhead: From the town of Bergland, drive north 2.0 miles on M-64 and turn right (east) on old M-64 (gravel). Drive east and north 3.9 miles on old M-64. There, turn right (east) on FR 326 and drive 0.7 mile to the North Country Trail (NCT). About 100 yards west of the NCT crossing, a wide shoulder offers parking. GPS: 46.664719, -89.545033

Special considerations: Note that the spur trail from FR 326 to the Hack Site is a path that has thin wear marks but viable trail marking (vertical white paint blazes). A few spots on the NCT are similar. This loop includes a mile of road walking on FR 326, a quiet forest lane. Use caution on the viewpoints, many of which are atop sheer cliffs.

The Hike

I was stunned when I first saw the Trap Hills. Huge, mesmerizing views; a beautiful older forest; and soul-satisfying solitude mile after mile. Part of the attraction was the long views—oceans of trees, forest stretching 50 miles or so to the far-off horizon. Better yet was the sheer mystery of the place, the feeling that, in the Trap Hills, exploration would reap rich rewards. The open, older forest invited rambling, and I kept finding new overlooks with memorable views—high-rock balconies where the lichen didn't show a single scuff mark from boots. Forest glens, chock-full of subtle ambience, were tucked into the hollows.

This hike offers a convincing sample of the Trap Hills' charms in a bite-size loop. Energetic hikers looking for a few more miles can venture east on the NCT (see options). Or you may want to sample a classic Trap Hills pastime—looking for new viewpoints. Typically the trail runs a stone's throw "inland," usually north, of the bluff's edge. While walking the trail scan for openings in the forest canopy in the direction of the bluff's rim and investigate.

Begin your outing where the NCT crosses FR 326. Walk southeast, uphill, on the NCT, a narrow but defined footpath entering the woods. Steadily climbing, the path passes a curious reddish boulder before approaching the top of a knoll. A rock

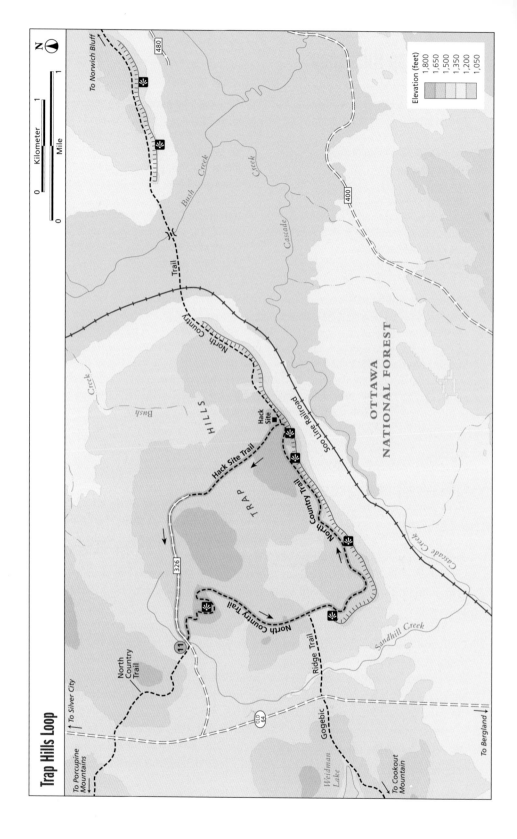

Trap Hills Loop

Elevation (feet)
1,800
1,650
1,500
1,350
1,200
1,050

N

Kilometer
0   1
Mile
0   1

To Norwich Bluff

480

Bush Creek

Cascade Creek

400

OTTAWA
NATIONAL FOREST

Bush Creek

TRAP HILLS

Hack Site

Hack Site Trail

North Country Trail

Soo Line Railroad

North Country Trail

Cascade Creek

326

11

North Country Trail

North Country Trail

Ridge Trail

Gogebic

OLD
64

Sandhill Creek

Weidman Lake

To Silver City

To Porcupine Mountains

To Cookout Mountain

To Bergland

outcrop offers northwest views—the Bergland fire tower 2 miles off and broad ridges of the Porcupine Mountains beyond.

Descending the knoll's east side, the NCT swings southward. First it crosses a small valley, then a low ridge, and finally drops to an intersection with the Gogebic Ridge Trail at Mile 1.6. Bear left (south) on the NCT as the Gogebic Ridge Trail goes right (west).

Continue on the NCT, first rock hopping a small creek and then ascending steeply through an older maple forest. At the top of that hill, watch for a rock outcrop about 15 feet to the right (northwest) of the trail. That ledge offers a worthwhile view to the northwest.

Heading southeast, the NCT nears the southern corner of the Trap Hills' high plateau, swings northeast, and begins a miles-long run in that direction. About a half-mile later, the trail nears the bluff's edge, and an open slope below the trail, partially screened by stunted trees, offers expansive views.

Continue hiking northeast on the NCT as it dips to a saddle and then ascends in a southerly direction. Topping out, the trail passes over grassy bedrock near a south-facing corner of a knoll, and a faint spur trail leads southwest thirty paces. There, a rock outcrop offers long views to the southwest, where a corner of Lake Gogebic peeks out from what seems to be an endless scene of undulating ridge and forest.

Resume walking northeast on the NCT. About a quarter-mile later the path again nears the edge of the bluff. A faint spur trail leads south and downhill 50 feet to striking views. A ledge-top opening here, roughly 80 feet wide and clear of trees, offers sweeping vistas southeast, south, and southwest. These are stunning views. However, a little less than a half-mile farther east are vistas that rival these. Walk east, passing over the top of the knoll marked 1,772 on maps (the highest point on this headland). As the trail nears the 4.1-mile point, it comes near the bluff's edge. For the first and only time on this hike a narrow opening allows you to stand on the trail and see the views without any partial obstruction from trees. Explore the viewpoint, enjoy the huge views, but also make a note of this spot.

As you resume hiking northeastward, count your paces. One hundred sixty-five paces later, at a point where the NCT swings north, is a trail junction (Mile 4.1). Turn sharply left (northwest) on a narrow path known as the Hack Site Trail, marked by white blazes, as the NCT goes right (north). "Hack Site" refers to the release of peregrine falcon chicks on the cliff top nearby. "Hacking" places young falcon chicks on an artificial structure on the top of a cliff that would be a suitable habitat. Human attendants feed them until they are old enough to fly and hunt for themselves. Check the website of the NCT Association (www.northcountrytrail.org/pwf) to see pictures of the hack box that was previously here. Whether or not the falcons interest you, those pictures serve as a superb preview of this hike and its views.

Peregrine falcons are flying stun guns. They knock out their prey with a light-ninglike dive, reaching well above 100 miles per hour in their attack.

Follow the Hack Site Trail north 0.9 mile, through pleasant forest, to FR 326 (Mile 5.0). Then walk north and west, 1.1 downhill miles on FR 326, to the NCT Trailhead (Mile 6.1).

Options: Hiking east on the NCT is an attractive addition. From the junction of the NCT and the Hack Site Trail (listed as Mile 0.0 for this description) walk east on the NCT, at first somewhat near the bluff's edge then further "inland," north. The forest is fine, and the trail leads in a long descent to the Soo Line Railroad tracks at Mile 1.5. Walk east across the tracks and the Bush Creek trail bridge at Mile 1.9. Continue to follow the trail eastward, slowly ascending on an overgrown lane before the trail once again becomes a path and ascends steeply east.

Another escarpment, not as high as the Hack Site cliffs but with a strategic location that makes it well worth exploring, is now south of the NCT. Scan the woods south of the trail for a domelike rock wall, a little less than 1 mile east of Bush Creek. A little scouting will reveal safe routes to scramble to the top of the rock, a location I call "Domeland" (Mile 2.8). This is an extensive mosaic of bedrock slabs and vegetation. Views west show the immense grayness of the Hack Site crag across the Bush Creek valley. Lake Superior's sparkling blue water and the forested ridges of the Porkies are visible to the northwest. When you're ready, retrace your steps to the Hack Site Trail.

One other option is well worth mentioning: a hike from FR 326 east along the NCT to FR 400, a total of 9.3 miles.

Miles and Directions

0.0 NCT Trailhead on FR 326.

1.6 Gogebic Ridge Trail junction.

4.1 Hack Site Trail junction.

5.0 FR 326.

6.1 NCT Trailhead on FR 326.

12 Trap Hills Traverse

Highlights: Spectacular views from a parade of viewpoints, quiet forest, and solitude
Location: Trap Hills, 4 miles north of Bergland
Type of hike: One-way shuttle backpack
Distance: 28.3 miles
Difficulty: Difficult*
Fees and permits: None, but consider a donation to the North Country Trail Association, www.northcountrytrail.org
Best months: May through October
Camping: Backpack camping is allowed along the trail, within zero-impact guidelines, on Forest Service land where blue markers are present. Vertical paint blazes indicate private land, where there is no camping (Whisky Hollow and 3 miles east, Lookout Mountain). Bergland Township Park, 5 miles south of the trailhead, has 15 campsites.
Maps: USGS Bergland NE (inc.), Matchwood NW (inc.), Oak Bluff (inc.), Rockland (inc.) quads; North Country Trail Maps TMI14, Cascade Falls to Ironwood, and TMI13, Alberta to Cascade Falls
Trail contact: Ottawa National Forest, (906) 358-4724, www.fs.usda.gov/ottawa; North Country Trail Association website, www.north countrytrail.org/pwf

Finding the trailhead: From the town of Bergland, drive north 2.0 miles on M-64 and turn right (east) on Old M-64 (gravel). Drive 2.9 miles east and north on Old M-64 to the Gogebic Ridge Trail trailhead. GPS: 46.650865, -89.552152

Special considerations: Parts of the North Country Trail (NCT) have thin wear marks but viable trail marking. Use caution on the viewpoints, many of which are atop sheer cliffs. Hikers may want to budget some time to explore Old Victoria. This restored historic mining village is adjacent to the hike's end. Also note the presence of an NCT trail shelter at Old Victoria, 0.9 trail mile east of the end of the hike. That shelter's location makes it useful for pre- or post-hike stays.

The Hike

Among all the attractions of this route, and there are many, one thing stands out in my memory of this trip—broad views. A string of rock outcrops offer sweeping vistas of what seem to be endless forest. Better yet are the sight lines along the ridgeline route, where I could spot a far-off cliff from which I'd enjoyed the sunrise the day before—or look farther east to where I would be the next morning. Sleeping on those high-rock balconies, watching the morning and evening light touch far-off ridges, was the icing on the cake.

Of course you do have to walk between the viewpoints, but that part of the route is hardly disappointing. Much of the Trap Hills forest is older second growth and a pleasure to the eye. Small streams cut mossy clefts in the escarpment. The trail passes dozens of rocky nooks that beg to be explored, and solitude is there for the taking.

The bottom line for backpackers is this: If you are looking for an energetic, adventurous, and highly rewarding 3-day outing, take a long look at this one. Three days would be reasonable, but more would be better if you enjoy exploring along the way.

Trap Hills Traverse; Norwich Bluff; Norwich Bluff to Victoria

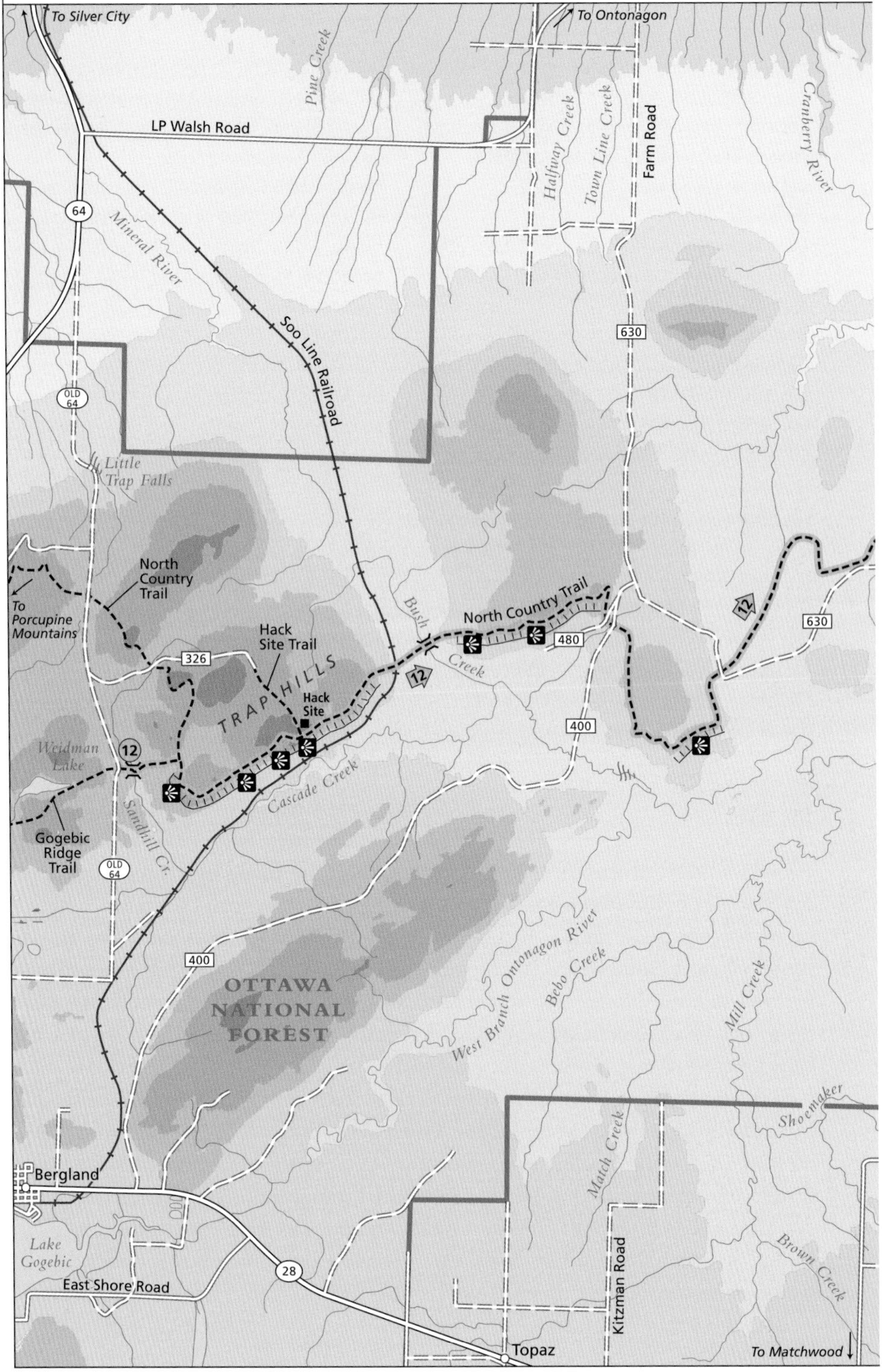

To Silver City

To Ontonagon

Pine Creek

LP Walsh Road

Halfway Creek

Town Line Creek

Farm Road

Cranberry River

64

Mineral River

Soo Line Railroad

630

OLD 64

Little Trap Falls

North Country Trail

To Porcupine Mountains

Bush Creek

North Country Trail

12

630

326

Hack Site Trail

TRAP HILLS

Hack Site

480

12

400

Weidman Lake

12

Gogebic Ridge Trail

OLD 64

Sandhill Cr.

Cascade Creek

400

OTTAWA NATIONAL FOREST

West Branch Ontonagon River

Bebo Creek

Mill Creek

Shoemaker

Bergland

Match Creek

Lake Gogebic

Kitzman Road

Brown Creek

East Shore Road

28

Topaz

To Matchwood

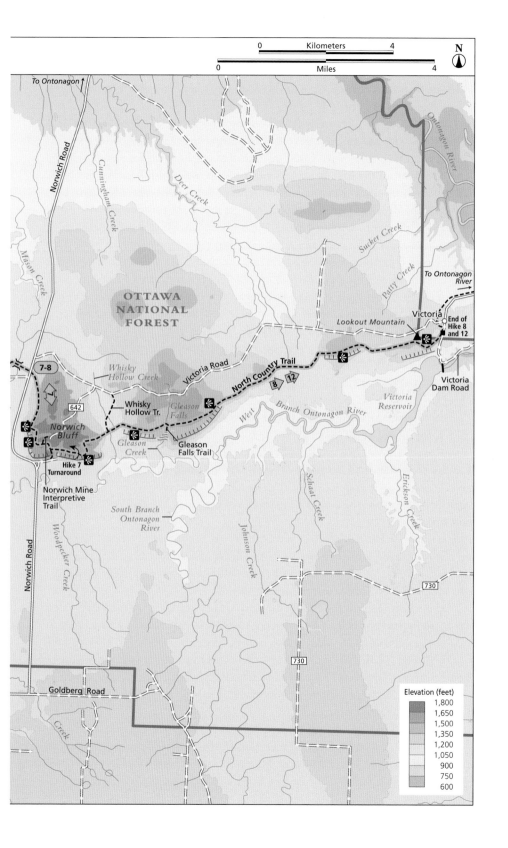

Two days would be a bit of a rushed trip, with little time to enjoy the sights. Note that Hikes 7 and 8 in this book cover some of the same ground as this one, so if you're looking for a shorter version of this hike, take a look at either Norwich Bluff or Norwich Bluff to Victoria.

Begin by hiking east from Old M-64 on the Gogebic Ridge Trail and follow it to its junction with the NCT at Mile 0.8. Turn right (east) and follow the NCT as it ascends through a fine maple forest. As the climb ends watch for a rock outcrop 15 feet northwest of the trail that offers views to the northwest. Typically the NCT runs a stone's throw away from the bluff's edge, but sharp-eyed hikers will have little trouble spotting the openings in the forest canopy that mark the viewpoints.

The NCT then runs southeast, passes the southern corner of the Trap Hills' high plateau, and begins a miles-long run northeast. About a half-mile later, an open slope below the trail offers long views south, before the path dips to a saddle. East of that saddle the path ascends steadily, reaching notable views a little over a half-mile later, where a faint spur trail leads 50 feet south, down the slope to a broad open cliff top. A ledge top opening here, roughly 80 feet wide and clear of trees, offers sweeping vistas southeast, south, and southwest. These are stunning views. However, a little less than half of a mile farther east are vistas that rival these. Walk east, passing over the top of the knoll marked 1,772 on maps (the highest point on this headland). As the trail nears the 4.1-mile point, it comes near the bluff's edge. For the first and only time on this hike, a narrow opening allows you to stand on the trail and see the views without any partial obstruction from trees. Explore the viewpoint and enjoy the huge views, but also make a note of this spot.

On a good day you may notice a headland with a sharp south face, 6 miles due east as the crow flies. That headland is Norwich Bluff, and after you have followed the NCT east for 14 trail miles you will be standing on that spot. When you do reach Norwich Bluff, look to the west. The gray crag of the Hack Site cliff, where you are now, is striking.

Return to the NCT. Hike 165 paces east to an unmarked junction (Mile 3.3) with a white-blazed trail running north a mile to the end of FR 326. This trail, known as the Hack Site Trail, refers to the release of young peregrine falcons on the nearby cliff, a process known as "hacking."

Continue northeast on the NCT as it turns a tad "inland" from the bluff's edge, crosses a saddle, and eases into a long descent to the Soo Line Railroad tracks at Mile 4.8. Cross the railroad tracks and a bridge over Bush Creek at Mile 5.1. About a mile east of the bridge, the trail ascends sharply and begins to parallel a series of rock slabs and domes south of the trail. That swath of bedrock is well worth exploring and offers views west across Bush Creek to the Hack Site cliffs, as well as north to Lake Superior and the Porcupine Mountains.

After enjoying the views continue walking east. Soon a rock ledge along the trail offers views south and west. The trail then runs northeast a bit before turning south then southeast and crossing FR 480 at Mile 8.5, and FR 400 at Mile 8.6. Follow the trail east and south. After swinging east, the trail runs along the crest of a "whaleback" stretch of bedrock, offering long views south as well as east to Norwich Bluff and beyond. Descending off that rock ridge, the NCT turns north and crosses FR 630 at Mile 12.0.

Walk east from FR 630, entering a flat gap in the ridgeline. The trail turns north for a bit and winds its way east to the marshy headwaters of Mason Creek and shortly thereafter to Norwich Road at Mile 15.7.

Norwich Road, paved but remarkably quiet, marks the trail's approach to an escarpment that offers some of the best views in the Trap Hills—Norwich Bluff. Hike southeast, following the NCT as it steadily ascends that bluff's western slopes. Two rock slabs near its southwestern corner offer views north to Lake Superior and the Porcupine Mountains, as well as west to the Hack Site.

Seeing the backwoods in moonlight is just one of many reasons to hike the longer trails.

Follow the NCT as it turns east to cross Norwich Bluff's convoluted south face, reaching a junction at Mile 17.7. Go straight (east) as a spur trail goes left (north) to FR 642, as the trail dips into a hollow and arrives at a corner of the headland that boasts spectacular views at about Mile 18.9. One hundred feet south of the trail, down a piney slope, a broad opening from the top of the cliff offers sweeping views. Unencumbered by screening ridges, the views stretch 50 miles or so.

Moving on, follow the NCT as it swings north and drops to a junction, unmarked when I saw it, with the Whisky Hollow Trail at Mile 19.9. Go straight (east), past the Whisky Hollow Trail, which goes left (north). Next the NCT quickly passes Whisky Hollow Creek and ascends to a series of bedrock ledges that offer broad views south and west to Norwich Bluff.

Following a ridge east the trail arrives at a junction with the Gleason Falls Trail at Mile 21.2. Turn right (south) onto the narrow Gleason Falls Trail and follow a ledge on the sidewall of Gleason Creek's steep little gorge to Gleason Falls (Mile 21.3). The 20-foot waterfall has a minimal flow except in wet spells, but the setting, a mossy cleft, is well worthwhile. Retrace your steps to the NCT at Mile 21.4 and turn right (east).

Running steadily eastward the NCT ascends a ridge, reaching a broad rock dome that offers a 180-degree view at about Mile 22.6. The trail then descends eastward, crosses several small drainages, and skirts a rock dome on talus slopes at Mile 24.2.

East of the talus slopes, the NCT crosses a mile-long stretch that is relatively flat. The mellow topography ends abruptly when the path takes a steep route to the top of the ridge marked point 1,490t on topographic maps (Mile 25.9). Eye-catching views and long sight lines open to the south, and the Trap Hills ridgeline leads west.

Now descending, the trail drops into a gap in the ridgeline before ascending to the west end of the ridge that includes the viewpoint known as Lookout Mountain. The NCT reaches that landmark vista at Mile 27.9, a good time and place to savor the views before the hike ends. Below, Victoria Reservoir's blue waters nest in forested green hills. To finish the hike follow the NCT northeast, descending 0.4 mile to Victoria Dam Road at Mile 28.3.

Miles and Directions

0.0   Gogebic Ridge Trailhead on Old M-64.

0.8   Junction with NCT.

3.3   Hack Site Trail junction, viewpoint nearby.

4.8   Soo Line Railroad tracks.

5.1   Bush Creek.

8.5   FR 480.

8.6   FR 400.

12.0   FR 630.

15.7   Norwich Road.

17.7   Junction with spur trail to FR 642.

18.9   Southeast corner of Norwich Bluff, viewpoint.

19.5   Junction with Whisky Hollow Trail.

19.9   Whisky Hollow Creek.

21.2   Junction with Gleason Falls Trail.

21.3   Gleason Falls.

21.4   Junction with Gleason Falls Trail.

22.6   Ridge east of Gleason Creek, viewpoint.

24.2   Talus slopes.

25.9   Summit (1,490 feet), viewpoint.

27.9   Lookout Mountain.

28.3   Victoria Dam Road.

13 Union River Cascades Loop

Highlights: A compact collection of small waterfalls, waterslides, and cascades plus a fascinating look at the history of copper mining in the Upper Peninsula

Location: Porcupine Mountains Wilderness State Park (PMWSP)

Type of hike: Loop

Distance: 1.0 mile

Difficulty: Moderate

Fees and permits: Michigan DNR Recreation Passport

Best months: May through October

Camping: PMWSP's Union Bay Campground, 3 miles northwest of the trailhead, has 100 campsites.

Maps: USGS Government Peak (inc.), White Pine (inc.) quads

Trail contact: PMWSP, (906) 885-5275

Finding the trailhead: From the intersection with M-107 in PMWSP, drive south on South Boundary Road a little less than 2 miles. Turn right (west) into the parking area for the Union Mine Interpretive Trail. GPS: 46.793950, -89.627224

Special considerations: Water levels affect the whitewater show here. The Union River's gurgling cascades maintain their charm even in low-water periods. However, the Little Union River Gorge's spectacular waterfall show tends to be a "now and then" event. The *Porcupine Mountains Companion,* a well-grounded reference by Michael Rafferty and Robert Sprague, describes one of these waterfalls, when it is flowing, as the highest in the park, with a 30-foot drop. During dry spells the gorge's mossy nooks and crannies are memorable, but the stream's flow is barely a trickle.

The Hike

Every time I visit the Union River, my usual brisk hiking pace slows to a halt. It is a place reminiscent of an art gallery with a theme of falling water, and it seems counterproductive to rush from display to display.

Begin your hike at the Union Mine Trailhead. Note that a series of numbered posts suggest a clockwise tour of this loop trail. If you enjoy learning a bit about history with your hiking (as I do), follow the loop in this direction. The informational signs along the way point out crumbled mine shafts and original roads, along with journal excerpts from some of those early miners. On the other hand, if you're hiking this trail solely for the remarkable cascades, consider hiking the trail in reverse, and therefore upstream, for better viewing of the falls. Triangular blue and white trail markers are easy to follow in either direction. The directions provided here follow the trail in reverse (counterclockwise). At the southwest corner of the trailhead's parking area, a path runs south and enters the woods. Hike south then east on that path, reaching South Boundary Road at Mile 0.1. Cross the road to its east side and follow the trail into the woods.

To the south of the trail, the mossy cleft known as the Little Union River Gorge begins with a rock wall that is the park's highest waterfall, when it is flowing. Continue hiking east, following the Union Mine Trail along the rim of the shady canyon;

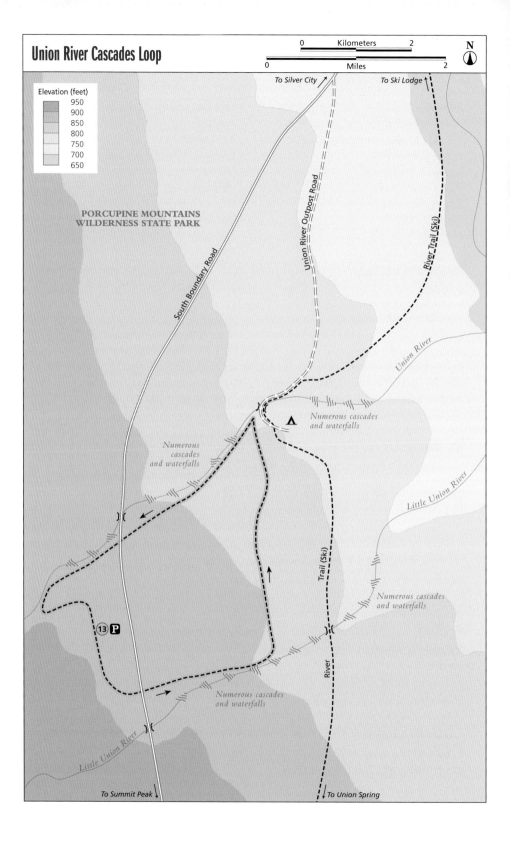

Union River Cascades Loop

Elevation (feet)
950
900
850
800
750
700
650

0 Kilometers 2
0 Miles 2

N

To Silver City
To Ski Lodge

PORCUPINE MOUNTAINS
WILDERNESS STATE PARK

South Boundary Road

Union River Outpost Road

River Trail (Ski)

Union River

Numerous cascades
and waterfalls

Numerous
cascades
and waterfalls

Little Union River

13 P

Trail (Ski)

Numerous cascades
and waterfalls

River

Numerous cascades
and waterfalls

Little Union River

To Summit Peak
To Union Spring

One of many delightful cascades on the Union River.

a giant hemlock marks a turn in the watercourse. At Mile 0.3 of the hike, a trail marker notes an old mining dig, and the path swings north.

Hike north on the Union Mine Trail, arriving at Union River (Mile 0.6) just west of the Union River Outpost Road's bridge. The path swings southwest here, paralleling the stream and a long, charming waterslide. Continue hiking west, upstream, as the river forms a series of cascades.

Cross South Boundary Road at Mile 0.8, following the Union Mine Trail southwest to one last water show. Note a rectangular cutout in the rocks where miners altered a 4-foot drop to accommodate a water wheel.

From that last cascade the trail turns south then quickly east, returning to the trailhead at Mile 1.0.

Option: Hikers with confidence in their off-trail hiking skills will find rich rewards if they opt to expand the Union Mine Trail Loop. Downstream of the trail both streams offer notable scenery, cascades, and solitude. This alternative would start at Mile 0.3 of the hike described above. Hike east, along the north side of the Little Union River Gorge (instead of following the Union Mine Trail north).

Miles and Directions

0.0   Union Mine Trailhead.

0.1   First crossing of South Boundary Road.

0.3   Trail leaves Little Union River Gorge.

0.6   Trail meets Union River.

0.8   Second crossing of South Boundary Road.

1.0   Union Mine Trailhead.

Iron River/Watersmeet Area Hikes

A lthough there are only four hikes in this area, these lakes and waterfalls surrounded by the Ottawa National Forest are well worth a trip. New to this edition of the guide, Bond Falls and O-Kun-de-Kun Falls are not the largest falls (though Bond Falls has an impressive 50-foot drop), but both could rate among the most picturesque spots in the Upper Peninsula.

The Ottawa National Forest is dotted with lakes, and a hike around Clark Lake or Deer Island Lake will offer a sampling of some of the finest and most secluded areas within the sprawling 16,000-acre tract of virgin forest.

Iron River to the south and Watersmeet to the north are both small towns. Iron River is the larger of the two with a population of about 3,000. For supplies in Iron River, visit Bigari Ace Hardware. Don't let the name fool you, the locals know that Bigari's is more like an old-fashioned general store, and it's the place to go for hiking and camping gear in Iron River.

Watersmeet is an even smaller town, with about 1,400 people in the township. It is appropriately named, as the surrounding Ottawa National Forest boasts over 500 named lakes and 2,000 miles of rivers and streams. Stop by the locally owned Sylvania Outfitters for gear and supplies.

Bigari Ace Hardware
605 Selden Rd.
Iron River, MI 49935
(906) 265-9614

Iron County, Michigan Chamber of Commerce
50 E. Genesee St.
Iron River, MI 49935
(906) 265-3822
www.tryiron.org

Sylvania Outfitters
E23423 US 2
Watersmeet, MI 49969
(906) 358-3766

Watersmeet Chamber of Commerce
PO Box 593
Watersmeet, MI 49969
(906) 358-9961
www.watersmeet.org

14 Bond Falls

Highlights: A sparkling falls of 50 feet hopping down a series of steps
Location: 12 miles north of Watersmeet
Type of hike: Loop with a short stem
Distance: 0.75 mile
Difficulty: Easy, with one difficult section
Fees and permits: Michigan DNR Recreation Passport

Best months: May through October
Camping: The Upper Peninsula Power Company maintains 26 campsites around the Bond Falls Basin, just south of the falls.
Maps: USGS Watersmeet quad (inc.)
Trail contact: Baraga State Park, (906) 353-6558

Finding the trailhead: From Watersmeet, drive approximately 9.5 miles north on US 45. Turn right (east) onto Bond Falls Road and drive about 3 miles before turning left onto Scenic Overlook Drive. The trailhead is at the northeast corner of the parking area. GPS: 46.409880, -89.134615
Special considerations: Most of this hike is on boardwalk, pavement, or gravel pathways. However, one section on the east side of the falls includes a steep, potentially slippery incline and an unmarked forest path. Because this area of the river is controlled by a dam, water levels can change rapidly, indicated by a siren. Keep these things in mind as you choose your route.

The Hike

This is a short hike, at only three-quarters of a mile, but Bond Falls is a spectacular sight, and worth a short walk. At just under 50 feet, the drop is impressive, and the opportunity to walk a path within touching distance of this massive powerhouse is too tempting to skip. The Bond Falls Scenic Site is owned by the Michigan DNR, but the area around the upper falls is maintained in part by the Upper Peninsula Power Company, who own the dam just upriver. Don't believe, however, that this falls is somehow tame because it is controlled. Rather, think of this as an example of what humans can accomplish when we work in conjunction with nature, rather than against it.

Begin your hike at the northeast corner of the parking area. Follow the paved walkway about 430 feet until a T-junction at a boardwalk. Here you will have immediate views of Bond Falls as it tumbles down 50 feet on either side of an island growing a small forest right in the middle of the falls. Take some time to admire the views.

When you are ready, take the boardwalk to your left and follow it around to the east for more views as it crosses over the Ontonagon River just downstream of the falls. The boardwalk turns to the right and ends at a short set of stairs leading to a trail at about 820 feet. Follow this trail south as it approaches a steep climb. Here decide whether or not this climb is for you. If not, return to the boardwalk and ascend the falls on the west side, which is made easier by a steep set of cement stairs. If you choose to make the climb, follow the worn path to the top and follow the trail as it heads south and east into the forest. If you're looking for solitude on this hike, this is

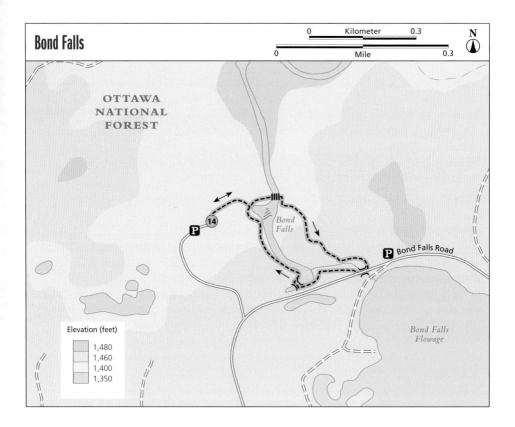

OTTAWA
NATIONAL
FOREST

P   14

Bond
Falls

P Bond Falls Road

Bond Falls
Flowage

Elevation (feet)

1,480
1,460
1,400
1,350

where you are most likely to find it. On my last visit, I startled a doe, who leapt away about 10 feet and then turned to watch me until I disappeared back into the woods. Be aware that the trail here is unmarked and often faint. Keep the sound of the river on your right as the trail roughly follows its path as it curves to the east at about 0.25 mile. This is a pleasant forest walk through maple, birch, and pine, with the rushing sound, if not always a view, of the river to keep you company. In about 500 feet, you will begin to see the river again, at least the smaller arm that rushes through the dam system. Walk around this (south), to the stairs leading up to the road and bridge. Cross the bridge to the "island" that sits between the two branches of the river flowing out of the Bond Falls Basin. There is a picnic area here, and the Bond Falls Outpost store. On your right, leave the road for the trail and cross a footbridge over the second branch of the river, at about the 0.5-mile mark. From here, the gravel trail follows the west side of the river as it descends through a series of small drops, generally referred to as the Upper Falls. These are as charming in their way as the main attraction, the water above each drop calm enough to clearly reflect the scenes of blue sky and fall colors in their surface.

As you reach the main falls again, steep cement stairs ease the descent, but be aware that water from the falls can make these stairs slippery. Stop at a viewing

The western half of Bond Falls tumbling down 50 feet of stairs

platform halfway down and you can literally reach out and touch the falling water. When you're ready, descend the rest of the stairs and return to the boardwalk. Follow this to the north and back to your starting point. Note that several openings in the boardwalks allow visitors to get a closer look at the falls from the banks, and to follow short trails downstream. Explore these at your leisure.

Miles and Directions

- **0.0** Bond Falls Interpretive Station and Trailhead.
- **0.4** Bond Falls Road Bridge.
- **0.5** Footbridge over western branch of river.
- **0.63** Stairs along western falls.
- **0.75** Trailhead.

15 Clark Lake Loop

Highlights: One of the largest stands of virgin forest in the upper Midwest and a quiet, non-motorized lake
Location: 8 miles southwest of Watersmeet
Type of hike: Loop
Distance: 7.6 miles
Difficulty: Moderate
Fees and permits: A daily fee per vehicle is collected May 15 through September 30. Season passes are also available. Camping fees are per night for designated backcountry campsites. There are no fees for day hikes, but registration is requested.

Best months: May through October
Camping: Six designated backcountry campsites border this route. A permit is required to use them. The Sylvania Campground, a half-mile east of the trailhead, has 48 drive-in campsites.
Maps: USGS Black Oak Lake (inc.) quad; Sylvania Wilderness Trail Map (Ottawa National Forest)
Trail contact: Sylvania Wilderness, (906) 358-4404, www.fs.usda.gov/ottawa

Finding the trailhead: From Watersmeet, drive 4.1 miles west on US 2 and turn left (south) on Gogebic CR 535. Drive 4 miles south and turn left (south) onto Sylvania's entrance road. Stop at the A-frame office. Drive south 0.2 mile and turn right (west), following signs to the boat launch on Clark Lake. Drive west 1 mile and turn left (south) on Thousand Island Lake Road. Drive another 0.3 mile to the boat launch and trailhead. GPS: 46.238692, -89.329352
Special considerations: This hike travels through an outstanding wilderness area. Treat it with respect.

The Hike

When hikers stand at the north end of Clark Lake, with its picnic area and boat ramp, they could easily imagine they were at any one of a number of northern lakes. By the time they arrive at the south end of the lake however, it is obvious they are someplace special—the core of a wilderness area sheltering 17,000 acres of virgin forest.

Paul Bunyan's ax swung hard and wide across our northern forests in the late 1800s. Sylvania is one of a handful of large chunks of old-growth forest that escaped that onslaught, and this hike takes you through notable stands of hemlock, sugar maple, and white pine elders. Two-hundred-year-old trees are common, and some hardy specimens here are 400 years old.

Begin your circuit of Clark Lake on the southeast corner of the boat ramp parking lot where a sign indicates the beginning of the Clark Lake Trail. Follow the trail southeast as it skirts the shoreline, rounding bays and cutting across piney peninsulas. After a little more than a mile, it ducks inland to make its way around aptly named Golden Silence Lake, a placid pond.

Along the way the myth that Midwest forests are thick and brushy dies. Sylvania's forest, like most old-growth, tends to be open and parklike under its tall

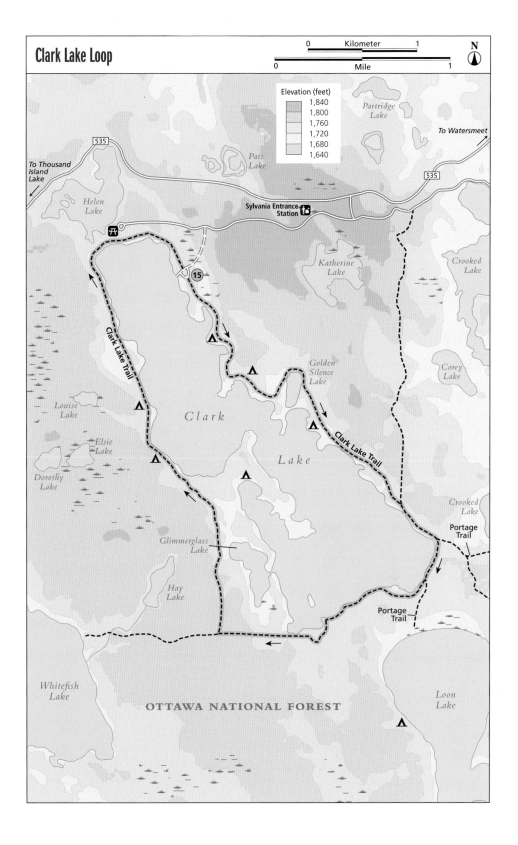

Clark Lake Loop

Elevation (feet)
1,840
1,800
1,760
1,720
1,680
1,640

N

0   Kilometer   1
0   Mile   1

To Thousand Island Lake

535

Helen Lake

Pats Lake

Partridge Lake

To Watersmeet

535

Sylvania Entrance Station

Katherine Lake

Crooked Lake

15

Clark Lake Trail

Louise Lake

Elsie Lake

Dorothy Lake

Clark

Golden Silence Lake

Corey Lake

Lake

Clark Lake Trail

Crooked Lake

Portage Trail

Glimmerglass Lake

Hay Lake

Portage Trail

Whitefish Lake

OTTAWA NATIONAL FOREST

Loon Lake

canopy. Below, the ground shows the pleasant lumpiness of fallen trees, aging into mulch and duff.

Continue following the path southeast and bear right (southeast) onto an old road at Mile 2.2. Walk along that old road to a meadow at Mile 2.4, the far eastern corner of Clark Lake. Stay straight (southeast) as a portage trail crosses, and 5 feet later turn right (southwest) on a path that crosses the meadow. This path quickly enters the woods and joins an old road that runs southwest near Clark Lake's southern shore. Stay straight (southwest) a quarter-mile later, as a portage trail crosses. That old road remains close to the lake for almost 1.5 miles before beginning a straight, westward course. Watch for a key signed intersection at Mile 4.3. Turn right (north) on a footpath that is faint at times but features abundant blue blazes.

Walk north, following the path through the forest for a mile before emerging once again on Clark Lake's shoreline. Another mile of shoreline walking brings you to the picnic area and beach at the north end of the lake at Mile 6.9. From there just continue another half-mile along the shoreline to the boat ramp and trailhead at Mile 7.4.

Miles and Directions

- **0.0** Trailhead.
- **0.9** Golden Silence Lake.
- **2.4** Clark Lake east end junction.
- **4.3** Clark Lake Trail.
- **6.9** Beach and picnic area.
- **7.4** Trailhead.

16 Deer Island Lake

Highlights: A quiet trail through one of the largest stands of virgin forest in the upper Midwest; loons on wilderness lakes
Location: 6 miles south of Watersmeet
Type of hike: Lollipop
Distance: 21.2 miles
Difficulty: Difficult*
Fees and permits: Camping fees are $16 per night for designated backcountry campsites. There are no fees for day hikes, but self-registration at the trailhead is requested.

Best months: May through October
Camping: Backcountry camping within the Sylvania Wilderness is allowed only at designated sites. A permit is required.
Maps: USGS Black Oak Lake (inc.) and Land O'Lakes (inc.) quads; Sylvania Wilderness Map (Ottawa National Forest)
Trail contact: Sylvania Wilderness, (906) 358-4404, www.fs.usda.gov/ottawa

Finding the trailhead: From Watersmeet, drive 8 miles south on US 45 south to Vilas CR B in Land O' Lakes, Wisconsin. Turn right onto CR B and drive over 0.5 mile through Land O' Lakes to Airport Road (Gogebic CR 539 as it crosses into Michigan). Turn right onto Airport Road. After 250 feet, Airport Road curves sharply to the left and becomes East Duck Lake Road. This road curves to the right as it enters Michigan and becomes CR 539. Drive about 0.25 mile and turn left onto Fischer Road. Drive west almost 0.5 mile to the end of Fischer Road and park at the end of the lane. GPS: 46.167176, -89.230196
Special considerations: This hike travels through an outstanding wilderness area. Treat it with respect.

The Hike

Sylvania, with its 17,000 acres of virgin forest and thirty-six named lakes, is no stranger to savvy nature lovers. Most of those folks, though, enter the area from the north, paddling canoes. Few of Sylvania's visitors know of the quiet footpath that enters from the southeast near Land O'Lakes. This trail quickly takes hikers into one of the most remote corners of the wilderness—the Deer Island Lake area. For ambitious hikers that is just the beginning. If you continue walking northwest and round Clark Lake on its loop, you create a prime route. For a brief moment, at the north end of Clark Lake, there are some minor signs of civilization. Other than that this hike is a 21.2-mile-long walking tour of old-growth forest and pristine lakes.

Start the hike by walking west from the Land O'Lakes trailhead. Follow the path northwest, arriving at a junction with an old woods road just east of Deer Island Lake's south end, at Mile 3.2. This is a key intersection and unmarked when I saw it. Turn right (northeast) and follow the old road north. About 1 mile later go straight (north), ignoring a spur that goes left to the north end of Deer Island Lake.

Follow the old road as it swings northwest, offering a last glimpse of Deer Island Lake, and arrives at an intersection with the Mountain Lake Trail at Mile 5.6. Turn

Deer Island Lake

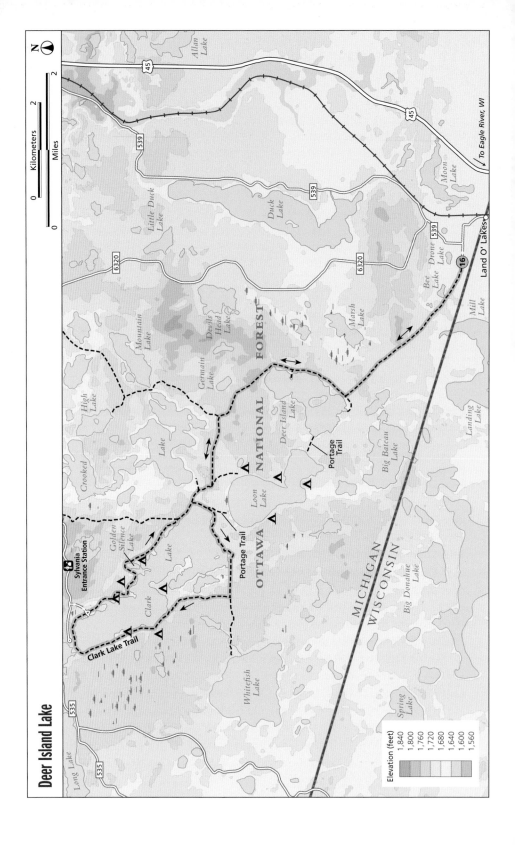

Elevation (feet)

1,840
1,800
1,760
1,720
1,680
1,640
1,600
1,560

N

Kilometers

0   2

Miles

0   2

Allan Lake

45

539

To Eagle River, WI

Little Duck Lake

Duck Lake

539

Moon Lake

6320

539

Land O' Lakes

6320

Bee & Drone Lake

16

Mill Lake

Mountain Lake

Devils Head Lake

Marsh Lake

NATIONAL FOREST

High Lake

Germain Lake

Deer Island Lake

Landing Lake

Crooked Lake

Portage Trail

Big Bateau Lake

Golden Silence Lake

Loon Lake

OTTAWA

Sylvania Entrance Station

Clark Lake

Portage Trail

MICHIGAN

WISCONSIN

Big Donahue Lake

Clark Lake Trail

Clark

535

Whitefish Lake

Spring Lake

Long Lake

535

Colorful mushrooms often hide in the moist undergrowth.

left (west), following another old road to yet another intersection north of Loon Lake, at Mile 6.5. Turn right (northwest) and walk to a meadow at the far eastern end of Clark Lake (Mile 6.8). Turn left (southwest), following a path that enters the woods and joins an old woods road running southwest near Clark Lake's southern shore. Stay straight (southwest) a quarter-mile later, as a portage trail crosses.

The old road remains close to the lake for almost 1.5 miles before beginning a straight, westward course. Watch for a signed intersection at Mile 8.7. Turn right (north) onto the Clark Lake Trail, a footpath that is faint at times but features abundant blue blazes. Walk north, following the path through a forest for a mile, before emerging once again on Clark Lake's shoreline. Another mile of northward walking brings you to a picnic area. Walk eastward, past a swimming beach and along a trail that curls southward to a boat ramp at Mile 12. At the southeast corner of the boat ramp parking area, a sign marks the Clark Lake Trail.

Follow the Clark Lake Trail southeast as it skirts the shoreline, rounding bays and cutting across piney peninsulas. After a little more than a mile, the trail ducks inland to make its way around aptly named Golden Silence Lake, a sylvan pond.

Continue following the path southeast and bear right (southeast) at a junction with an old road at Mile 14.2. Walk along that old road to the meadow at the far eastern corner of Clark Lake (Mile 14.4), the same spot we saw at Mile 6.8. From here retrace your steps of the first part of the hike to return to the Land O'Lakes trailhead.

Options: This route has two attractive options. The first involves following the described route to Mile 6.8, the eastern corner of Clark Lake. From that point hike southwest on the Clark Lake Trail another 0.3 mile, and turn left (south) on the portage trail leading to Loon Lake. Walk south a quarter-mile to Loon Lake's shore, then east along a sandy beach. As the shore curves south, look for an informal path in the open woods that parallels the lakeshore. Follow that path and Loon Lake's east shore south and east for 2 miles to the portage trail that leads to Deer Island Lake. Hike southeast a quarter-mile on the portage trail to Deer Island Lake. There, a three-quarter-mile off-trail segment begins. Hike south through open woods, keeping Deer Island Lake in sight to your left (northeast), to the Deer Island Lake Trail junction that you saw at Mile 3.2. Total distance for this hike, out-and-back from Land O' Lakes, would be about 13.5 miles.

Backpackers looking for an optimum base camp would do well to consider a multinight stay at the Mallard designated campsite on the north end of Loon Lake. That location puts you in excellent position to do the Clark Lake Trail loop as a day trip, as well as explore north to Mountain Lake or west to Whitefish Lake. This plan would require a 6-mile backpack on the first and last day.

Miles and Directions

0.0   Land O'Lakes trailhead.

3.2   Deer Island Lake junction.

5.6   Mountain Lake Trail junction.

6.8   Clark Lake junction.

8.7   Clark Lake Trail (turn north).

11.3   Beach and picnic area, Clark Lake.

12.0   Boat ramp, Clark Lake.

12.9   Golden Silence Lake.

14.4   Clark Lake junction.

21.2   Land O' Lakes trailhead.

17 O-Kun-de-Kun Falls

Highlights: A quiet backwoods waterfall
Location: 25 miles north of Watersmeet
Type of hike: Out-and-back
Distance: 2.8 miles
Difficulty: Moderate
Fees and permits: None, but consider a donation to the North Country Trail Association, www.northcountrytrail.org

Best months: May through October
Camping: Dispersed camping is allowed in the Ottawa National Forest within guidelines. There is 1 campsite at O-Kun-de-Kun Falls.
Maps: USGS Rockland quad (inc.)
Trail contact: Ottawa National Forest, (906) 358-4724, North Country Trail Association, (866) 445-3628

Finding the trailhead: From Watersmeet, drive approximately 25 miles north on US 45. Turn right (east) into the parking area for the O-Kun-de-Kun Falls Trailhead about half a mile after crossing the Baltimore River.
Special considerations: This is actually an easy hike, except for the mud. Much of the time, this is a particularly wet trail. Narrow boardwalks do ease the way over some rougher areas, but keep this in mind during especially wet periods. GPS: 46.646989, -89.175653

The Hike

O-Kun-de-Kun Falls is a fairly overlooked spot in an area with many waterfalls to choose from. Because of this, you're likely to have the trail to yourself, and to my mind, this waterfall has a great deal to recommend it; it drops 25 feet over the edge of undercut sandstone slabs, framed above by tall pine and below by the earthy browns of sandstone. It is also one of the few falls that is just as worthwhile to view during low-water episodes, as this allows walking on the smooth sandstone for closer views of the impressive drop.

Begin your hike at the North Country Trail parking area off of US 45. Follow the gravel path northeast to its junction with the North Country Trail and a signboard for O-Kun-de-Kun Falls. Turn right on this trail and continue heading northeast. The trail here is narrow and muddy, but some boardwalks ease the way over the roughest areas. At about Mile 0.4, cross an ATV trail and continue heading northeast on the NCT. If you don't let the boggy trail bother you, this is a pleasant woodsy walk. Eventually, after the first mile, sight lines open up a little to your right (south), especially in fall, and you can catch glimpses of the Baltimore River valley. Soon after this, you'll begin to hear the river and soon notice a waterfall peeking through the trees down the steep slope. These are, as far as I know, unnamed falls. There are unofficial trails leading down, navigable for agile hikers. Continue heading northwest on the trail as it descends gradually into the river valley. At about Mile 1.3, O-Kun-de-Kun Falls appears on the right, with easy paths to view the verge and then the base. Walk on the trail or on the smooth bedrock along the river to

O-Kun-de-Kun Falls

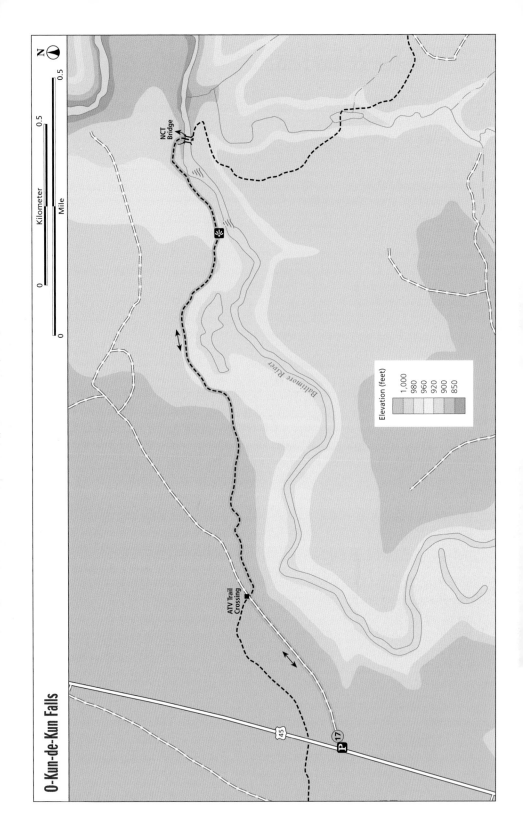

Elevation (feet)

1,000
980
960
920
900
850

Baltimore River

NCT
Bridge

ATV Trail
Crossing

45

P 17

N

Kilometer

Mile

0   0.5   0.5

reach the NCT Bridge at Mile 1.4. Spend some time exploring the river here before retracing your steps back to the trailhead.

Miles and Directions

0.0 O-Kun-de-Kun Falls NCT Trailhead.

0.4 ATV Trail crossing.

1.1 Unnamed falls.

1.3 O-Kun-de-Kun Falls.

1.4 NCT Bridge over Baltimore River.

2.8 Trailhead.

O-Kun-de-Kun Falls surrounded by a striking mix of pine and autumn colors

Houghton/Copper Harbor Area Hikes

The Keweenaw Peninsula is a long ridge of land pointing out into Lake Superior. The hikes in this area aren't long, but they are certainly worth the drive (which is glorious in its own right). Horseshoe Harbor is a particular favorite of mine, with its weathered rock ridges towering over Lake Superior on one side and miles of undisturbed forest on the other. Don't underestimate Canyon Falls, a mistake I made because the trailhead is at a rest area. The riverside hike to the falls and beyond is rewarding and unexpected.

Some hikes in this section aren't in the Keweenaw Peninsula, but they are closer to Houghton than any other urban center. Craig Lake, one of the original drop sites for the moose reintroduction project, is a beautiful place (even if you don't spot a moose), chosen for moose and for the guide because it is extremely secluded.

Houghton and its sister city Hancock are the gateway to the Keweenaw. The entire peninsula has a rich mining history, especially Calumet (north of Houghton), which was once such a boomtown that it was in the running to be Michigan's state capital. If you're inclined to explore under the earth as well as on its surface, you can take a mine tour 300 feet underground at Quincy Mine in Hancock. For gear and supplies in Houghton, try the locally owned Year Round Gear or Downwind Sports.

At the northernmost point of the Keweenaw sits the picturesque community of Copper Harbor. Fort Wilkins State Park has an extensive campground, as well as a completely reconstructed 19th-century fort on the banks of the lovely Lake Fanny Hooe. During peak season, the fort is interactive, with actors in period costume to tell visitors about daily life at the fort. For supplies in Copper Harbor, stop by The Gas Light General Store. This is the epitome of the small town general store, with a little bit of everything from the local brew (Brickside Brewery right across the street), to hardware and cold weather clothing.

If you take M-26 out of Copper Harbor, you'll pass through the quaint lakeside towns of Eagle River and Eagle Harbor. Between the two, next to a roadside waterfall called Jacob's Falls, you will stumble upon something unexpected—a stunning Benedictine monastery with gold onion domes. This is the home of the Holy

Transfiguration Skete. Just down the road, the monks run a small business called The Jampot, selling jams and baked goods made primarily from locally harvested foods. In summer, the lines are out the door of this humble building, and the jams, breads, and desserts are worth the wait.

Downwind Sports
308 Shelden Ave.
Houghton, MI 49931
(906) 482-2500
www.downwindsports.com

Year Round Gear
220 Shelden Ave.
Houghton, MI 49931
(906) 828-9191
www.yearroundgear.com

The Gas Light General Store
39 Gratiot St.
Copper Harbor, MI 49918
(906) 289-4652

18 Bare Bluff

Highlights: Unimpeded views of the Keweenaw Peninsula and Lake Superior from a notable viewpoint. On a good day the views stretch to the Huron Mountains, 40 miles south.
Location: Keweenaw Peninsula, 5 miles south of Copper Harbor
Type of hike: Out-and-back
Distance: 2.6 miles
Difficulty: Moderate*

Fees and permits: None, but consider a donation to the Michigan Nature Association
Best months: May through October
Camping: Fort Wilkins State Park, 5 miles north of the trailhead, has 159 campsites.
Map: USGS Lake Medora quad (inc.)
Trail contact: Michigan Nature Association, (866) 223-2231, www.michigannature.org

Finding the trailhead: From Copper Harbor, drive about 11 miles west on US 41. Turn left onto Gay–Lac La Belle Road and drive about 4.3 miles to Lac La Belle. From there, stay on Lac La Belle–Bete Grise Road as it curves to the left. Continue 2.9 miles east on Bete Grise Road. Then, turn left (northeast) onto Smith Fisheries Road. Note that Smith Fisheries Road is signed as "Private." However, use of the road to access the Sanctuary is permitted. Drive east 2.5 miles on that road to a logging pullout on the road's east side and park there. GPS: 47.397187, -87.911603
Special considerations: Bare Bluff is part of the Russell and Miriam Grinnell Memorial Nature Sanctuary, a private nature preserve, which is the property of the Michigan Nature Association (MNA). Treat it well; read the MNA guidelines on the blue sign. Hikers visiting during the late spring/early summer nesting season should be aware that merlins (a falcon species) could be nesting nearby, perhaps on a ledge below the cliff top. Proceed in a cautious, respectful manner— both for the birds' sake and your own. Merlins can be very aggressive. Be aware that the viewpoint is the top of a high cliff.

The Hike

East of Bete Grise the pavement ends, the shoreline turns forbiddingly rocky, and one of the truly great U.P. landscapes—a back of beyond known to locals as the Tip of the Keweenaw—begins. Here woodlands stretch shore to shore, accented by rock-topped ridges, lakes, and cascading streams flowing to the big lake. It's a swath of wild country penetrated by only a few seasonal roads, and reminiscent of Isle Royale. Fortunately recent efforts by The Nature Conservancy translate into ongoing protection for large chunks of the tip. Earlier the MNA purchased a few key tracts.

Bare Bluff, a memorable viewpoint, is one of those MNA properties. An airy cliff top on its south summit, some 500 feet above Lake Superior's waters, offers sweeping vistas that are among the finest in the U.P.

Hikers familiar with Sugar Loaf, the well-known lookout just west of Marquette, may find a comparison useful. Picture a similar vantage point, but on a wild Keweenaw shoreline, a narrow footpath leading to the heights, and not a soul around.

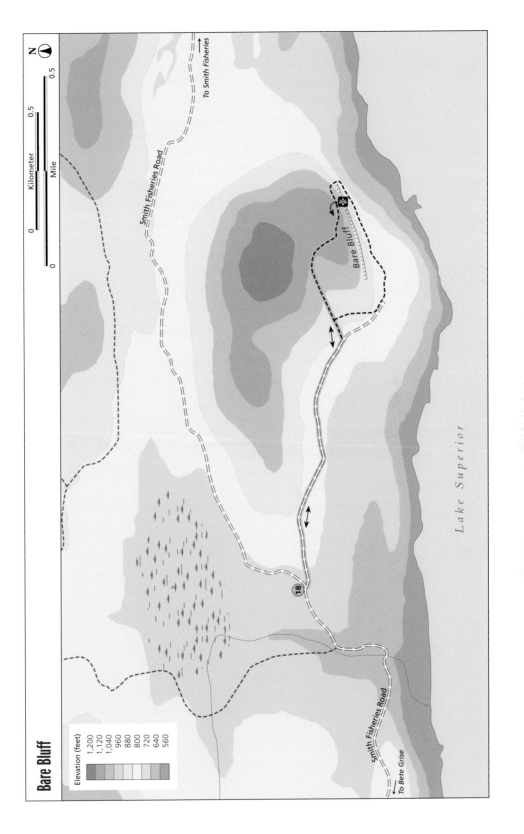

Bare Bluff

Elevation (feet)
1,200
1,120
1,040
960
880
800
720
640
560

Smith Fisheries Road

To Smith Fisheries

Bare Bluff

18

Smith Fisheries Road

To Bete Grise

Lake Superior

N

Kilometer
0   0.5

Mile
0   0.5

Begin your hike by walking east on the unnamed logging road. During my visit I found an active logging operation here, and the contrast with the idyllic spot beyond could not have been greater. Persevere: Bare Bluff is well worth it.

Continue walking east on the logging road to Mile 0.7, where a blue MNA signboard on the left (east) side of the road marks a trail running east into the woods, as the logging road swings downhill to the right (south). Take a moment to read the guidelines on the MNA signboard. Then walk east on that trail for 150 paces; there a MNA map board marks a trail junction at Mile 0.8. Turn left (north) and follow that path, marked by both blue and yellow diamonds, uphill. Steadily ascending, the trail swings east, becoming a tad faint but marked by yellow and orange flagging, just before it emerges onto the bedrock of the lookout at Mile 1.3.

There a stunted maple and oak forest ends at a high ledge, offering magnificent views. To the east the scalloped shoreline stretches past the tumbling whitewater of the Montreal River to Keystone Point, and then Keweenaw Point, the tip of the tip. Look west and Bete Grise's beaches bracket the mouth of the Little Gratiot River, Lac La Belle, and Point Isabelle beyond.

I was there on a day of some humidity and could easily see Keweenaw Point some 6 miles off, but haze obscured Manitou Island a few miles beyond. On a good day the Huron Mountains, 40 miles south across Keweenaw Bay, appear on the southern horizon.

Miles and Directions

0.0   Trailhead at logging landing.

0.7   Trail begins at Michigan Nature Association sign.

0.8   Trail junction.

1.3   Bare Bluff Overlook; turnaround point.

2.6   Trailhead at logging landing.

19 Canyon Falls

Highlights: Waterfalls and a rocky gorge
Location: 1 mile south of Alberta
Type of hike: Out-and-back
Distance: 1.8 miles
Difficulty: The official trail is easy; the second segment is difficult.
Fees and permits: None
Best months: May through October

Camping: Big Lake State Forest Campground, 10 miles west of the trailhead, has 12 campsites.
Map: USGS Vermilac quad
Trail contact: Michigan Department of Natural Resources, (906) 353-6651, www.michigan .gov/dnr

Finding the trailhead: From Houghton, drive 41 miles south on US 41 and turn right (west) into the trailhead parking area, about 1.1 miles past Alberta. GPS: 46.626749, -88.471220
Special considerations: Use caution on wet rocks near the river. The first part of this hike follows an official, maintained trail. The second part ventures off-trail, along segments of an old trail. This second section is very rewarding but requires good judgment. Some of this walking takes place atop massive slabs of bedrock, and some crevices are present in those rock slabs. Moss or leaves cover some of these crevices, creating the possibility of serious injury. Be alert.

The Hike

Aptly named Canyon Falls is a spectacularly scenic area that can be as mild—or as wild—as you want it to be. An official, constructed trail leads to the namesake waterfall, which is a beauty. As that path ends, the gorge area begins, offering nimble hikers an adventurous outing along its rim.

Begin your hike at the marked trailhead at the southwest corner of the Canyon Falls roadside park. Walk southwest on a broad, graveled path, the Canyon Falls Trail. About 400 paces from the parking area, the trail nears the Sturgeon River and its swift water. A series of low ledge drops—most just a few inches and one waist high—adds to the current's velocity as it nears Canyon Falls. This stretch of river is worth taking your time over. There are several spots to wander onto rock shelves and get a closer look at the river's swirls and eddies. As always, use caution on potentially wet and slippery footing.

The river cascades down 15-foot-high Canyon Falls (Mile 0.4) into a rocky slot, locally known as the Gorge. Follow the fence to the right (west) of the waterfall for the best viewing of the falls and a tantalizing look downstream into the rapids and rock walls of the Gorge. Turn around here if maintained trails are your preference. An opening in the railing allows you to step down to a lower ledge and an even better view of Canyon Falls and the canyon below.

If the rim of the Gorge area interests you, take note of a long and low block of rock just west of this railing area. Work your way to the north end (your right as you are facing it) of that rock, then west past its end. There you will see a path, an old

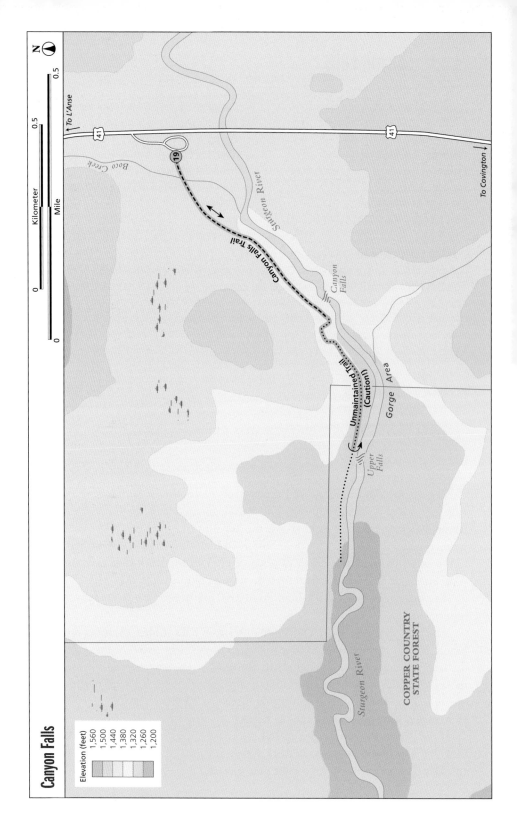

Canyon Falls

Elevation (feet)
1,560
1,500
1,440
1,380
1,320
1,260
1,200

To L'Anse

To Covington

Boco Creek

Sturgeon River

Canyon Falls Trail

Canyon Falls

Unmaintained Trail (Caution!)

Gorge Area

Upper Falls

Sturgeon River

COPPER COUNTRY STATE FOREST

N

Kilometer
0   0.5   0.5

Mile
0   0.5

Canyon Falls. The Sturgeon River drops into the picturesque cleft known as the Gorge.

trail that leads west, onto the rim of the Gorge. This rim is an almost magical place. It seems as if you stepped through a window and into wilderness. Below you the river churns between huge boulders and gray rock walls 30 feet high. Above, pine needles carpet the bedrock as the path continues southwest and west.

Almost 1 mile west of the trailhead, the walls of the Gorge lower and the river charges into one last whitewater display. Upper Falls is a huge ramp, a waterslide that rides a tilting bedrock strata and splits in two just before its final drop. A pleasant break spot, this is also the turnaround point for the hike.

Miles and Directions

- **0.0** Trailhead.
- **0.4** Canyon Falls.
- **0.9** Upper Falls; turnaround point.
- **1.8** Trailhead.

20 Craig Lake

Highlights: A remote lake, marsh and stream, and quiet forest
Location: 10 miles northwest of Michigamme
Type of hike: Loop
Distance: 7.9 miles
Difficulty: Moderate
Fees and permits: Michigan DNR Recreation Passport
Best months: May through October

Camping: Craig Lake State Park offers rustic backcountry camping, within zero-impact guidelines. A permit is required, which can be obtained from Van Riper State Park. Sandy Beach campsite, 0.5 mile east of the trailhead, has 3 tent pads.
Maps: USGS Mount Curwood (inc.), Three Lakes (inc.) quads
Trail contact: Van Riper State Park, (906) 339-4461

Finding the trailhead: From Michigamme, drive 1.4 miles west on US 41 and turn right (north) on Craig Lake Road. Drive 3.0 miles on that road and turn left (northwest) continuing on Craig Lake Road. Follow that road, which is at times rough, 3.4 miles. At a T-junction, turn right onto North Nestoria Road and drive about 200 feet to a parking area on the left. GPS: 46.599356, -88.189598

Special considerations: For identification purposes, some trail intersections on the map are designated by an alphabetical code (Junction A, for example).

The Hike

Craig Lake comes with an attitude check. Persist through 6 miles of rough, bumpy road that winds its way to the trailhead, and the rewards will begin as soon as you shut off the ignition. Odds are, that will be the last mechanical sound you'll hear during your visit to Michigan's most remote state park.

Round a gate at the parking area's east end and you enter a non-motorized zone, a designated state wilderness area. Craig Lake State Park's 6,984 acres feature two lakes—Craig Lake and Crooked Lake, each nearly 2 miles in length—and a mosaic of marshes, streams, and quiet forest. Seeing loons and eagles is pretty much a sure thing. Members of the U.P.'s resurgent moose population put in an appearance now and then as well.

A loop trail circles the park's namesake lake, visiting the lake's quiet north end, the park's back of beyond. The 8-mile circuit tour also offers a short side-trip to remote Clair Lake.

Begin your hike by walking on a gated dirt road 310 paces east from the parking area to an intersection designated Junction A (Mile 0.2). Go straight (north), as the eastern segment of the Craig Lake Trail (also the North Country Trail, or NCT, here) splits off to the right (east).

Continue hiking north and northwest on the dirt road. You will pass a put-in and a bay of sparkling Craig Lake and arrive at Junction B at Mile 0.4. Go straight

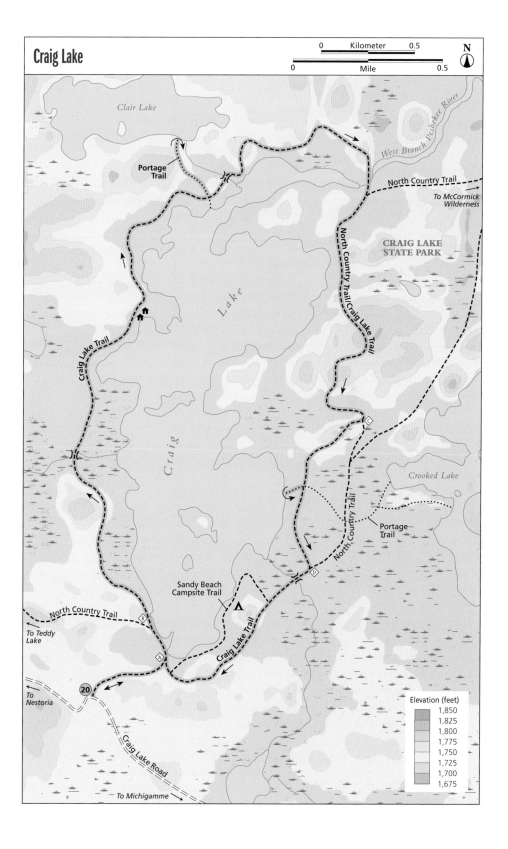

Craig Lake

0   Kilometer   0.5

0   Mile   0.5

N

Clair Lake

Portage
Trail

West Branch Peshekee River

North Country Trail

To McCormick
Wilderness

CRAIG LAKE
STATE PARK

North Country Trail/Craig Lake Trail

Lake

Craig Lake Trail

Craig

Crooked Lake

North Country Trail

Portage
Trail

North Country Trail

Sandy Beach
Campsite Trail

Craig Lake Trail

North Country Trail

To Teddy
Lake

To Nestoria

20

Craig Lake Road

To Michigamme

Elevation (feet)

| 1,850 |
| 1,825 |
| 1,800 |
| 1,775 |
| 1,750 |
| 1,725 |
| 1,700 |
| 1,675 |

Craig Lake's remote and sparkling waters, where loons linger and a portage ramp eases the carry to Crooked Lake

(northwest), as the NCT departs left (west). About 1 mile north of that intersection, the Craig Lake Trail, which is still a dirt road, utilizes a sturdy bridge to pass over a large marshy creek. This is a good place to scan for herons and other wildlife. Next the trail arrives at a clearing by the lake and a lodge (available for rental) left from the days when Frederick Miller, of the brewing family, owned Craig Lake. Check the north side of the lodge's clearing for the trail's continuation, as it becomes a path entering the woods. The path winds its way, occasionally nearing the lake's rocky shore, and reaches a junction with the Clair Lake Portage Trail at Mile 2.7. Turn left (north) and hike 0.2 mile to sample Clair Lake's quiet ambience or perhaps its excellent smallmouth bass fishery.

Retrace your steps south and turn left (east) on the Craig Lake Trail (Mile 3.1). Hike east, crossing a sturdy bridge over Clair Lake's little outlet stream and arriving at a rock outcrop that offers narrow views of Craig Lake's northeast inlet. Then the path wanders east, swinging north a bit to skirt wetlands before arriving at Craig Lake's outlet (Mile 4.3), a branch of the Peshekee River.

Cross the outlet to its south side on a sturdy, 30-inch-wide log. I was startled as several smallmouth bass, one a hefty 18 inches long, attempted to jump up in the riffle below the log. Hike south, following the Craig Lake Trail as it nears Craig Lake's northeast bay, dips and rolls through some hilly terrain, and arrives at Junction C at

Mile 5.6. Turn right (west), following a sign for Craig Lake, as another trail goes south (signed for Crooked Lake and the NCT). Follow the Craig Lake Trail southwest to a junction with the Crooked Lake Portage Trail at Mile 6.2. Turn right (west) and walk ninety paces to Craig Lake, where a constructed portage ramp leads up a slope from the shoreline. Loons were offshore during my visit. This is a pleasant break spot.

Retrace your ninety steps eastward and turn right (south) on the Craig Lake Trail. Hike south and southeast to Junction D at Mile 6.9. Turn right (south), as the NCT and Crooked Lake Trail come in from the left (north). Hike south and west on the Craig Lake Trail (now part of the NCT and a jeep trail in width), crossing a sturdy bridge over a large inlet creek. Go straight (southwest) at Mile 7.2 as a spur goes right (northwest) to a camping area on the lakeshore.

Continue hiking southwest on the Craig Lake Trail, arriving at Junction A at Mile 7.7. Turn left (southwest) and walk some 310 paces to the trailhead parking area.

Miles and Directions

0.0 Trailhead.

0.2 Junction A.

0.4 Junction B.

2.0 Cabin Meadow.

2.7 Clair Lake Portage Trail junction.

2.9 Clair Lake.

3.1 Clair Lake Portage Trail junction.

4.3 Craig Lake outlet.

5.6 Junction C.

6.2 Crooked Lake Portage Trail junction.

6.3 Craig Lake shore.

6.4 Crooked Lake Portage Trail junction.

6.9 Junction D.

7.2 Campsite spur.

7.7 Junction A.

7.9 Trailhead.

21 Estivant Pines Loop

Highlights: A notable stand of virgin white pines
Location: 2 miles south of Copper Harbor
Type of hike: Lollipop
Distance: 2.0 miles
Difficulty: Moderate
Fees and permits: None, but consider a donation to the Michigan Nature Association

Best months: May through October
Camping: Fort Wilkins Park at Copper Harbor has 159 campsites.
Maps: USGS Lake Medora, Fort Wilkins quads (inc.); "Estivant Pines Sanctuary Guide" (available at Copper Harbor visitor center)
Trail contact: Michigan Nature Association, (866) 223-2231, www.michigannature.org

Finding the trailhead: From Copper Harbor, drive south 1 mile, on paved Second Street/Lake Manganese Road. At that point turn left (east) onto a graded gravel road (now following signs to Estivant Pines), also known as Lake Manganese Road. After driving 0.9 mile on the gravel road, turn right (south) on an unnamed dirt road, part of an intersection triangle of roads. After less than 0.1 mile, turn right (west) on another dirt road, Burma Road, and drive 0.4 mile west to the trailhead parking area, on the left (south) side of the road. GPS: 47.44606, -87.87722
Special considerations: This hike travels through the Estivant Pines Nature Sanctuary, a property of the Michigan Nature Association. This is a special place—treat it well. Read the guidelines on the signboard at the trailhead.

The Hike

Some of the finest specimens of virgin white pines in Michigan are here, a haunting remnant of the vast swaths that once stretched across northern Michigan. These ancient trees, a few elders reaching 400 years, stand in groves scattered across the sanctuary's 510 acres.

Begin your hike from the south end of the trailhead parking area. Walk south on the broad trail 0.2 mile to a signed trail junction (designated Junction A for identification purposes on the map). Disregard the Memorial Grove Trail to your left (east) and continue walking straight (south), reaching another junction at Mile 0.4 (designated Junction B on the map). There turn right (west) on a narrower footpath, the Cathedral Loop Trail.

Hike west—rocks and roots sometimes challenging—on the Cathedral Loop Trail. The trail loops around to the south, passes a hollowed out white pine snag, and reaches its namesake, the Cathedral Grove, at Mile 0.8. Giant white pines line the trail here, loaning their aura to what may well be the most contemplative locale of the hike.

When you are ready, continue hiking on the Cathedral Loop Trail, now heading north and reaching the junction with the Memorial Grove Trail at Mile 1.0 (designated Junction C on the map). Turn right (east) here and hike eastward on the Memorial Grove Trail, reaching that grove at Mile 1.4.

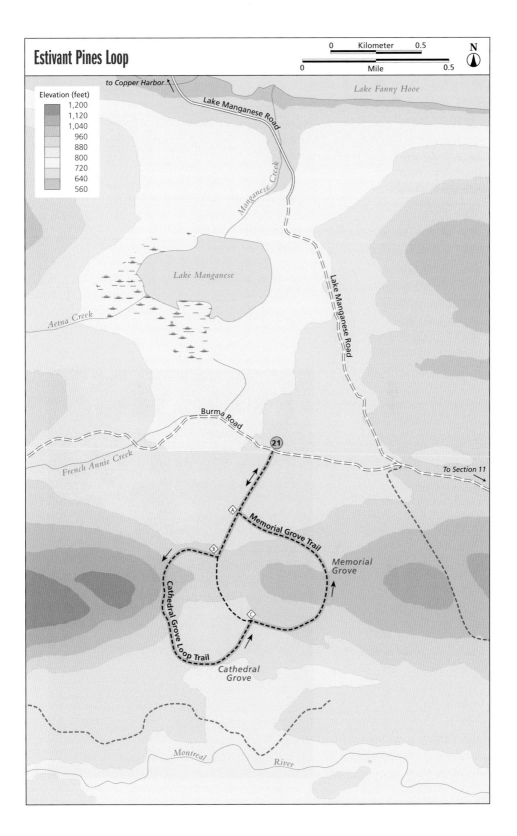

Estivant Pines Loop

Elevation (feet)
1,200
1,120
1,040
960
880
800
720
640
560

0   Kilometer   0.5

0   Mile   0.5

N

to Copper Harbor

Lake Fanny Hooe

Lake Manganese Road

Manganese Creek

Lake Manganese

Aetna Creek

Lake Manganese Road

Burma Road

French Annie Creek

21

To Section 11

A

Memorial Grove Trail

B

Memorial Grove

C

Cathedral Grove Loop Trail

Cathedral Grove

Montreal   River

At about Mile 1.6 of the hike, a rounded boulder emerges in the center of a small clearing surrounded by old-growth pines. This is a perfect place to sit for a while with only the ancient forest for company. It's easy to imagine, in this spot, how Michigan must have looked before the logging era.

Follow the Memorial Grove Trail, from its namesake stand, as it loops north then west and meets Junction A at Mile 1.8. There turn right (north), returning to the trailhead and the end of the hike at Mile 2.0.

Miles and Directions

0.0 Trailhead.

0.2 Memorial Trail junction (north), Junction A.

0.4 Cathedral Loop Trail junction, Junction B.

0.8 Cathedral Grove.

1.0 Memorial Trail junction (south), Junction C.

1.4 Memorial Grove.

1.8 Junction A.

2.0 Trailhead.

Virgin white pines surround a quiet clearing on the Memorial Grove Trail.

22 Horseshoe Harbor

Highlights: A spectacular bedrock shoreline on the north shore of the Keweenaw Peninsula
Location: 5 miles east of Copper Harbor
Type of hike: Out-and-back
Distance: 1.6 miles
Difficulty: Moderate*
Fees and permits: None, but consider a contribution to The Nature Conservancy

Best months: May through October
Camping: Fort Wilkins State Park, 3 miles west of the trailhead, has 159 campsites.
Map: USGS Fort Wilkins quad (inc.)
Trail contact: The Nature Conservancy, (906) 225-0399, www.tnc.org

Finding the trailhead: From Copper Harbor drive east 2.3 miles on US 41 to the end of the pavement. Continue east for 0.8 mile on a graded dirt road known as the Mandan Loop Road. Then turn left (north) on a narrow, dirt two-track road known as the Horseshoe Harbor Road. Drive that road 1.2 miles north and east to the trailhead. Parking pullouts are on the south side of the road. GPS: 47.46918, -87.80292

Special considerations: Horseshoe Harbor Road is not suitable for all vehicles, especially during wet periods, as pools and mud make several places difficult, and turnarounds are not always possible. Consider parking along Mandan Loop Road and hiking the extra 1.2 miles into the trailhead. This hike travels through the Mary Macdonald Preserve at Horseshoe Harbor, a property of The Nature Conservancy. This is a special place—treat it well. Read the guidelines on the signboard at the trailhead.

The Hike

A certain aura, a whiff of raw fury, hangs on the shoreline here. Even on a benign summer day, the stark reefs of eroded conglomerate rock seem to speak of the epic storms of November.

While the U.P. and the Keweenaw have other notable wave-washed shores, this one, with its exposed location and striking rock architecture, is a worthy contender for ranking as an icon.

Begin your visit by walking north on a broad and rocky trail that starts opposite the trailhead's parking pullouts. After a woodsy 0.3 mile, the trail emerges onto a rock cobble beach, the Lake Superior shore.

Before you a string of bedrock islands shelters a cove, a rough rectangle in shape, and a quarter-mile wide. A passing bald eagle swooped down to claim one of these rocks during my August visit. At the northwest end of the inlet, the reef of bedrock that forms the islands rises into a ridge 15 feet high.

Walk north along the cobble beach to that bedrock wall at Mile 0.4, and then west along its base. A gravelly flat beneath, and just south of the rock, offers passage west. During high-water episodes, long ponds form on this side of the ridge, making passage difficult. If you're comfortable climbing the ridge, consider walking along the

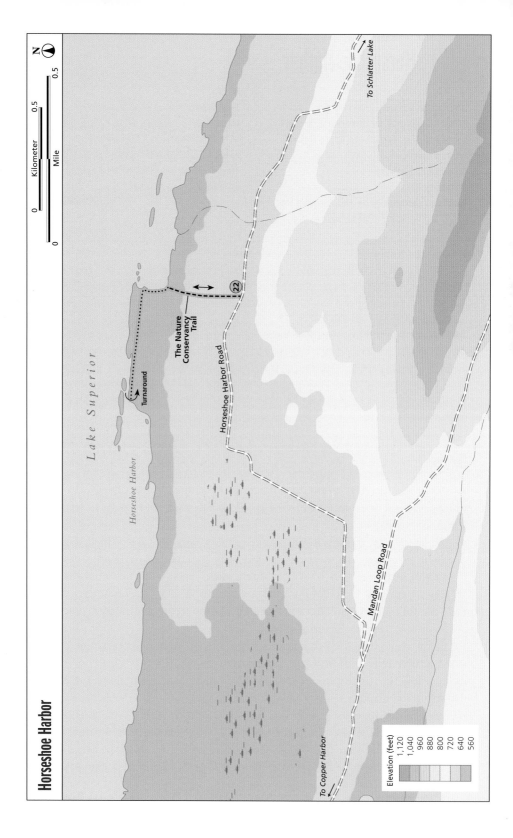

Horseshoe Harbor

Lake Superior

Horseshoe Harbor

Turnaround

The Nature
Conservancy
Trail

22

Horseshoe Harbor Road

Mandan Loop Road

To Schlatter Lake

To Copper Harbor

N

Kilometer
0   0.5

Mile
0   0.5

Elevation (feet)

1,120
1,040
960
880
800
720
640
560

A bald eagle perched on the ancient bedrock along the rugged Horseshoe Harbor coast

top for the entire length. There, orange and green lichens, able to thrive on the most wind-exposed spots, accent the rock. Nooks and crannies shelter miniature flower gardens, reminiscent of the last tiny patches of greenery on a high mountain. Access to the ridge is easiest from the beach, and the views of Lake Superior are spectacular. Far out in the lake, you might be lucky enough to spot one of the long freighters that haul ore across the Great Lakes.

Continue hiking west to Mile 0.8, where the rock reef once again becomes a string of islands, and the shoreline curls south, forming another bay. This makes a good turnaround spot for the hike.

Miles and Directions

0.0 Trailhead.

0.3 Beach.

0.4 Bedrock rib.

0.8 West end of bedrock rib; turnaround point.

1.6 Trailhead.

23 Isle Royale

Highlights: Solitude in the least visited national park; moose; truly wild landscapes of bedrock, Lake Superior, and dense forest
Location: 50 miles northwest of Copper Harbor, in Lake Superior
Type of hike: Two loops which can be combined or hiked separately
Distance: 8.0 miles
Difficulty: Moderate for distance; the hiking is easy
Fees and permits: Registration required upon arrival for all camping. A $4 per day use fee is charged on the ferry, separately from the ferry charge (cash or check only). Fees for the ferry vary depending on which service you use.
Best months: May through mid-September
Camping: Camping is allowed on Isle Royale at designated campsites. Registration and itinerary required on arrival.
Map: USGS Rock Harbor Lodge, Belle Harbor quads (inc.); Isle Royale National Park trail map
Trail contact: Isle Royale National Park Headquarters, (906) 482-0984

Finding the trailhead: These two hikes begin at the Rock Harbor Visitor's Center. GPS: 48.146024, -88.486258
Special considerations: Access to Isle Royale is either by ferry from Houghton or Copper Harbor, or by sea plane from Houghton. Prices and schedules vary, so research departure times and dates. At the beginning and end of the season, ferries do not run every day, and sometimes only twice weekly. Potable water is only available at the Rock Harbor and Windigo visitor areas, and water from any other source must be boiled due to tapeworms. Iodine and UV filters are not sufficient. There are no bears on Isle Royale, so precautions against them are not necessary.

The Hike

Isle Royale is the epitome of untamed wilderness in the Upper Peninsula. To reach it requires a lengthy ferry ride across miles of Lake Superior's deeps. If you're willing to do the extra planning required for a trip here, you will be well rewarded. This island is an environment unlike any other available in the Midwest, boasting 612 species of lichens (about 200 more than any other national park) and thirty-two species of orchids. The island also supports a thriving moose population and a small wolf pack, but has no white-tailed deer or bears. Moose sightings here are not uncommon. Geologically, the island is made from the same rock formation as the Keweenaw Peninsula. Think of it like this: If you cupped your palm, and filled it with water, the Keweenaw would be the pad of your thumb, while the tips of your fingers would be Isle Royale. Your hand is the bedrock curving under Lake Superior and poking out tilted slabs of rock on either end to form islands and peninsulas. The rock here is old and weathered, worn into intriguing formations, with tipped layers creating "fingers" of land between long inlets of Lake Superior water.

Isle Royale

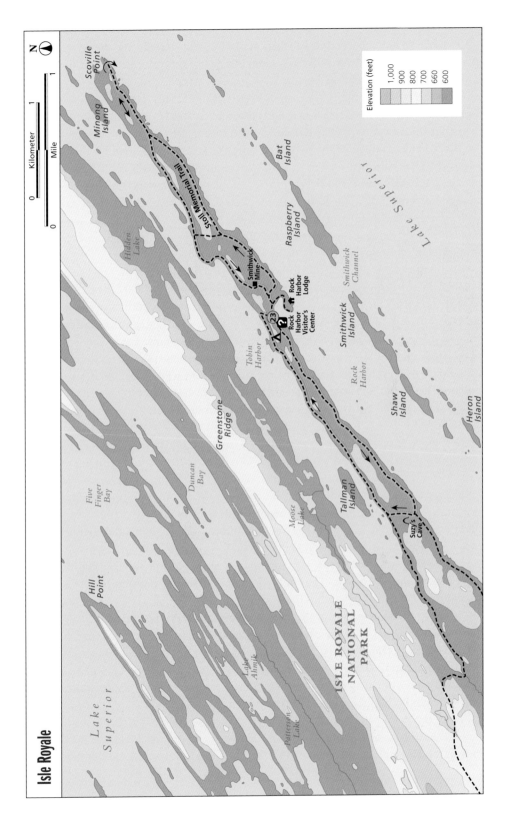

This hike is just a tiny sample of what's available on Isle Royale, and meant to get you started, no matter your skill level. From Rock Harbor, you can explore much farther into the interior of the island.

Begin your hike at the Rock Harbor Visitor's Center. This hike consists of two loops, a total of 8.0 miles, which you can complete separately or combine into one long loop. From the Visitor's Center, head northeast along the marina pathway toward the Rock Harbor Lodge. At the restaurant, turn left, following the signs for the Stoll Memorial Trail. This first section of trail, until about the 1.0-mile mark, is a well-marked interpretive trail. After leaving the Rock Harbor Lodge area, the trail moves steadily northeast, back and forth between shaded forest trails and bedrock ridges with a view of Lake Superior and another ridge of islands to the southeast. Juniper bushes flourish among the rocky crags, and in the forest, the hanging fruticose lichens bring to mind the Spanish moss of much warmer climates.

At the 1.0-mile mark, you enter a designated wilderness area, and the trail becomes rougher, but still easily navigable. On top of the rock outcrops, the trail can be difficult to spot, but watch for rock cairns or an arrow painted onto the surface of the rock. At Mile 1.7 of the hike, a junction appears. Mark the spot, but continue northeast another 0.5 mile on a spur trail to Scoville Point. The rocky point here is scoured by wind, water, and ice, but a few trees still hold out on the point. The views from here are impressive in every direction, with Lake Superior a bit wild on the southeast side, but in sheltered Tobin Harbor on the northwest, the passive water turns to intriguing greens and teals and lets you see clear to the bottom of the lake (it looks shallower than it is).

When you're ready, retrace your steps to the trail junction at Mile 2.7. Turn right (northwest) to take the northern half of the loop back to the Visitor's Center. This is a shady forest trail skirting the shore of the long inlet of Tobin Harbor. If you didn't know this was part of Lake Superior, you might mistake it for an inland lake. It has that quiet, peaceful feeling that Lake Superior, in all of its massive strength, doesn't often exhibit. At Mile 3.2, rejoin the Stoll Memorial Trail, staying on the right hand trail as the Stoll Loop connector trail branches off to your left (south). At about Mile 4.0 of the hike, you will pass a set of fenced off mine pits. Interpretive signs here explain the significance of mining on Isle Royale. Follow this trail another 0.2 mile back to the Rock Harbor Visitor's Center.

To begin the second loop of this hike, head southwest on the trail to Three Mile Campground, which begins just behind the Visitor's Center. This is a fairly easy hike on obvious trails. On my last visit, I was lucky enough to encounter a bull moose not a quarter-mile up the trail. While moose encounters can be dangerous, this particular male was unconcerned by my presence, and I spent several amazing minutes watching him go about his business (which was mostly eating).

From the main path behind the Visitor's Center, turn left (southwest) onto the trail that leads past the shelters of the Rock Harbor Campground. Similar to the first loop, this trail is a pleasant combination of rocks and forest. However, on this stretch, the shoreline trail is often much closer to Lake Superior, and even descends to a small rocky beach area at about Mile 0.6. Follow this pleasant trail for about 1.8 miles to a signed junction with the trail to Suzy's Cave. Ascend the rocks to the cave at about Mile 1.9. Suzy's Cave was formed by wave action when Lake Superior's water levels were much higher. The story goes that the cave was named for Suzy Tooker, a child who often canoed from nearby Tooker's Island about 100 years ago.

After exploring the cave, follow the trail around and to the north as it descends the ridge and meets a junction with the Tobin Harbor Trail at Mile 2.0. Turn right onto this trail, heading northeast, and follow it along the shores of Tobin Harbor as it returns to the Rock Harbor Visitor's Center at Mile 3.8.

Miles and Directions

Scoville Point Loop

- **0.0** Rock Harbor Visitor's Center.
- **0.2** Beginning of Stoll Memorial Trail.
- **1.0** Enter Scoville Point Wilderness Area.
- **1.7** Trail junction to Scoville Point spur.
- **2.2** Scoville Point.
- **2.7** Trail junction.
- **3.2** Stoll Memorial Trail junction.
- **4.0** Historic mine site.
- **4.2** Rock Harbor Visitor's Center.

Suzy's Cave Loop

- **0.0** Rock Harbor Visitor's Center.
- **0.6** Rocky beach.
- **1.8** Trail junction to Suzy's Cave.
- **1.9** Suzy's Cave.
- **2.0** Junction with Tobin Harbor Trail.
- **3.8** Rock Harbor Visitor's Center.

24 Tibbets Falls/Oren Krumm Shelter

Highlights: Rapids and quiet water of the Sturgeon River, Tibbets Falls, and a pleasant backcountry shelter and campsite

Location: 53 miles south of Houghton, 5 miles northwest of Covington

Type of hike: Out-and-back

Distance: 3.6 miles

Difficulty: Moderate

Fees and permits: None, but consider a donation to the North Country Trail Association

Best months: May through October

Camping: The Oren Krumm Shelter and 2 developed backcountry campsites are at this

hike's turnaround point. Big Lake State Forest Campground, 4 miles north of the trailhead, has 12 campsites.

Maps: USGS Covington quad (inc.); North Country Trail Map TMI13, Alberta to Cascade Falls

Trail contact: Michigan Department of Natural Resources, (906) 353-6651; www.michigan.gov/dnr; the Peter Wolfe Chapter of the North Country Trail website, www.northcountrytrail.org/pwf

Finding the trailhead: From Houghton, drive about 44 miles south on US 41 to the intersection with M-28/US 141 S. Turn right onto M-28/US 141 S and drive west 6 miles to Plains Road. Turn right (north) on Plains Road and drive 3 miles, just past the bridge over the Sturgeon River. Park on the broad shoulder on the east side of the road. GPS: 46.584184, -88.576179

Special considerations: Parts of the North Country Trail (NCT) on this hike can be under water during high-water episodes.

The Hike

The Sturgeon River is the central figure in scenes that play out as you move through each new vignette along its shores. The river is first a rapidly flowing rush of background music, then a wild whitewater show, and finally a wide and still portrait of solitude, all in rapid succession.

Begin your visit just north of the Sturgeon River bridge on the west side of Plains Road. Thirty paces north of the bridge, a white-blazed spur trail of the North Country Trail enters a narrow opening in the trees. Walk west on that thin but well-defined path.

Continue straight (west) at Mile 0.4 as the NCT enters from the right (north) and the white-blazed spur trail ends. Walk west on the NCT, listening to the swiftly running river to the south. The trail swings south, following the river as it curves into a large oxbow bend. At the southernmost point of that bend, Kelsey Creek enters from the opposite (south) side and marks the beginning of an extensive stretch of rapids.

Both the river and the trail then curve north, reaching Tibbets Falls at Mile 1.1. Slate ledges extend across the river here, and the falls consist of a series of drops over those ledges.

Tibbets Falls/Oren Krumm Shelter

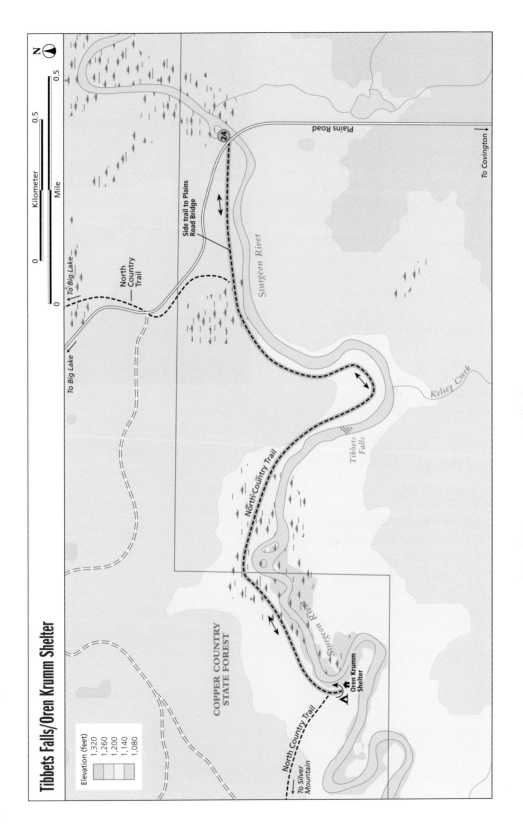

Elevation (feet)
1,320
1,260
1,200
1,140
1,080

N

Kilometer
0   0.5
Mile
0   0.5

To Big Lake

North Country Trail

Side trail to Plains Road Bridge

Sturgeon River

Plains Road

To Covington

To Big Lake

North Country Trail

Tibbets Falls

Kelsey Creek

COPPER COUNTRY STATE FOREST

Sturgeon River

North Country Trail

Oren Krumm Shelter

North Country Trail
To Silver Mountain

24

Continue hiking northwest on the NCT as it follows the river downstream. One last whitewater scene plays out as the river is funneled into a 10-foot-wide chute before bouncing left on the bedrock slabs.

After this last drop, the river current mellows and slows, and the trail enters a stretch of floodplain forest with beaver cuttings nearby. The flat ends and the shelter appears on a 20-foot-high riverbank. The last 0.3 mile of forest before the shelter, and the shelter itself, were burned down in a 2007 wildfire that claimed over 1,100 acres, mostly to the north and west of the site. The Oren Krumm Shelter was rebuilt soon after, and the ecosystem was rejuvenated by this natural part of the cycle that helps sustain life in the forest.

To go to the shelter, turn left (south) at Mile 1.7, as the NCT goes right (west). Walk south 0.1 mile and you will be at the Oren Krumm Shelter. A fire pit, with rustic seating, overlooks the river—a perfect break spot before turning around and hiking back to the trailhead.

Impressive whitewater stretches of the wide Sturgeon River

Miles and Directions

- **0.0** Trailhead at Plains Road.
- **0.4** North Country Trail junction.
- **1.1** Tibbets Falls.
- **1.7** Junction with shelter spur.
- **1.8** Oren Krumm Shelter; turnaround point.
- **3.6** Trailhead at Plains Road.

25 White Deer Lake

Highlights: A quiet, remote wilderness; forest; lakes; cliffs; and history
Location: 10 miles northwest of Champion
Type of hike: Out-and-back
Distance: 7.8 miles
Difficulty: Moderate
Fees and permits: None
Best months: May through October

Camping: Backpack camping is allowed along the trail within zero-impact guidelines. Van Riper State Park, 10 miles south of the trailhead, has 188 campsites.
Map: USGS Summit Lake quad
Trail contact: Ottawa National Forest, (906) 852-3500, www.fs.fed.us/r9/ottawa

Finding the trailhead: From Champion drive 2.3 miles west on M-28 and turn right (north) on Marquette CR 607 (also known as the Peshekee Grade). Drive 9.1 miles north on CR 607, and turn right (north) into the trailhead parking area. GPS: 46.641423, -88.046809
Special considerations: CR 607 is paved, but quite buckled in places, and almost as rough as some unpaved roads. This hike passes through the McCormick Wilderness, a special place. Treat it well.

The Hike

The McCormick Tract is a living vision of what the land was like when it was whole—and what it could be again. Logging hit many of the acres within this backwoods almost a century ago, but time since then has been kind. The McCormick family, descendants of the inventor of the reaping machine, bought land here for a family retreat. These days the McCormick Tract is a federal wilderness and a notable example of a forest's ability to heal itself, if allowed to do so.

Decorating the broad swath of forest is a mosaic of sparkling lakes, clear-running streams, and rock outcrops. A few miles of trails penetrate the remote interior of this 16,000-acre wilderness.

Begin your hike by walking east from the trailhead on the White Deer Lake Trail, immediately crossing a sturdy bridge over the Peshekee River. The trail follows the old road, now overgrown in spots, which went to the McCormick family lodge at White Deer Lake.

Once past the Peshekee the trail turns north, running through a scrubby stretch, and then threads its way between a cliffy headland and the marshy waters of Baraga Creek. At Mile 1.0, the trail crosses Camp 11 Creek, typically an easy rock hop, and runs northeast to the unmarked junction with the Lower Baraga Lake Trail at Mile 1.2. From this direction, the spur path, almost a 180-degree turn to your left, can be easy to miss. It is 450 paces past the creek crossing. Make a mental note of its location for your return trip.

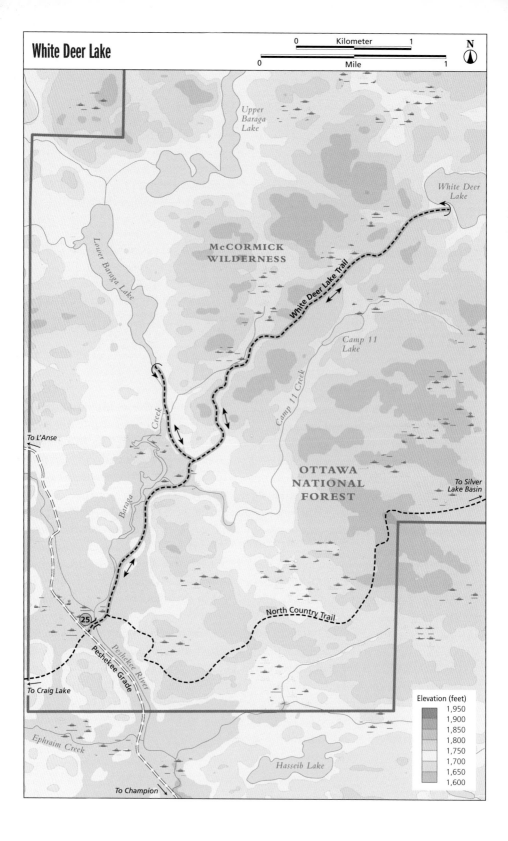

0   Kilometer   1

0   Mile   1

N

Upper
Baraga
Lake

White Deer
Lake

McCORMICK
WILDERNESS

White Deer Lake Trail

Lower Baraga Lake

Camp 11
Lake

Camp 11 Creek

Creek

OTTAWA
NATIONAL
FOREST

To L'Anse

To Silver
Lake Basin

Baraga

North Country Trail

25

To Craig Lake

Peshekee River

Peshekee Grade

Ephraim Creek

Hasseib Lake

To Champion

Elevation (feet)

1,950
1,900
1,850
1,800
1,750
1,700
1,650
1,600

Crossing the Peshekee River in autumn, on the trail to White Deer Lake

Continue hiking northeast on the White Deer Lake Trail. Soon the path ascends a slope, and the ambience of the McCormick forest begins. Maples are the upland hardwood here, and the forest is open and older, untouched by logging for nearly a century.

About a half-mile later the trail dips to run along a marshy section, framed by cliff-hugging white pines. Now returning to the rolling hardwood hills, the path runs northeast to White Deer Lake (Mile 3.2). Just before reaching the lake, the White Deer Lake Trail passes a flat, open spot, where remnants of the foundations of the McCormick lodge buildings remain. You can also see vestiges of foundations of the old McCormick buildings on an island just offshore. In the early 1900s an extensive trail system branched out from this spot. One of those constructed paths, the Bentley Trail, led to the Huron Mountain Club on the Lake Superior shore. Today it is possible to find traces of those old paths here and there in the McCormick backcountry, but they are relics of trails long gone. Off-trail hikers that know of the old trails' locations see them as valuable route clues, fascinating hints of the life of those who walked this land before us.

White Deer Lake is now a peaceful spot. Loons dive for minnows in the shallows around the island; their wailing calls echo across the water at twilight. Eagles pass overhead, and the hustle and bustle of modern life seems far away.

When you are ready retrace your steps to the junction with the Lower Baraga Lake Trail, Mile 5.2 of the outing. Turn right (west) and follow the narrow path as it swings north through the woods. About a quarter-mile later, the path nears Baraga Creek, a scene of subtle but powerful beauty and a nice spot to linger.

Resume hiking north, arriving at the outlet of Lower Baraga Lake at Mile 5.8. Lower Baraga Lake is a mile long, and the outlet is on a narrow, out-of-the-way arm of the lake. I would suggest hiking another 0.1 mile for a better view. A faint path makes its way along the eastern shoreline to a peninsula, Mile 5.9 of the hike.

Retrace your steps to the outlet (Mile 6.0) and south on the Lower Baraga Lake Trail to the junction with the White Deer Lake Trail at Mile 6.6. Turn right (southwest) onto the White Deer Lake Trail, hiking to Camp 11 Creek (Mile 6.8) and back to the trailhead.

Miles and Directions

0.0 Trailhead.

1.0 Camp 11 Creek.

1.2 Lower Baraga Lake Trail junction.

3.2 White Deer Lake.

5.2 Lower Baraga Lake Trail junction.

5.8 Lower Baraga Lake outlet.

5.9 Peninsula on Lower Baraga Lake.

6.0 Lower Baraga Lake outlet.

6.6 Lower Baraga Lake Trail junction.

6.8 Camp 11 Creek.

7.8 Trailhead.

Marquette Area Hikes

arquette is the largest town in the Upper Peninsula, with a population over 20,000. Northern Michigan University and a lively tourist industry support a thriving culture of art and history. The town features several museums, including the Marquette Regional History Center and the Maritime Museum, as well as popular summer festivals like Art on the Rocks and a fall craft beer fest. Further, Marquette is home to several conservation organizations: The Nature Conservancy U.P. offices are here, as well as The Superior Watershed Conservancy and Land Trust, and Save the Wild U.P., a local grassroots organization.

On Presque Isle, a wooded park jutting out into Lake Superior, explore "the black rocks," an ancient lava flow crowning the north end of the peninsula, and cliff dive into a sheltered bay. Also, stop by the local artist galleries and the Moosewood Nature Center, or have a picnic and watch one of the huge freighters being loaded with iron ore from the unique pocket dock.

Hikes in this area feature rocky peaks with sweeping views of Lake Superior, inland lakes where migratory birds, beaver, and deer are frequent visitors, and forest paths through endless blueberry patches. Wolf howls are sometimes heard in the distance. Marquette also has its share of splendid waterfalls; Little Garlic Falls is a local favorite, but you're still likely to have the trail to yourself. These hikes highlight the best that the area has to offer for any experience level.

Marquette County Travel & Visitors Bureau
337 W. Washington St.
Marquette, MI 49855
(800) 544-4321, (906) 228-7749
www.travelmarquettemichigan.com

Michigan Welcome Center
2201 US 41
Marquette, MI 49855

Downwind Sports
514 N. 3rd St.
Marquette, MI 49855
(906) 226-7112
www.downwindsports.com

Marquette Food Co-op
502 W. Washington St.
Marquette, MI 49855
(906) 225-0671
http://marquettefood.coop

26 Blueberry Ridge

Highlights: A sprawling forest walk on summertime ski trails, surrounded by blueberry patches
Location: 6 miles south of Marquette
Type of hike: Lollipop
Distance: 5.6 miles
Difficulty: Easy
Fees and permits: Michigan DNR Recreation Passport

Best months: May through October
Camping: Marquette's Tourist Park campground, about 8.5 miles north of the trailhead, has 110 campsites.
Maps: USGS Sands quad (inc.)
Trail contact: Michigan DNR, (906) 346-9201, www.michigan.gov/dnr

Finding the trailhead: From the intersection of US 41 and CR 553 in Marquette, drive south on CR 553 approximately 6.5 miles to a parking area on the left (east) side of the road. GPS: 46.460974, -87.424428

The Hike

Blueberry Ridge is a classic walk in the woods on summer cross-country ski trails. The paths are wide and level, and although there are hills, the rolling rhythm isn't tedious. The forest here is dominated by white, red, and Scotch pine, oak, and birch, while the groundcover (as you might guess) is thick with blueberry bushes. If you're here in late July or early August, you can gather quarts of berries without moving far off the trail.

This path navigates through portions of different loops, with the goal of hiking as far from traffic noise as possible. Trail junctions are numbered and well marked with arrows and maps.

From the parking area head south (right) on the Crossroads Loop trail. The first half-mile runs through a small area that shows signs of recent logging and curves east into open oak woodlands. It was along this stretch that I found evidence of a wolf utilizing the trail as well. Although similar to domestic dog tracks, wolf tracks are notable by their size, deep nail trenches, and placement one in front of the other. Scat filled with fur is another good indicator.

At Mile 0.8 is an unmarked junction for a connector trail to the Husky Loop. Take the right fork, heading south. At Mile 1.2 is another junction, marker 5, where four trails meet. Continue straight through the junction, as the Husky Loop turns east (left). After a quick 0.1 mile, there is yet another junction, this time marker 7. Turn left onto the Superior Loop trail, now heading northeast.

After junction 7, there is a mile-long stretch of quiet trail. The Superior Loop has slightly more rugged terrain, but it is also the farthest trail from nearby County Roads 553 and 480. This length of trail heads northeast before curving south and then east as it approaches trail marker 8 at Mile 2.3. At this junction, turn south (right) to stay on

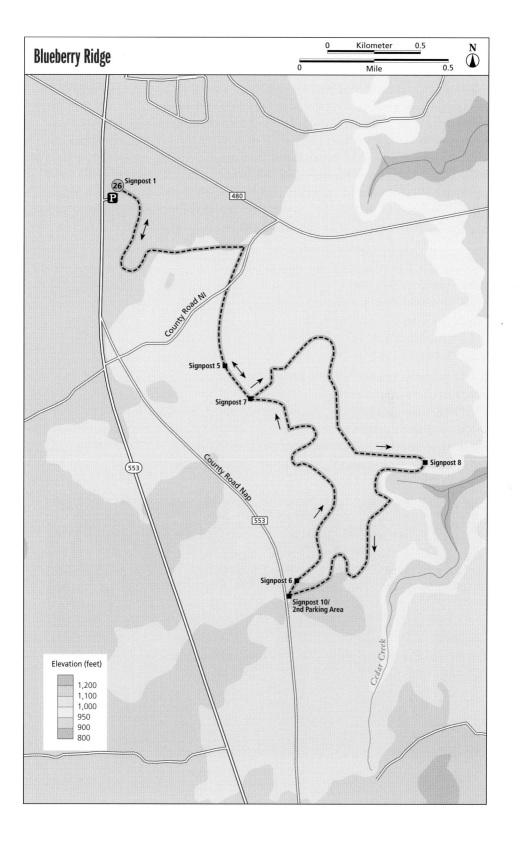

Blueberry Ridge

Elevation (feet)
1,200
1,100
1,000
950
900
800

the Superior Loop, as the Wildcat Loop continues east. The trail quickly turns around and heads west again before curving to the south around Cedar Creek. After another uninterrupted mile, the trail passes marker 10, a second parking area and trailhead, and then swings north (still on the Superior Loop) to marker 6, a junction with the Wolverine Loop at Mile 3.3. Take the right (east) fork, to stay on the Superior Loop. One more quiet mile will find you back at marker 7 (Mile 4.3), this time approaching from the southeast. Take the middle of the three trails, heading northwest, to cross back to the Husky Loop. Marker 5 and the Husky Loop is a quick 0.1 mile. Once again, take the middle of three options, still heading northwest, to retrace your path on the Husky Loop. At Mile 4.8, take the left fork of the unmarked Husky/Crossroads junction and retrace your steps back to the trailhead at Mile 5.6.

Miles and Directions

0.0 Trailhead at trail marker 1.

0.8 Crossroads/Husky trail junction.

1.2 Trail marker 5 junction.

1.3 Trail marker 7 junction.

2.3 Trail marker 8 junction.

3.2 Trail marker 10, secondary parking area.

3.3 Trail marker 6 junction.

4.3 Trail marker 7 junction.

4.4 Trail marker 5 junction.

4.8 Crossroads/Husky trail junction.

5.6 Trailhead at trail marker 1.

Pine, birch, and oak trees dominate the scenery along the Blueberry Ridge Trails.

27 Echo Lake

Highlights: A deep and mysterious inland lake and a high viewpoint
Location: 8 miles north of Marquette
Type of hike: Out-and-back with a short spur
Distance: 2.4 miles
Difficulty: Moderate
Fees and permits: None, but consider a donation to The Nature Conservancy

Best months: May through October
Camping: Marquette's Tourist Park, 7.5 miles south of the trailhead, has 110 campsites.
Map: USGS Buckroe quad (inc.)
Trail contact: The Nature Conservancy, (906) 225-0399, www.nature.org

Finding the trailhead: From the intersection of Hawley Street and Sugarloaf Avenue in Marquette, drive 7.5 miles north on CR 550 and turn left onto an unmarked two-track road. Drive approximately 1.5 miles on this road to a small parking area and gate. GPS: 46.643091, -87.535536
Special considerations: The two-track road can be impassable during wet periods, and difficult anytime for two-wheel-drive vehicles. On my last visit, I parked about a half-mile down the road from the gate and walked in—not an unpleasant addition to the hike.

The Hike

As many times as I've visited Echo Lake, I still have the sense that the lake itself is unknowable. At its deepest point, the lake is 70 feet deep, which means that, roughly, a seven-story building could hide beneath its surface. I continue to find this fact fascinating. Often mergansers drift across the lake's surface and if you're here after dark, you may be lucky enough to hear wolves howling from somewhere nearby. Deer tracks dot the marshy areas on the north shore. Sugar maples, hemlock, and oak trees dominate the forest, and bedrock looms dramatically over and into the lake.

Begin your hike at the gated trailhead and follow the wide road west as it curves slightly north and then more directly south. At a sign for The Nature Conservancy, turn right and follow the path uphill. At 0.5 mile, the trail reaches the lake and boat launch. Turn right and follow the lakeshore trail around to Mile 0.6, where the overlook trail branches off to the right. Follow the overlook trail northwest as it begins to ascend, at first gradually, before it turns sharply southwest and becomes steeper as it makes its way first west and then northeast around the outcrop. The forest closer to the lake is dominated by hemlock, but as the trail climbs, oak begins to take over. In fall, the trail can be covered in leaves, but is still relatively easy to pick out. Use caution though, as thick leaf cover can disguise loose rocks and errant tree roots. The trail reaches the high point at Mile 1.0. Although not as high as nearby Hogback and Sugarloaf Mountains, this spot offers more solitude and a lovely view of Echo Lake framed by both of those peaks.

When you're ready, retrace your steps back to the overlook trailhead (Mile 1.4), and turn right. Follow the trail around to viewpoints on the lakeshore (Mile 1.5) and

Echo Lake

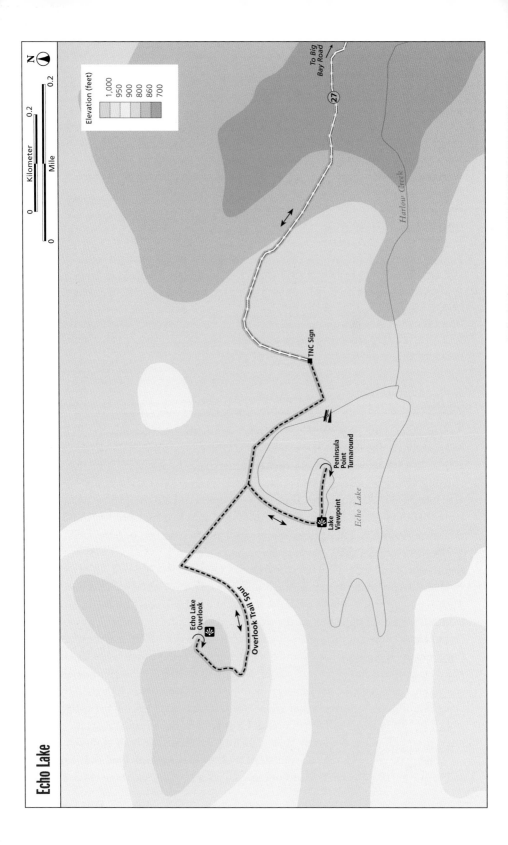

Echo Lake from the rocky shore of the lake viewpoint

peninsula (Mile 1.6). This is not a "beach" lake, and the water is clear enough that the rock shelves sinking almost straight down into the depths are clearly visible for a few feet. Take your time to appreciate this unique place, and when you're ready, retrace your steps back to the trailhead, bypassing the overlook trail at Mile 1.8.

Option: For experienced and agile hikers, it is possible to circumnavigate the lake. This is an attractive option because it offers a view of three "finger lakes" just to the west. Keep in mind that this is a difficult off-trail hike along ridges and slopes with loose rock. It is not recommended for those not used to off-trail hiking. A compass is also recommended, as you will not be able to keep the lake in sight at all times. From the boat launch area, a thin trail heads south on a ridgeline above the eastern shore. The trail quickly disappears though, and you have to forge your own route around the rest of the lake.

Miles and Directions

- **0.0** Gated Trailhead.
- **0.4** Kayak/canoe launch.
- **0.6** Overlook Trailhead.
- **1.0** Overlook.
- **1.4** Overlook Trailhead.
- **1.5** Shoreline viewpoint.
- **1.6** Peninsula point; turnaround point.
- **2.4** Gated Trailhead.

28 Falls of the Yellow Dog

Highlights: A remote series of cascades in a beautiful forest setting
Location: 20 miles west of Big Bay
Type of hike: Out-and-back
Distance: 4.8 miles
Difficulty: Difficult*
Fees and permits: None
Best months: May through October

Camping: Backpack camping is allowed along the trail within zero-impact guidelines. Big Eric's Bridge State Forest Campground, 14 miles northwest of the trailhead, has 20 campsites.
Map: USGS Bulldog Lake quad (inc.)
Trail contact: Ottawa National Forest, (906) 852-3500, www.fs.usda.gov/ottawa

Finding the trailhead: This is a remote trailhead. Consider the advantages of having an accurate map and compass with you in your vehicle. Presume that intersections mentioned are unmarked. Most vehicles, handled with care, can make this drive under good conditions. Poor conditions may make this route impassable.

From the town of Big Bay, drive 2 miles south on Marquette CR 550 (paved) and make a right (south) on Marquette CR 510 (graded dirt). Follow that road southwest 3.2 miles and turn right (west) on Triple A Road (graded dirt).

Drive west and south on Triple A Road. After 3.1 miles bear left (south), continuing on Triple A Road as Northwestern Road goes right (west). Drive another 10.9 miles, first south and then steadily west, on Triple A Road to Anderson's Corner (approx. 46.758478, -87.973840).

Go straight (west) as Ford Road goes right (north). After going west past Anderson's Corner, Triple A Road curves south. Follow that curve south and, after driving 0.5 mile from Anderson's Corner, go straight (south), ignoring a hand-painted dead end sign as Triple A Road goes right (west) (approx. 46.752098, -87.976423).

Continue driving south another 1.5 miles and bear left (south), entering a two-track lane (approx. 46.734781, -87.976014), as the road swings right (west) and uphill. Follow that lane south 0.1 mile to the marked trailhead on the McCormick Wilderness boundary. GPS: 46.733282, -87.975073

Special considerations: This hike passes through the McCormick Wilderness, a special place. Treat it well. The trail leads to the two branches of the Yellow Dog River. Travel off-trail or along faint, rough paths is necessary upstream to view the cascades and waterfalls on both streams.

The Hike

The headwaters country of the Yellow Dog River holds a hallowed spot in U.P. lore. Approached only by a long, dusty drive, the whole upper drainage resides within a wilderness area, the McCormick Tract. There, on a high plateau inhabited by a remarkable forest, the waters of White Deer Lake, Lake Margaret, and dozens of brooks flow north. At the north end of that plateau, the pace quickens. That pristine water tumbles downward hundreds of vertical feet in the cascades known as the Falls of the Yellow Dog. This hike visits these waterfalls on two separate branches of the river, a mile apart.

Falls of the Yellow Dog

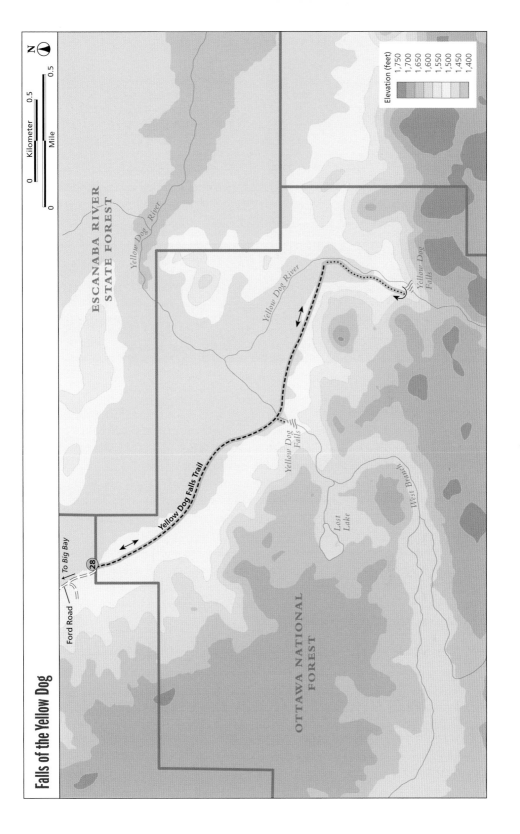

ESCANABA RIVER STATE FOREST

OTTAWA NATIONAL FOREST

Yellow Dog River

Yellow Dog River

Yellow Dog Falls

Yellow Dog Falls

Yellow Dog Falls Trail

Ford Road

To Big Bay

28

Lost Lake

West Branch

N

Kilometer
0   0.5

Mile
0   0.5

Elevation (feet)
1,750
1,700
1,650
1,600
1,550
1,500
1,450
1,400

Trails lined with wildflowers are not uncommon in the U.P.

Start your hike by walking south from the trailhead on an overgrown woods road that quickly becomes a footpath. The path is pleasant. The forest is older and charming with maple and beech and a scattering of hemlock groves.

After a mile the trail reaches the West Branch of the Yellow Dog River. Turn right (south) and work your way upstream about 150 feet to where the cascades begin. A long sliding cascade on a large rock slab is the main feature here, but small waterfalls and cascades continue upstream.

When you are ready retrace your steps north, downstream, to the trail (Mile 1.2). I crossed the West Branch on a log, slippery with moss, with vital assistance from my trekking poles. Follow the path east as it ascends a short, rocky stretch near the West Branch. The path continues to run east, at times a bit faint, and reaches the main branch of the Yellow Dog River at Mile 2.0.

The cascades here are farther off the trail, and rougher to get to, than the West Branch's waterfalls. That said, I think they are exceptionally appealing and worthwhile.

Work your way upstream along the west bank of the river. The river is pleasant here, but there is a good quarter-mile to go before the cascade show begins. Watch for a remnant from the days when this land was the retreat of the McCormick family: two wooden bridges bracketing a small island in the stream.

Just south of those bridges, the valley narrows, the pitch of the stream steepens, and the cascades begin. It is quite a show—a long series of drops as the Yellow Dog River bounces down more than 150 vertical feet in less than a quarter-mile.

Footing is often rough, and somehow that seems appropriate. This is a place to take your time and soak in the sights and sounds of an exceptional stream in a notable forest setting. The top of the cascades (Mile 2.4) is the turnaround point for this hike.

Miles and Directions

0.0 Trailhead.

1.0 Trail crosses West Branch of the Yellow Dog River.

1.1 Top of cascades on West Branch of the Yellow Dog River.

1.2 Trail crosses West Branch of the Yellow Dog River.

2.0 Yellow Dog River (main branch).

2.4 Top of cascades on Yellow Dog River (main branch), turnaround point.

4.8 Trailhead.

29 Hogback Mountain

Highlights: The highest point in the Marquette area, stunning views of Lake Superior and surrounding forests
Location: 4 miles northwest of Marquette
Type of hike: Out-and-back
Distance: 4.6 miles
Difficulty: Difficult
Fees and permits: Michigan DNR Recreation Passport

Best months: May through October
Camping: Marquette's Tourist Park, 5 miles southeast of the trailhead, has 110 campsites.
Maps: USGS Marquette quad (inc.)
Trail contact: Michigan DNR, (906) 346-9201, www.michigan.gov/dnr; North Country Trail Association, (866) HIKENCT (445-3628), www.northcountrytrail.org

Finding the trailhead: From the intersection of Hawley and Sugarloaf in Marquette, drive just over 4.5 miles north on CR 550 to a parking area on the left, known locally as the gravel pit. GPS: 46.615271, -87.468624
Special considerations: Although most of this route is moderate hiking, the last mile to the peak can be difficult, involving steep ascents and some scrambling up potentially slippery rock faces. Further, several old trails cross this area, so a compass is always a good addition.

The Hike

Hogback Mountain is a local favorite. Especially for people new to the area, arriving at the top comes with a sense of accomplishment for having conquered Marquette's highest point. From Hogback's rocky promontory the northern forest seems endless in three directions. Only to the east do the trees give way to the deep blues of Lake Superior stretching off to the horizon. Although you can't always expect solitude here, the trip is still worth it. On one recent visit, a young musician was masterfully playing bagpipes while staring off into the distance.

Begin your hike at the gravel pit parking area. Just about 100 feet south and up a hill, there's a small paved lot and a sign for the Harlow Lake Pathway. Take this trail (to the right) as it heads away from the road and into the forest. Almost immediately you will come to another junction and a sign with a map of the surrounding trails. Take the left fork of this trail and continue to another unmarked junction of three trails. The middle and left hand trails will both take you to the same place; the middle trail navigates around the north side of a large rock outcrop, while the left branch takes you back toward the road and around the southeast face of the outcrop. While the north side (middle trail) is longer, the path through the forest is more pleasant than its counterpart along the road. Taking the middle path, the trail runs east and then south (0.2 mile) before turning east again to skirt the southern edges of a three-quarter-mile-long series of rocky spurs. The trail here is marked with vertical slashes of blue paint. Although some are faint, the trail is generally worn and easy to follow.

Hogback Mountain

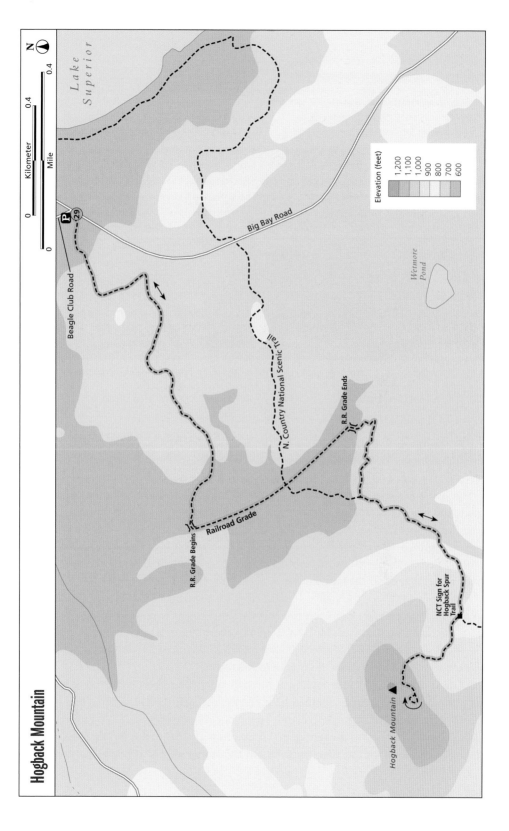

Beagle Club Road

P 29

Big Bay Road

Wetmore Pond

N. Country National Scenic Trail

R.R. Grade Ends

R.R. Grade Begins

Railroad Grade

NCT Sign for Hogback Spur Trail

Hogback Mountain

Lake Superior

N

Kilometer

0   0.4   0.4

0   Mile

Elevation (feet)

1,200
1,100
1,000
900
800
700
600

View of the fall colors of seemingly endless forest from the rocky peak of Hogback Mountain

Before the first mile, the forest on the left side of the trail starts to thin, and through the trees dense shrubs begin to take over. The trail winds between a more open, wetland area on the left and the rocky spurs on the right before crossing a short bridge and emerging on an old railroad grade at Mile 1.0. Turn left onto the railroad grade and follow it south for about 0.5 mile. The hiking on this grade is pleasant, surrounded by speckled alders and a small stream that parallels the west side. The grade is so overgrown that its previous purpose is not obvious. Only an occasional worn railroad tie, almost buried by dirt and new growth, gives any indication that this was once something other than a hiking trail.

At about Mile 1.5, the railroad grade crosses a segment of the North Country Trail (NCT). Turn right onto this trail, crossing the stream on a short bridge. From here, the trail is marked with blue NCT trail markers. This is also the point at which the route meets up with the more popular trail from Wetmore Landing, so expect to share space with more people from here to the top.

The surroundings change rapidly, as the trail enters into open cedar forest. Even on a sunny day, the light is dimmed here, filtered through the tall canopy. The trail runs briefly south, before turning sharply to the northwest for about 0.2 of a mile and then gradually curving southwest again. Up to this point, the trail is mostly level, but here it begins to ascend, at first gradually, but later more steeply as it approaches the mountain. At Mile 1.9, a NCT sign points the way (straight ahead) to the Hogback spur trail. From here to the top, the trail is labeled with vertical white markers.

Although there is less than 0.4 mile from here to the top, this is the most difficult segment of the climb. Parts of the trail ascend slopes covered with loose rocks, while at other points, it's necessary to pick your way up small, but nearly vertical, rock spurs. These obstacles are navigable, with enough footholds and sturdy roots to help ease the way up. As the trail continues up, previews of spectacular landscapes begin to appear through the trees. A last scramble over a smooth rock surface leads to the peak of Hogback and the turnaround point for the hike at Mile 2.3, but take plenty of time at the top to appreciate the views before heading back down.

Miles and Directions

0.0 Trailhead at "gravel pit" parking area.
1.0 Junction with railroad grade.
1.5 Junction with North Country Trail.
1.9 Junction with NCT Hogback spur trail.
2.3 Hogback Mountain peak.
4.6 Trailhead.

30 Laughing Whitefish Falls

Highlights: A famous waterfall, quiet woods, and a hidden chasm
Location: 10 miles west of Chatham
Type of hike: Out-and-back, with 2 stems
Distance: 3.4 miles
Difficulty: Moderate*
Fees and permits: None, but consider a donation to the North Country Trail Association, www.northcountrytrail.org

Best months: May through October
Camping: Forest Lake State Forest Campground, 16 miles east of the trailhead, has 23 campsites.
Maps: USGS Sand River quad (inc.); North Country Trail Map TMI11, Au Train Lake to Little Garlic Falls
Trail contact: Michigan Department of Natural Resources, (906) 339-4461

Finding the trailhead: From Chatham, drive 7.7 miles west on M-94 and turn right (north) on North Sundell Road. Drive 2.3 miles north and turn right (east) into the Laughing Whitefish Falls Scenic Area. Drive 0.4 mile east to the trailhead. GPS: 46.382222, -87.077306
Special considerations: This hike takes place within the Laughing Whitefish Falls State Natural Area. Please treat this special area well. This area is laced with old logging trails. Watch carefully for trail markers as it's easy to miss the little-used spur trails.

The Hike

Laughing Whitefish Falls, plunging 100 feet into a scenic gorge, earns mention as one of the most spectacular waterfalls in Michigan. Picture a 15-foot free fall that sets the stage for the main act, an 80-foot-high bridal train of whitewater tumbling down a rock apron. The striated texture of the rock bounces a zillion small ripples skyward, each sparkling in midday light.

Below the falls the river settles into a scenic gorge, lined with springs, mossy corners, and old-growth white pine and hemlock. A fine maple-beech forest graces the plateau above.

Take a moment to read the educational signboard at the north end of the trailhead parking loop, then hike north on the broad Laughing Whitefish Falls Trail. Go straight (east) at Mile 0.3, as a spur trail of the NCT goes left (north). Continue walking east, descending past a brook gurgling over small ledge drops; a fern garden is nearby.

The falls kind of sneak up on you. A railing appears at Mile 0.6, the river flowing beside it to the right. As you approach, a huge hole opens beyond the railing, to the north, and spray and sound announce the waterfall.

A set of sturdy stairs leads some 150 steps to a viewing platform at the bottom of the falls. This is the best place to view the flowing symmetry of the Laughing Whitefish Falls. Descend the stairs, past intimate views of mossy nooks and crannies, to the viewing platform. This is a superb place for a break.

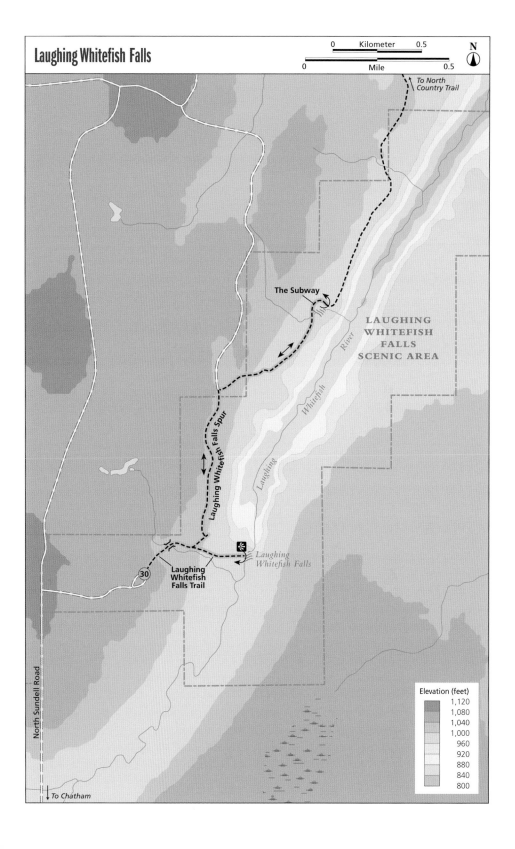

Laughing Whitefish Falls

0   Kilometer   0.5

0   Mile   0.5

N

To North
Country Trail

The Subway

LAUGHING
WHITEFISH
FALLS
SCENIC AREA

Laughing Whitefish Falls Spur

Whitefish

River

Laughing

30

Laughing
Whitefish
Falls Trail

*Laughing
Whitefish Falls*

North Sundell Road

To Chatham

Elevation (feet)
1,120
1,080
1,040
1,000
960
920
880
840
800

Laughing Whitefish Falls' initial 15-foot drop leading to an 80-foot bridal veil of whitewater

When you are ready ascend the stairs and retrace your footsteps to the junction with a spur trail of the NCT, at Mile 0.9 of the hike. Turn right (north) onto the spur trail. A narrow path leads north and fifty paces later becomes an old woods road. This trail is marked with vertical white blazes and blue diamonds. After following the old woods road for about 0.7 mile, the NCT spur trail turns right (east) on a narrow, faint path. Especially in spring, this trail is unworn and nearly invisible. Navigate by following the vertical white blazes.

Follow this path east and north. At Mile 2.0 it curls around the lip of a small, but striking, canyon scene. A brook feeds a thin little waterfall, a 25-foot drop that features cascades, both top and bottom, bracketing an 8-foot free fall. An undercut stretch below the falls led me to label this the "Subway." Beyond, hemlocks line the brook's descent to the river.

I was here during a wet spell. The brook was flowing nicely, and I stayed for a while. The little cove was good company. I couldn't help wondering what other gems lay hidden nearby, tucked in the corners of the Laughing Whitefish River's gorge. To return to the trailhead, retrace your steps south, arriving at Laughing Whitefish Falls Trail at Mile 3.1. Turn right (west) and walk 0.3 mile to the trailhead.

Option: The spur trail continues heading north from the Subway. Because I got temporarily lost on the logging trails on my last trip, I discovered some lovely stretches of North Country Trail downstream, where the river widens and slows, several times with the help of well-constructed beaver dams. About a mile north of the Subway, the spur trail rejoins the east-west NCT and crosses the river. If you choose to lengthen your hike, this is a good turnaround point.

Miles and Directions

0.0 Trailhead.

0.3 Junction with North Country Trail (NCT) spur.

0.6 Laughing Whitefish Falls.

0.9 Junction with NCT spur.

2.0 The Subway, a rock overhang.

3.1 Junction with Laughing Whitefish Falls Trail.

3.4 Trailhead.

31 Little Garlic River

Highlights: Little Garlic River and its cascades, attractive forest, ancient hemlocks
Location: 10 miles northwest of Marquette
Type of hike: Out-and-back
Distance: 8.0 miles
Difficulty: Moderate
Fees and permits: None, but consider a donation to the North Country Trail Association, www .northcountrytrail.org

Best months: May through October
Camping: Marquette Tourist Park, 11 miles south of the trailhead, has 110 campsites.
Maps: USGS Negaunee quad (inc.); North Country Trail Association Map TMI11, Au Train Lake to Little Garlic Falls
Trail contact: Michigan Department of Natural Resources, (906) 346-9201, www.michigan .gov/dnr

Finding the trailhead: From the intersection of Sugarloaf Avenue and Hawley Street, on Marquette's north side, drive west and north 10.4 miles on Marquette CR 550. Turn left (south) into the trailhead parking area (just west of the bridge over the Little Garlic River). GPS: 46.674122, -87.543037

The Hike

Little Garlic River is one of those quiet hikes that steadily grows on you, one subtle scene at a time. The Little Garlic River, a pristine brook trout stream that the trail follows, and the surrounding forest are a pleasure to the eye. Four serene miles from the trailhead, the path arrives at Little Garlic Falls, a scenic stretch of cascades, rapids, and swift water running through a rocky cleft.

Begin your visit along the Little Garlic River by hiking south from the trailhead on the North Country Trail (NCT), through a damp fern garden. The river is just 30 feet to the east. Soon the riverbank rises into a bluff, and the trail ascends into a fine beech-maple forest. About 1 mile from the trailhead, the NCT passes through an ancient stand of hemlocks and a short spur trail leads south, onto a sharp promontory, high above the river.

Continue hiking southwest on the NCT as it descends to run along the river, rises once more to cross a bluff, and returns to river level. As the terrain flattens out, the trail crosses Harrison Road (dirt) at Mile 2.9, and reenters the woods, passing a line of mossy boulders each the size of a small truck.

Now running northwest, the trail passes through open forest. A rock dome shows to the north. After utilizing a plank bridge to cross a marshy spot, the trail winds over several open rock slabs before turning southwest and reaching Little Garlic Falls at Mile 4.0.

I was at Little Garlic Falls at a low-water time and discovered a charming setting beyond the end of the official trail. I worked my way upstream along the north side

Little Garlic River

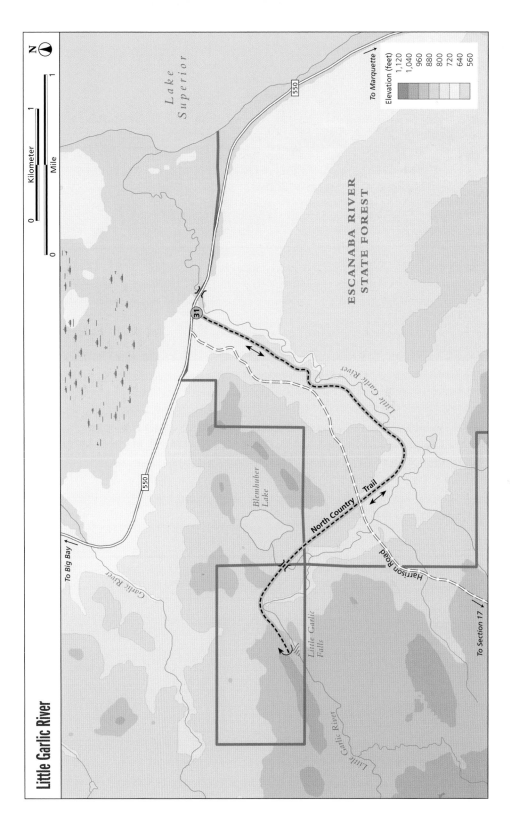

Lake Superior

ESCANABA RIVER STATE FOREST

Blemhuber Lake

Garlic River

Little Garlic River

Little Garlic Falls

North Country Trail

Harrison Road

To Big Bay

To Marquette

To Section 17

550

550

31

N

Elevation (feet)
1,120
1,040
960
880
800
720
640
560

Kilometer
0   1

Mile
0   1

Little Garlic Falls, gurgling cascades in a charming forest setting

for fifty paces and found a memorable scene: a cascade dropping 4 feet into a pool bordered by a 30-foot-high cliff.

Option: Nimble hikers may want to cross to the stream's south shore if conditions allow. I was able to rock hop across, finding a faint path leading upstream for 400 yards. Even at low water the small river retained its charm, rippling over rock slabs and gurgling its way downstream.

Miles and Directions

0.0 Trailhead.

2.9 Harrison Road.

4.0 Little Garlic Falls; turnaround point.

8.0 Trailhead.

32 Morgan Creek/Carp River Falls

Highlights: Two impressive waterfalls and long stretches of charming forest close to Marquette

Location: 2.5 miles south of Marquette

Type of hike: Out-and-back with a short spur

Distance: 4.1 miles

Difficulty: Easy, with a couple of moderate slopes

Fees and permits: None, but consider a donation to one of the local groups who helped

build bridges over Morgan Creek (Lake Superior Watershed Partnership or the Boy Scouts of America)

Best months: May to October

Camping: Marquette's Tourist Park, with 110 campsites, is 4.5 miles from the trailhead.

Map: USGS Marquette quad (inc.)

Trail contact: Noquemanon Trail Network, (906) 235-6861

Finding the trailhead: From Marquette, drive about 2.5 miles south on CR 553. Just before reaching the Marquette Mountain Ski Area, turn right at a dirt road (Marquette Mountain Road, but not signed) just after the first short section of metal railing. Park on the road, or drive in and park in one of many small turn-offs. GPS: 46.510587, -87.415305

Special considerations: During dry periods, any good two-wheel-drive vehicle should be able to drive at least 0.5 mile on Marquette Mountain Road. At other times, four-wheel drive is recommended. The walk in along the forest road is pleasant and not heavily trafficked, especially in September, so I recommend parking on CR 553 and hiking in.

The Hike

The Morgan Creek and Carp River areas feature some lovely scenery without a long trek into the backwoods. For hikers who are not yet comfortable leaving civilization far behind, this hike offers a backwoods feel close to home. My last visit here was in early fall, and throughout the hike I was accompanied by a gentle cascade of maple and birch leaves in dazzling reds and yellows.

Begin your hike heading west on Marquette Mountain Road, on the west side of CR 553 just before Marquette Mountain Ski Area. Although most vehicles can drive this packed dirt road, it's a pleasant hike in among the maples, birches, and cedars, and the road sees only infrequent vehicle use. At about 0.75 mile, the road curves to the south, bringing it closer to the Carp River. After the first mile, you'll leave behind the sound of traffic from 553 and soon the rushing water of the river will become audible from down the steep slope to your left, as the road curves west again. You should also be able to glimpse whitewater through the trees. Several trails wind over the slopes here, but these are generally for mountain biking. However, there are several narrow, unmarked trails leading down to the river. Be aware that these are on steep slopes, so exercise caution if you choose to navigate one. A little past 1.25 miles, you'll come upon several parking pullouts and a trail to your right (south) signed as "Unnamed Morgan Creek Falls." Just past the sign is a short set of stairs leading down, followed by a bridge over Morgan Creek. The

Morgan Creek/Carp River Falls

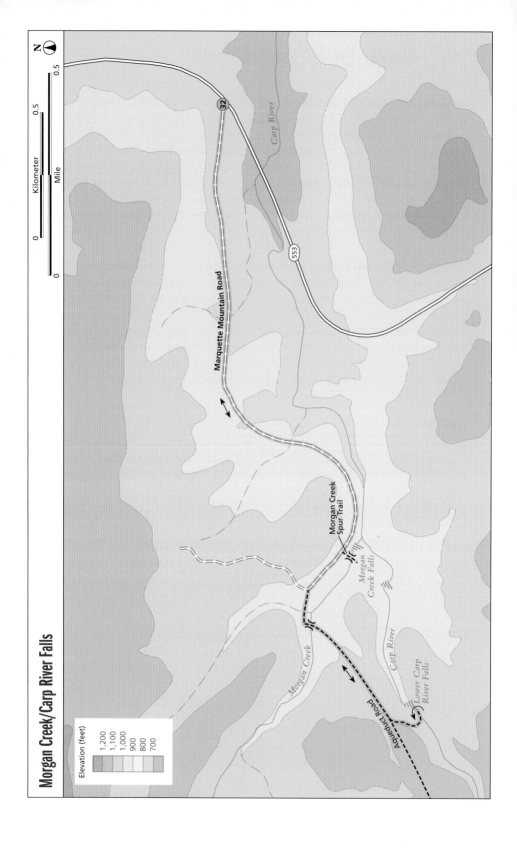

Elevation (feet)
1,200
1,100
1,000
900
800
700

Marquette Mountain Road

Morgan Creek
Spur Trail

Morgan Creek Falls

Morgan Creek

Carp River

Lower Carp
River Falls

Aqueduct Road

Carp River

32

553

N

Kilometer
0   0.5   0.5
Mile
0   0.5

Fall colors just beginning to appear around Morgan Creek Falls

bridge is just upstream from the falls. After crossing, make your way down and to the left (east) for the best viewing of this 20-foot drop, just before Morgan Creek joins the Carp River.

When you're ready, re-cross the bridge and ascend the stairs back to the road. Continue west on Marquette Mountain Road as it curve to the northwest. At Mile 1.5, a road will branch off to your left as Marquette Mountain Road curves west. Continue on Marquette Mountain Road for about 260 feet. Keep an eye out to your left for a bridge crossing Morgan Creek. At about Mile 1.56, a short, steep trail heading southwest connects to a Noquemanon access trail running parallel to (and sometimes on top of) an old aqueduct pipe. Less than 100 feet away from the road, cross Morgan Creek on a bridge built on top of this pipe. The trail here begins to ascend gradually. Continue ascending as another Noquemanon bike trail signed "Yellow" descends to your left. At about Mile 1.9, the trail levels. Continue about 200 feet to another wide two-track on your left. A short ramp of metal and cement, likely left from logging efforts, marks the correct path. Head south on this trail, which also descends into the Carp River valley, and the sound of whitewater will lead you on to the Carp River Falls at Mile 2.12. These falls are considerably larger than Morgan Creek, but more difficult to view. Be aware that some ledges here are undercut by the river and the thick cover of white pine needles is slippery. Still, this is a worthwhile place to spend some time, to listen to the rushing and admire the endless fall of water. This is the most secluded spot on this hike, cut off from the noise of civilization by the earth and rock walls of the valley through which the Carp River runs. When you're ready, retrace your steps back to the trailhead.

Miles and Directions

0.0 Trailhead at CR 553.

1.27 Spur trail to Morgan Creek Falls.

1.29 Morgan Creek Falls.

1.56 Aqueduct Trail.

1.58 Bridge over Morgan Creek.

1.95 Carp River Falls Trail.

2.12 Carp River Falls.

4.1 Trailhead.

33 Whitefish Lake Preserve

Highlights: Quiet inland lake views, wildlife, and boulder-strewn forests
Location: 15 miles east of Marquette
Type of hike: Loop with a short stem
Distance: 1.1 miles
Difficulty: Easy
Fees and permits: None
Best months: May through October

Camping: Laughing Whitefish Campground, 8 miles north of the preserve
Maps: USGS Sand River quad (inc.); The Nature Conservancy's George Shiras III Discovery Trail map
Trail contact: The Nature Conservancy, (906) 225-0399, www.nature.org

Finding the trailhead: From Marquette, drive 4.7 miles south on US 41 to the intersection with M-28. Turn left onto M-28 and drive 14.7 miles to Deerton Road. Turn right onto Deerton Road and follow it 1.5 miles until it dead-ends at Deerton-Onota Road. Take Onota Road to the right for 0.1 mile before making a left turn onto Peter White Road. Drive 2.0 miles until Peter White Road branches to the left (watch for the sign). Continue on Peter White Road 0.9 mile to a small parking area on the left. GPS: 46.4313, -87.0459

Special considerations: Although this is a short hike with easy walking throughout, the trail itself doesn't see much use, so the first 0.5 mile can be tricky to navigate. Keep an eye out for the green and yellow The Nature Conservancy markers, which are posted frequently along the trail. Also, white-tailed deer are populous in this area, and hunting is allowed with a permit from The Nature Conservancy. If you're hiking in late fall, consider wearing bright clothes.

The Hike

The George Shiras III Discovery Trail encourages hikers to step back into history and consider not only the impact that we've had on the land over the last centuries, but also the impact that these places have had on us. The trail wanders along the lake plain under speckled alder shrubs and old-growth hemlocks before rising along an easy slope out of the lake plain and into boulder-strewn forests of young maple and beech. The diffuse green of sunlight through the leaves mingling with songbird tunes drifting down from above lends a fairy-tale air to the landscape here.

Begin your hike by walking northeast around the metal gate that fronts the parking area. On this first 300 feet to the bridge, you'll find yourself surrounded by speckled alder shrubs and multicolored wildflowers like St. John's wort, oxeye daisies, heal-all, and common yarrow. As you reach the footbridge, built on the wooden bones of an old logging bridge, take a few minutes to appreciate the clear views of the tannin-tinted river. Beavers utilize this area, and as you continue over the bridge, you may spot the telltale stumps of gnawed saplings. Almost immediately, the trail branches and you'll follow the right-hand fork (south) to begin the loop. Watch for the yellow and green diamonds of The Nature Conservancy trail markers as you wind around the roots of old-growth hemlocks along the shoreline. At about 0.15 mile, the trail turns

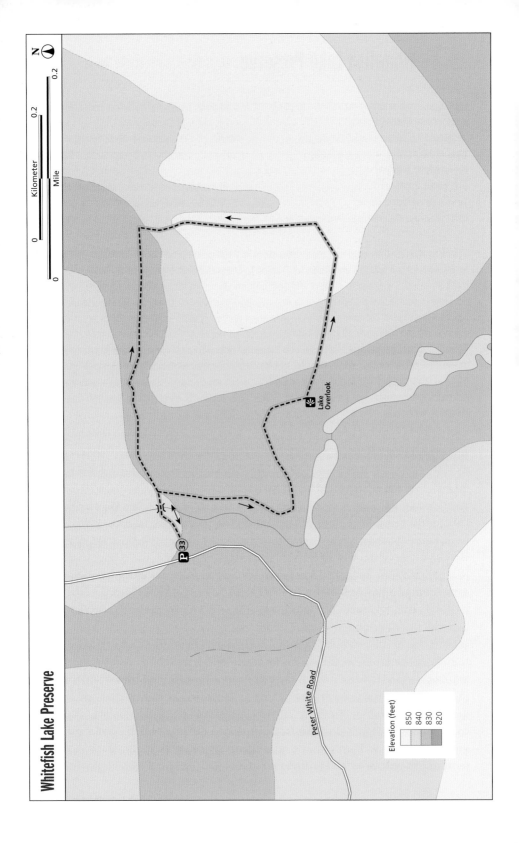

Whitefish Lake Preserve

Lake Overlook

Peter White Road

Elevation (feet)
850
840
830
820

Kilometer
0   0.2

Mile
0   0.2

N

Wild rice, cattails, and lily pads on Laughing Whitefish Lake

east, still following the river as it begins to widen into the north point of Laughing Whitefish Lake. The trail briefly ascends the hillside northeast before quickly turning southeast again and dropping back down to the lake plain to highlight a last clear view of the lake, where the shallow and sluggish water is thick with cattails and wild rice. It was from a canoe on these waters that early conservationist George Shiras III, after whom the trail is named, took the first photographs of wildlife at night. In 1906, those photographs, mostly of white-tailed deer, would become the first wildlife pictures to ever appear in *National Geographic* magazine.

From this point on, the trail turns its back to the lake and ascends out of the moist soils of the lake plain and into drier maple and beech forests. This section of trail can be particularly tricky, as leaf litter covers signs of previous wear. While taking your time to locate the next marker, also pause to take in the massive boulders that seem to rise from the moss and leaf litter into the diffuse green light seeping down through the canopy. The behemoth rocks were dropped here by glaciers as they receded at the end of the last ice age. A few are large enough to sustain their own small gardens of moss and ferns.

Continue to follow the trail markers east until about Mile 0.54, where the trail turns abruptly north as it widens into overgrown logging roads. It has been decades since logging took place here, and although you can still find the decaying stumps of immense trees poking out of the ground cover, the land is recovering nicely, and plant life is slowly reclaiming the open corridors. White-tailed deer use these trails as well, and you can often spot tracks in the mud. Woodpeckers, sandhill cranes, and wild turkeys also wander into these areas, and migratory neotropical songbirds pass through in spring and fall.

At about Mile 0.75, the trail turns west and continues straight back to the bridge and the parking area at Mile 1.1.

Miles and Directions

0.00 Trailhead at gate.

0.06 Bridge over Laughing Whitefish River.

0.38 Whitefish Lake overlook.

0.54 Logging road begins.

0.75 Trail turns west.

1.1 Trailhead.

Escanaba/Iron Mountain Area Hikes

A lthough there are only three hikes offered in this area, each offers a unique experience. The Cedar River Loop, a snowless incarnation of extensive cross-country skiing trails, offers quiet and easy walking in deep cedar woods. Piers Gorge presents a series of impressive falls along an unusually rowdy stretch of the Menominee River. New to this edition, the Bay de Noc–Grand Island Recreation Trail allows hikers to experience eye-catching forest and ridge landscapes while also contemplating the history of the Upper Peninsula, as the trail follows a historic Chippewa portage route between Lake Michigan and Lake Superior.

Escanaba is one of the larger towns in the U.P., with a population of around 12,000. If you're looking for a base of operations from which to begin your U.P. adventures, Escanaba might be a good place to start. Pioneer Trails Park features a campground on the Escanaba River with ninety-six campsites. The town also boasts an extensive lakeshore park and charming historic downtown area. It was also the setting for Jeff Daniels' quirky comedy about U.P. hunters, *Escanaba in Da Moonlight*.

It's easy to get confused in the Upper Peninsula, between Iron River, Ironwood, and Iron Mountain. Although they're all named for the iron ore that was extensively mined here in the late 1800s and early 1900s, each town has its own unique identity. The city has recently incorporated a project to revitalize the downtown area by encouraging local events and renovating historic buildings. On summer Saturdays, visit Iron Mountain's downtown farmers' market. For gear and supplies in Iron Mountain, stop by Northwoods Wilderness Outfitters.

Dunham's Sports
301 Lincoln Rd.
Escanaba, MI 49829
(906) 789-4007

Pioneer Trail Park
6822 US2-41 & M35
Gladstone, MI 49837
(906) 786-1020

Northwoods Wilderness Outfitters
N-4088 Pine Mountain Rd.
Iron Mountain, MI 49801
(906) 774-9009

34 Cedar River Loop

Highlights: Quiet forest and riverside scenes along the Cedar River
Location: 8 miles north of Cedar River, 30 miles southwest of Escanaba
Type of hike: Lollipop
Distance: 5.5 miles
Difficulty: Moderate
Fees and permits: None
Best months: May through October

Camping: Cedar River North State Forest Campground, 2 miles west of the trailhead, has 18 campsites.
Maps: USGS North Lake quad (inc.); Cedar River Pathway Map, Michigan Department of Natural Resources
Trail contact: Michigan Department of Natural Resources, (906) 786-2351, www.michigan .gov/dnr

Finding the trailhead: From the town of Cedar River, drive 1.6 miles north on M-35 and turn left (north) onto River Road (Menominee CR 551). (Alternately, from Escanaba, drive about 28 miles south on M-35 and turn right onto River Road.) Drive 5.8 miles north and turn left (west) onto the gravel lane signed for the Cedar River Pathway and Campground. Drive 0.1 mile west and park in the ski trail parking area. GPS: 45.500207, -87.385911

Special considerations: Parts of this trail are in low-lying areas and can be muddy or ponded to the point of impassibility, especially in May, and even early June, when the area is still overwhelmed by snowmelt.

The Hike

Cedar River Pathway is a classic walk in the woods on a cross-country ski trail that works well as a hiking trail. Along the way the route passes picturesque scenes along the placid Cedar River, hemlock groves, and a seemingly endless parade of pleasant woodland panoramas. Life, like the river's current, seems to flow slower here. This also seemed to be a good place for wildlife viewing in spring, as I was accompanied on my hike by a variety of songbirds. I also glimpsed a coyote loping off into the woods and a couple of garter snakes soaking up the late spring sun.

A series of numbered intersections marks the ski trails here, which are a series of loops. Note that this hike's route begins with trail marker 9, proceeds to 8, and then arrives at 2. At that point it travels in numerical sequence (2, 3, and so on), with the exception of marker 5, which is no longer present.

Begin your hike by walking west on the gravel lane that leads to the campground from the ski trail parking lot. Hike west to marker 9 (Mile 0.2) and turn right (north) on a 4-foot-wide ski lane to marker 8 (Mile 0.6). Turn left (west) and walk 0.3 mile to marker 2 (Mile 0.9). Turn right (northwest), following the Loop 2 ski trail through a cedar stand to a scenic bench on the banks of the Cedar River at about Mile 1.4. I was there on a mellow October day and found the break spot irresistible.

From the riverside bench continue walking north to marker 3 (Mile 1.8). Turn left (north), following the Loop 3 ski trail as it wanders west for a few peek-a-boo

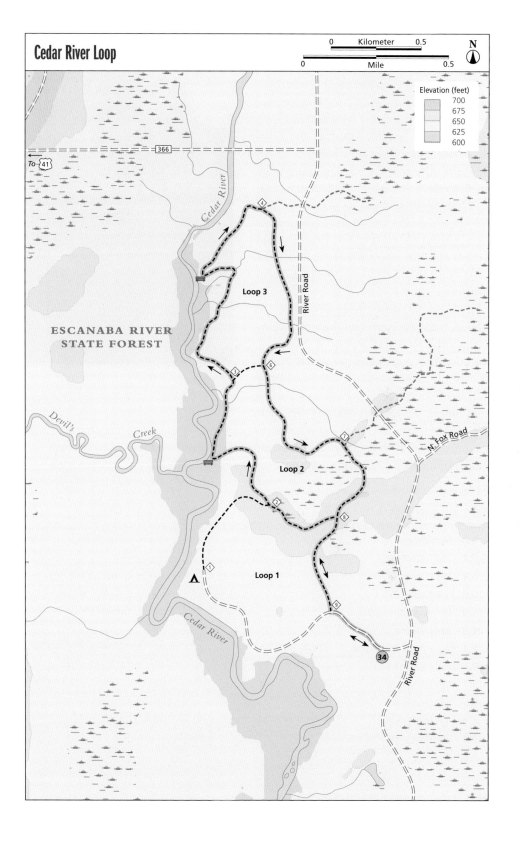

Cedar River Loop

Kilometer
0   0.5

Mile
0   0.5

N

Elevation (feet)
700
675
650
625
600

366

To 41

Cedar River

River Road

Loop 3

ESCANABA RIVER
STATE FOREST

Devil's   Creek

4

3

6

5

7

N. Fox Road

Loop 2

2

8

2

Loop 1

Λ

9

34

Cedar River

River Road

views of the river before swinging inland. A westward leg brings the trail back to the Cedar River for a final visit and another scenic bench, at about Mile 2.4. Next the trail runs northeast to marker 4 (Mile 2.8).

Turn right (south), following the Loop 3 ski trail south through a hemlock grove. The path, despite a few wiggles, runs steadily south to marker 6 (Mile 3.7). Turn left (east) and hike south and east to marker 7 (Mile 4.5). Bear right (southeast) and a few minutes later the trail rises onto a low ridge, perhaps 30 feet high, the major hill of the hike. After miles of flat to rolling terrain, the little ascent is striking.

Hike to marker 8 (Mile 4.9). Bear left (south), retracing your steps from the beginning of the outing to marker 9 (Mile 5.3). Turn left (east) and follow the gravel lane to the ski trail parking area, the hike's end (Mile 5.5).

One of a few clear views of the Cedar River, with pines crowding along the shore

Option: At markers #4 and #7, short side trails run east to River Road. If trail conditions are bad, as they can be in spring, especially, River Road provides a dry and quiet alternative. When I walked the road, it was deserted and pleasant, with songbirds darting back and forth through the open sunny area between the trees.

Miles and Directions

0.0 Trailhead.

0.2 Trail Marker #9.

0.6 Trail Marker #8.

0.9 Trail Marker #2.

1.4 First riverside bench.

1.8 Trail Marker #3.

2.4 Second riverside bench.

2.8 Trail Marker #4.

3.7 Trail Marker #6.

4.5 Trail Marker #7.

4.9 Trail Marker #8.

5.3 Trail Marker #9.

5.5 Trailhead.

35 Bay de Noc-Grand Island National Recreation Trail

Highlights: A quiet forest hike on a 40-mile-long historical trail
Location: 18 miles north of Escanaba
Type of hike: Out-and-back
Distance: 4.6 miles
Difficulty: Easy
Fees and permits: None

Best months: May through October
Camping: Camping is allowed at the trailhead, and Haymeadow Creek Campground, 7 miles north of the trailhead, has 5 campsites.
Maps: USGS Rapid River quad (inc.)
Trail contact: Hiawatha National Forest, (906) 786-4062, www.fs.usda.gov/hiawatha

Finding the trailhead: Drive 2 miles east from Rapid River on US 2 to CR 509. Turn left (southeast) on CR 509 and drive 0.6 mile. Turn left (north) and continue 1 mile on CR 509 to the trailhead on the left. GPS: 45.931615, -86.918465

The Hike

This is a straightforward hike on well-marked and age-worn trails. The complete trail, 40 miles long, stretches from Rapid River to M-94, near Munising. Running parallel to the Whitefish River, the trail recreates a portage route used by the Algonquian Noquet tribes traveling between Lake Michigan and Lake Superior. Later, early European fur traders and loggers used the trail until a road was constructed. In some places, the centuries of use are evident in the deeply worn trail.

The hike itself is a quiet and peaceful walk on level, sometimes sandy ground. I was here in October, and had the trail to myself. However, this is a multipurpose trail, so it is possible to encounter equestrians and bicyclers during busier summer months. The first 10 miles of the 40-mile-long trail maintain the relatively flat mixture of forest, open spaces, and stream crossings. After that, the trail begins to rise and fall with a hilly glacial landscape more typical of the central Upper Peninsula. The hike I've outlined here is short, but can easily be extended to whatever point feels comfortable.

Begin your hike at the trailhead parking area. Head north on the campground road about 200 feet to the trail on the right (east). Follow this trail steadily north as it passes through sun-speckled red pine and jack pine woods. After crossing an ATV trail at Mile 0.2, the trail passes through more open areas. Although these open areas are pretty, and interspersed with groups of pine saplings, the evidence of logging is sometimes obvious. There is still beauty here, though it may not be the awe-inspiring delight of old-growth forests. Rather, this is the beauty that comes from recovery. The trail, the land, and generations of trees were here before the Noquets forged this trail, and they will renew themselves in spite of human needs for resources. There is wildlife here as well. Woodpeckers were at work in the trees, tapping out rhythms that I could hear far down the trail. On my return trip, there were coyote footprints along the sandy trail that hadn't been there only an hour before, and the thought that

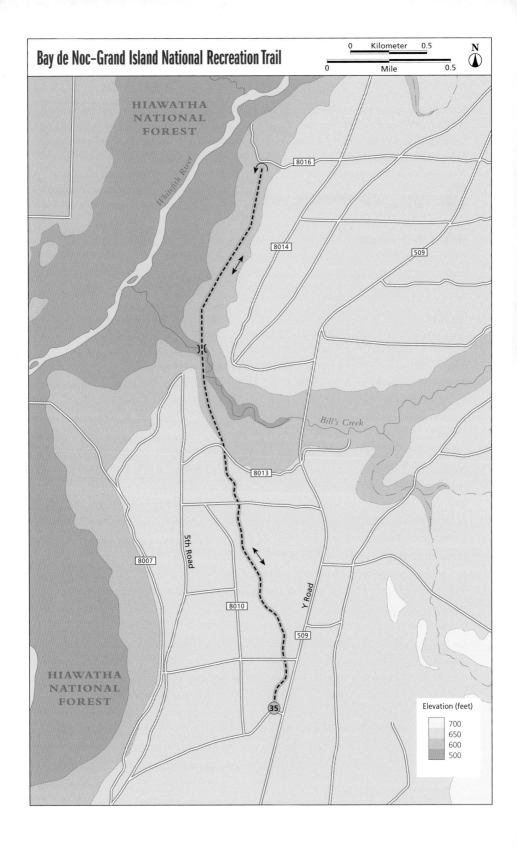

Bay de Noc-Grand Island National Recreation Trail

HIAWATHA
NATIONAL
FOREST

Whitefish River

8016

8014

509

Bill's Creek

8013

8007

5th Road

8010

Y Road

509

35

HIAWATHA
NATIONAL
FOREST

Kilometer

Mile

N

Elevation (feet)

700
650
600
500

New growth and open meadows demonstrate the tenacity of ecosystems recovering from logging and fire.

I was sharing the path with wild neighbors also made me optimistic about the future of the habitat here.

In the first 1.2 miles, the trail crosses three more deserted dirt roads at fairly regular intervals. Trees take over after this last road crossing, as the trail wanders through jack pine, red pine and aspen forest. At Mile 1.5, still running north, the trail crosses Bill's Creek and continues on to FR 8016 at Mile 2.3, the turnaround point for this hike.

Miles and Directions

- **0.0** Trailhead.
- **0.2** ATV trail crossing.
- **0.5** FR 8008 crossing.
- **0.8** Unnamed dirt road crossing.
- **1.2** FR 8013 crossing.
- **1.5** Bill's Creek bridge.
- **2.3** FR 8016, turnaround point.
- **4.6** Trailhead.

36 Piers Gorge

Highlights: A series of booming drops on the Menominee River, Misicot Falls earns a "don't miss" rating.
Location: 3 miles south of Norway
Type of hike: Out-and-back
Distance: 2.6 miles
Difficulty: Moderate
Fees and permits: None

Best months: May through October
Camping: Carney Lake State Forest Campground, 23 miles north of the trailhead, has 16 campsites.
Map: USGS Norway quad (inc.)
Trail contact: Dickinson County Area Partnership, (906) 774-2002, www.dickinson chamber.com

Finding the trailhead: From the town of Norway, drive south 1.9 miles on US 8 and turn right (west) on Piers Gorge Road. Drive 1.2 miles west to the trailhead. GPS: 45.759106, -87.941709
Special considerations: Use caution on wet rocks near the river.

The Hike

Most times the Menominee River runs deep and slow and stretches almost 100 yards across. At Piers Gorge it gets rowdy. Bedrock walls channel the flow into an 80-foot-wide sluice, part of a mile-long stretch of swift water and rapids topped off by a crescendo of thundering ledge drops. It is a striking scene of big water throwing its weight around, the roaring soundtrack a not-too-subtle warning to stand clear, or else.

Quieter scenes also play out here. One could spend hours musing over the current's patterns etched in the bedrock. The forest is a pleasure to the eye, and eagles and ospreys scan from above for an easy meal.

A relatively benign trail leads upstream from the trailhead, periodically marked by posts that announce first pier and so on. Branching off from these posts are much rougher trails that nimble hikers use to approach the river. "Piers" refer to bedrock reefs that extend into the current. The Third and Fourth Piers also possess names as waterfalls.

Begin your tour by walking west from the trailhead, quickly crossing two wood bridges that span a damp cedar stand bisected by a clear-running brook. The broad trail arrives at the First Pier's signpost at Mile 0.1. Hike south, off the maintained trail, for one hundred paces here and a broad bedrock dome borders the first whitewater, a 2-foot drop.

Return to the main trail and hike up a rocky rise, arriving at the post for the Second Pier at Mile 0.4. This one is louder, and if you hike twenty-five paces south, you learn why. Huge wave trains scour the river's southern shore, while a series of ledge drops inhabit the near side of the river.

Backtrack to the main trail and resume walking west, arriving at the Third Pier's post at Mile 0.5. The Third Pier is Misicot Falls, a 5-foot drop, followed by powerful

Piers Gorge

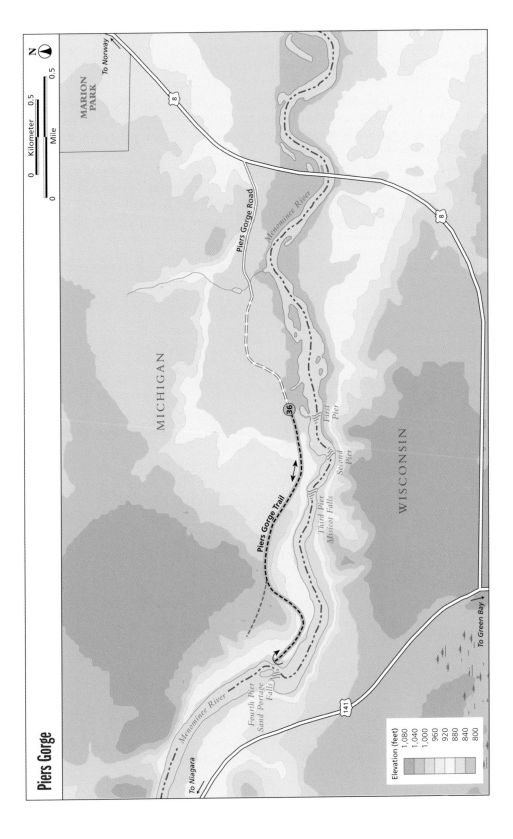

Elevation (feet)

1,080
1,040
1,000
960
920
880
840
800

MICHIGAN

WISCONSIN

MARION PARK

To Norway

To Niagara

To Green Bay

Menominee River

Piers Gorge Road

Piers Gorge Trail

First Pier

Second Pier

Third Pier
Misicot Falls

Fourth Pier
Sand Portage Falls

8

8

36

141

N

0   Kilometer   0.5

0   Mile   0.5

rapids featuring fearsome standing waves. A large, automobile-size boulder below the drop splits the wave trains, forming a foamy bulge. The trail here is perched on the hillside, offering a memorable high view of the falls and rapids.

When you are ready continue hiking west on the Piers Gorge Trail, arriving at a split at Mile 0.8, where a signpost points the way to the Fourth Pier. Bear left (southwest), walking a trail that becomes a narrow footpath and leads to the Fourth Pier's post at Mile 1.3.

The Fourth Pier, Sand Portage Falls, is a 5-foot cascade, a narrows between bedrock. Legend has this as the beginning of the Great Sand Portage, a prudent alternative to canoeing the rapids and a route that stretched from here to below the First Pier's unnamed falls. Knowing of the legend, I wondered who had used this portage and what stories they told of this place.

Miles and Directions

- **0.0** Trailhead.
- **0.1** First Pier.
- **0.4** Second Pier.
- **0.5** Third Pier, Misicot Falls.
- **0.8** Junction with path to Fourth Pier, Sand Portage Falls.
- **1.3** Fourth Pier, Sand Portage Falls; turnaround point.
- **2.6** Trailhead.

Munising Area Hikes

Without a doubt, Munising sits at the verge of some of the most breathtaking landscape in the U.P.: Pictured Rocks National Lakeshore. There's no denying the draw of the colorful sandstone cliffs, etched into fantastical shapes over ages of contact with Lake Superior's stubborn waves. Hiding in the forests behind the cliffs, lakes and waterfalls abound, while farther east along the shore, cliffs fall away and transition into rocky shoreline and then high sweeping sand dunes. Like the Porcupine Mountains, this is an area that one could easily spend weeks exploring.

Although most of the hikes offered here are within Pictured Rocks National Lakeshore, there are also a few gems outside of its boundaries. Grand Island, for example, is an almost uninhabited island rising like a statuesque queen out of Munising's bay. Also, the Rock River Falls are nestled into a corner of the Hiawatha National Forest, and are often overlooked by locals and tourists alike, but these falls are well worth the pleasant hike into a secluded area.

Munising is a lovely town fronted by Lake Superior and backed by high rolling hills. The Interagency Visitor Center, shared between the Hiawatha National Forest and Pictured Rocks, is a great place to get more information on the surrounding area.

Alger County Transit—ALTRAN
530 East Munising Avenue, P.O. Box 69
Munising, MI 49862
906-387-4845
www.altranbus.com/backpack.html

Munising Visitors Bureau
PO Box 421
Munising, MI 49862
(906) 387-1717

Pictured Rocks National Lakeshore/
Hiawatha National Forest
Interagency Visitor Center
400 East Munising Ave.
Munising, MI 49862-0040
(906) 387-3700

Shopko Hometown
E9916 M-28 East
Wetmore, MI 49895
(906) 387-2525

37 Au Sable Point/Log Slide

Highlights: Terraced bedrock, shipwrecks, a lighthouse, a historic log slide, sweeping high views of Lake Superior, and huge sand dunes
Location: 13 miles west of Grand Marais
Type of hike: Out-and-back
Distance: 7.0 miles
Difficulty: Moderate
Fees and permits: None for day hikes. There is a fee for backcountry camping permits within Pictured Rocks National Lakeshore (PRNL).

Best months: May through October
Camping: PRNL's Hurricane River Campground, at the trailhead, has 21 campsites.
Maps: USGS Au Sable Point and Grand Sable Lake quads (inc.)
Trail contact: PRNL, (906) 387-3700 or (906) 387-2607, www.nps.gov/piro

Finding the trailhead: From Munising, drive about 35 miles east on Alger CR H-58 and turn left (north) onto the Hurricane River Campground road. Drive a quarter-mile north on the campground spur road to the picnic area beside the mouth of the Hurricane River. Follow the signs for Au Sable Lighthouse Parking. GPS: 46.6656, -86.1670

Special considerations: This hike follows either the Lake Superior shoreline or the Lakeshore Trail, part of the North Country Trail (NCT). Shoreline routes can be glorious in fine weather, but windy and exposed in poor conditions.

The Hike

This hike is a charmer, with a bit of a daydreamlike feeling to it. First there's the stroll down the Lake Superior shoreline, a pleasant beach that turns to gently sloped sandstone bedrock scalloped by waves. Farther down the shore are the ribs of shipwrecks and the Au Sable Point Lighthouse. Then the route follows the Lakeshore Trail to a viewpoint perched 300 feet above the lake, a lookout with a sweeping view of the spectacular Grand Sable Dunes.

Begin at the picnic area just east of the mouth of the Hurricane River. Step down to the shoreline and walk east along the water's edge. As the beach nears a low bedrock cliff, the remains of an 1883 shipwreck, the *Mary Jarecki*, appear just below the waterline.

Continue walking east, now on sandstone bedrock, along a ledge-lined bluff green with moss and hanging gardens and dripping with small waterfalls. When water levels on Lake Superior are high, wading around one or two sandstone outcroppings may be necessary.

The remains of two more shipwrecks, the *Sitka* and the *Gale Staples*, lie just offshore 150 yards west of Au Sable Point. At low tide, parts of these ships actually lie on the beach, so watch your footing, as steel and wood rise out of the sand in unexpected places. Hike east from the wrecks, watching for log steps that lead up the bluff. Ascend those steps to the lighthouse complex, a collection of four buildings and the white tower. During the peak summer season, park rangers offer guided tours of the historic light station.

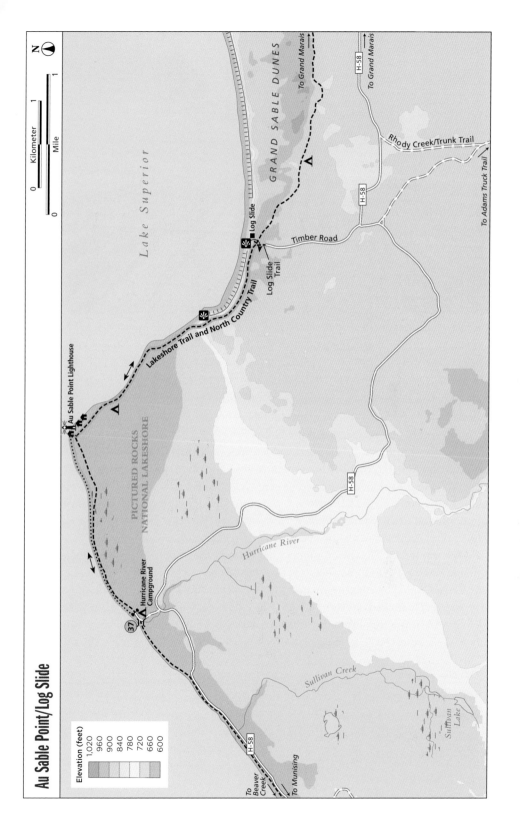

Au Sable Point/Log Slide

Elevation (feet)
1,020
960
900
840
780
720
660
600

N

0   Kilometer   1

0   Mile   1

Lake Superior

GRAND SABLE DUNES

To Grand Marais

To Grand Marais

H-58

Rhody Creek/Trunk Trail

To Adams Truck Trail

Log Slide

Timber Road

Log Slide Trail

H-58

Lakeshore Trail and North Country Trail

Au Sable Point Lighthouse

PICTURED ROCKS NATIONAL LAKESHORE

Hurricane River Campground

37

Hurricane River

H-58

Sullivan Creek

Sullivan Lake

To Beaver Creek

To Munising

Remains of the steamer Sitka *resting on the Lake Superior shoreline since wrecking in 1904*

The Lakeshore Trail (also a segment of the NCT) runs by the west side of the buildings. Hike that trail—a charming path just inland from the lakeshore—southeast as it ascends a wooded bluff. Along this stretch are several viewpoints that may well be the most spectacular perspective of the Grand Sable Dunes. The tall dunes and shoreline sweep east in a graceful arc; sand and tan tones are offset by the lake's deep blue.

Still climbing, the trail reaches a high plateau and runs east, arriving at the Log Slide at Mile 3.5. During the logging era workers slid the cut trees down a steep chute in the dunes to the lake below. A wide spur trail runs north one hundred paces to an overlook that offers sweeping views of Lake Superior and the Grand Sable Dunes. This is the hike's turnaround point.

Option: If Lake Superior is too rough for hiking the shoreline, or you're uncomfortable wading around obstacles, it is also possible to reach the light station via the old Coast Guard road that runs parallel to the shore. This is a pleasant walk through the woods on a packed dirt surface. Stairs descend to the beach at intervals, so you can still view the shipwrecks from the deeper beach areas. From the light station, continue on the Lakeshore/NCT as directed above.

Miles and Directions

0.0 Hurricane River mouth.

1.5 Au Sable Point Lighthouse.

3.5 Log Slide; turnaround point.

7.0 Hurricane River mouth.

38 Beaver Lake Loop

Highlights: A quiet inland lake, forest, wildlife, and beach along Lake Superior shoreline
Location: 20 miles northeast of Munising
Type of hike: Loop
Distance: 10.2 miles
Difficulty: Difficult due to distance; the hiking is moderate
Fees and permits: None for day hikes. There is a fee for backcountry camping permits within Pictured Rocks National Lakeshore (PRNL).

Best months: May through October
Camping: Backpack camping is allowed at designated sites within zero-impact guidelines. PRNL's Little Beaver Lake Campground, at the trailhead, has 8 campsites.
Map: USGS Trappers Lake quad
Trail contact: PRNL, (906) 387-3700 or (906) 387-2607, www.nps.gov/piro

Finding the trailhead: From Munising, drive 19 miles east on Alger CR H-58 and turn left (north) onto Little Beaver Lake Road (gravel). Drive 3 miles north on that road to the Little Beaver Lake Campground. GPS: 46.557937, -86.362836
Special considerations: This hike follows Twelvemile Beach and the Lakeshore Trail along the Pictured Rocks shoreline. As a shoreline route it can be glorious in fine weather, but windy and exposed in poor conditions. Many PRNL trails, with the exception of the Lakeshore Trail, have no official names. However, trail junctions tend to be well marked with directional arrows and mileage to landmarks, other trail junctions, and so on. Some intersections on the map have been designated Junction A, Junction B, and so on, to avoid confusion.

The Hike

East of Spray Falls, the Pictured Rocks cliffs that line the Lake Superior shoreline for 15 miles taper off and Twelvemile Beach begins. The vertical relief of the craggy coast moves inland and becomes the rim of the vast valley known as Beaver Basin.

Not only is Beaver Basin a noticeable healthy bulge in the long, skinny national lakeshore boundary lines, parts of the basin are the lakeshore's quietest corner. Moose wander through, sampling the greens at Trapper Lake; bald eagles and river otters like the fishing at Beaver Lake; and rare coaster brook trout run up Seven Mile Creek.

One dirt road touches the edge of the basin, leading to Little Beaver Lake. There, a loop hike begins that swings around Beaver Lake, winds through a swath of remote forest, and runs the wave-washed beach of Lake Superior for miles.

Begin your circuit at the south end of the Little Beaver Lake Campground by hiking south on the Beaver Lake Trail. That path weaves its way southeast, then east, reaching the shoreline of its namesake at about Mile 0.8. I was there on a morning when the lake was a giant reflecting pool. The stillness was broken only by a kingfisher and an eagle passing by. For about half a mile the trail stays a stone's throw from the shore, then moves inland a tad in an area of meadowlike old fields. Crossing

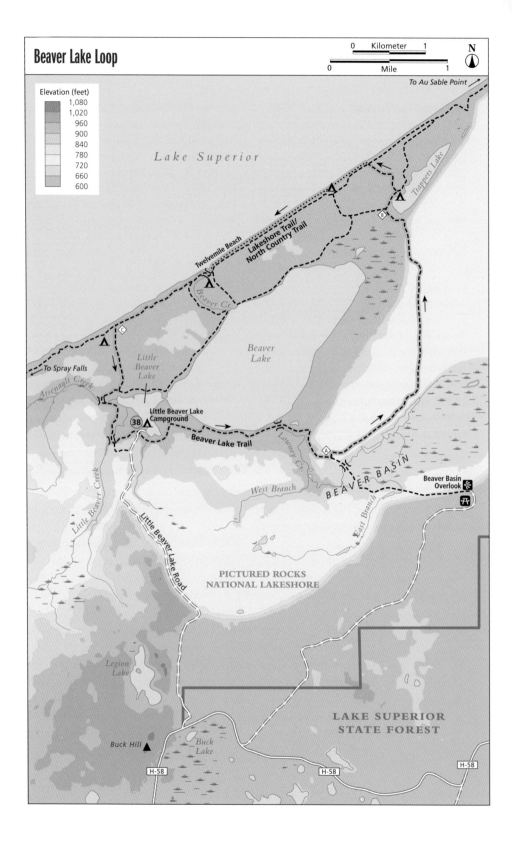

Beaver Lake Loop

0 — Kilometer — 1

0 — Mile — 1

N

Elevation (feet)
- 1,080
- 1,020
- 960
- 900
- 840
- 780
- 720
- 660
- 600

To Au Sable Point →

Lake Superior

Twelvemile Beach

Lakeshore Trail/
North Country Trail

Beaver Cr.

Trappers Lake

8

To Spray Falls →

Arsenault Creek

C

Little Beaver Lake

Beaver Lake

Little Beaver Lake Campground

38

Beaver Lake Trail

Lowney Cr.

A

BEAVER BASIN

Beaver Basin Overlook

Little Beaver Lake Creek

Little Beaver Lake Road

West Branch

East Branch

PICTURED ROCKS
NATIONAL LAKESHORE

Legion Lake

Buck Hill

Buck Lake

LAKE SUPERIOR
STATE FOREST

H-58

H-58

H-58

a bridge over Lowney Creek, the Beaver Lake Trail heads south and ascends to an intersection at Mile 2.4, designated Junction A.

Turn left (east), following a sign for Trappers Lake. The trail follows an old woods road northeast, along the forested rim of a low plateau that occupies a large wedge of Beaver Basin. About a mile northeast of Junction A, the trail begins an almost due north run to Trappers Lake. Finally it descends to an intersection just southwest of the lake at Mile 5.3, Junction B. Turn right (northeast) and follow the sandy trail 0.1 mile to the Trappers Lake campsite (Mile 5.4) and another intersection. Turn left (north) on a connector trail that runs northwest to Lake Superior.

Walk 0.5 mile northwest to an intersection with the Lakeshore Trail (Mile 5.9), on a bluff above Twelvemile Beach. Take a moment to savor the view from the 40-foot-tall bluff. Then descend a sandy ramp to the beach below and walk southwest toward the distant ramparts of Grand Portal Point, some 8 miles off.

Hike the shoreline to the mouth of Beaver Creek, then turn left (south) and follow a path along the creek a little less than 100 yards, pass a massive log jam, and arrive at a trail bridge at Mile 7.7. Cross the bridge to Beaver Creek's north side and follow the Lakeshore Trail west to an intersection at Mile 7.9. Turn right (west) there, following the Lakeshore Trail (also the North Country Trail) west as a trail that leads to Beaver Lake goes left (south).

Walk west on the Lakeshore Trail to an intersection at Mile 8.6, designated Junction C. Consider a break on the nearby bluff top (a few feet north) that overlooks Lake Superior, the last lake view on this hike. At Junction C turn left (south), as the Lakeshore Trail continues straight (west), and hike 0.6 mile to an intersection (Mile 9.2) above an inlet of Little Beaver Lake. Turn right (west), following a connector trail that crosses Arsenault Creek on a sturdy bridge, meanders past sandstone cliffs, and arrives at a junction just beyond Little Beaver Creek at Mile 9.9. Turn left (east), following the White Pine Nature Trail to the trailhead at Mile 10.2.

Miles and Directions

0.0   Little Beaver Lake trailhead.

0.8   Beaver Lake.

2.4   Junction A.

5.3   Junction B.

5.4   Trappers Lake campsite.

5.9   Lakeshore Trail/Twelvemile Beach.

7.7   Beaver Creek.

7.9   Beaver Creek junction.

8.6   Junction C.

9.2   Little Beaver Lake junction.

9.9   Little Beaver Creek junction.

10.2   Little Beaver Lake trailhead.

39 Bruno's Run Loop

Highlights: Undeveloped lakes, an ancient hemlock grove, quiet forest, and river
Location: 15 miles south of Munising
Type of hike: Loop
Distance: 8.6 miles
Difficulty: Moderate
Fees and permits: None
Best months: May through October

Camping: Hiawatha National Forest's Pete's Lake Campground, just east of the trailhead, has 41 campsites.
Maps: USGS quads Corner Lake, Tie Lakes; Hiawatha National Forest Bruno's Run handout map
Trail contact: Hiawatha National Forest's Munising Ranger District, (906) 387-3700, www.fs.usda.gov/hiawatha

Finding the trailhead: From Munising, drive 3.1 miles south and east on M-28 and turn right (south) on Alger CR H-13 (also known as Forest Highway 13). Drive 10.3 miles south and turn left (east) on FR 2173. Drive 0.5 mile east. Then turn right (south) on FR 2256 (Pete's Lake Campground Road). Drive 0.3 mile south and turn right (south) into the trailhead parking area. GPS: 46.229596, -86.601620

The Hike

Bruno's Run is a loop trail that has a pleasant rhythm about it. It goes like this: Walk a mile or so through fine forest. The terrain is sometimes rolling hills, but it's not grueling. All the while scan for flashy pileated woodpeckers and other forest delights. Then arrive at a quiet lakeshore and enjoy loons, eagles, breezes, and broad vistas. Repeat the lake rhythm seven times. Ditto the forest part, and throw in an ancient hemlock cathedral for good measure. Did I mention passing clear-running streams several times and enjoying an abundance of peace and quiet?

Begin your circuit tour by walking east through the Pete's Lake Campground. At the east end of the campground loop, a blue diamond marker and a hiker sign mark the path's beginning. Walk a woodsy 0.7 mile east and north and cross quiet FR 2173 to its east side.

Hike south and east. Nearby Grassy Lake is visible through the trees. Then walk along the lake's hemlock-lined shore. At the end of the shoreline stretch, the trail passes over the lake's outlet stream on a sturdy bridge. It then again crosses FR 2173 (at Mile 1.6) and immediately arrives at McKeever Lake. For the next half-mile, the Bruno's Run Trail winds along that lake's shore, finally swinging southwest, and crosses Deer Creek on another solid bridge.

Now running steadily westward, the path nears an arm of McKeever Lake, passes Wedge Lake, and curls around Dipper Lake. Next the trail crosses FR 2258 (Mile 4.0) and nears Indian River as it approaches Forest Highway H-13 at Mile 4.2. Pay attention here. Walk up the road's embankment and turn left (south). Walk 100 feet

Bruno's Run Loop

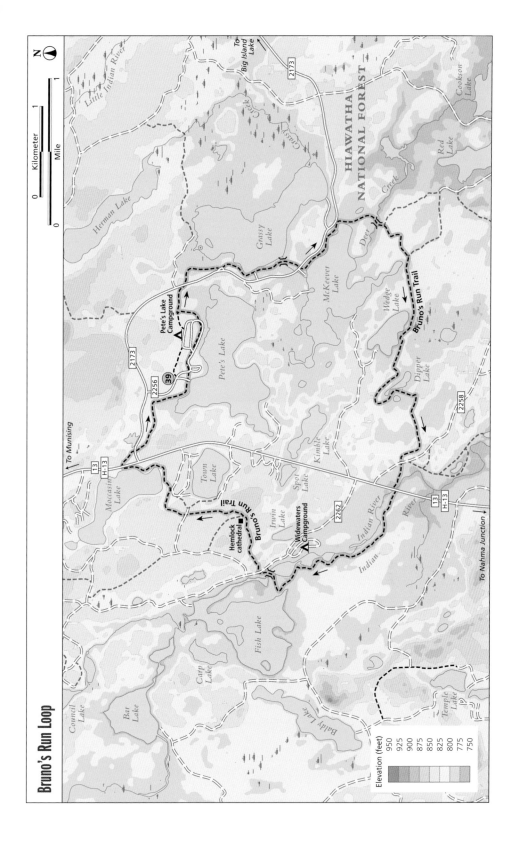

Elevation (feet)
950
925
900
875
850
825
800
775
750

Passing through the densely vegetated wetlands between Dipper Lake and its unnamed companion

south along the highway, utilizing the highway bridge to cross Indian River. Then turn right (northwest), descending the embankment to the trail.

Hike west, then northwest on the Bruno's Run Trail. The river broadens at a place aptly known as Widewaters, and the trail nears the shore and crosses the stream at Mile 5.7.

Hike east as the trail ascends a ridge and arrives at a grove of virgin hemlocks at Mile 6.1. Someone once told me, "Old-growth forest just has a way of making you feel good, making you feel that something is very right here." This is such a place, and a sign offers lyrical comment.

When you feel ready to move on, continue hiking east and north on the Bruno's Run Trail. An educational sign mentions that a trail segment here follows the grade of the Nahma and Northern Railway, a logging-era railroad.

A half-mile of trail along Moccasin Lake's shore precedes a second crossing of Forest Highway H-13 at Mile 7.1. Cross the highway to its east side. Then follow the trail into the woods, hiking southeast to a third crossing of FR 2173 at Mile 7.4. Cross that road and continue walking southeast on the Bruno's Run Trail, arriving at the trailhead at Mile 8.6.

Miles and Directions

0.0 Trailhead at Pete's Lake.

0.7 FR 2173 (first crossing).

1.6 FR 2173 (second crossing).

4.0 FR 2258.

4.2 Forest Highway H-13 (first crossing).

5.7 Indian River footbridge.

6.1 Hemlock cathedral.

7.1 Forest Highway H-13 (second crossing).

7.4 FR 2173 (third crossing).

8.6 Trailhead at Pete's Lake.

40 Chapel Loop

Highlights: Pictured Rocks cliffs, Grand Portal Point, Chapel Rock, and Chapel Falls
Location: 20 miles northeast of Munising
Type of hike: Loop
Distance: 9.7 miles
Difficulty: Moderate
Fees and permits: None for day hikes. There is a fee for backcountry camping permits within Pictured Rocks National Lakeshore (PRNL).

Best months: May through October
Camping: Backpack camping is allowed at designated sites within zero-impact guidelines. PRNL's Little Beaver Lake Campground, 15 miles east of the trailhead, has 8 campsites.
Map: USGS Grand Portal Point quad
Trail contact: PRNL, (906) 387-3700 or (906) 387-2607, www.nps.gov/piro

Finding the trailhead: From Munising, drive 13.9 miles east on Alger CR H-58 to Melstrand. Turn left onto Chapel Road (gravel) and drive 5.1 miles north to the Chapel trailhead. GPS: 46.519795, -86.462162

Special considerations: This hike follows the Lakeshore Trail, part of the North Country Trail (NCT), along the Pictured Rocks shoreline. As a shoreline route it can be glorious in fine weather, but windy and exposed in poor conditions. Sometimes the Lakeshore Trail runs right along the top of the cliffs, other times it is a stone's throw inland. Along the latter stretches unofficial spur paths often lead to the cliff tops and worthwhile views. Use caution near the edges of the cliffs. The Pictured Rocks cliffs consist of undercut and honeycombed sandstone. What you are standing on, if close to the cliff edge, may not be solid rock. Within Pictured Rocks National Lakeshore, many trails—with the exception of the Lakeshore Trail—have no official names. Trail junctions, however, tend to be well marked with directional arrows and mileage to landmarks, other trail junctions, and so on.

The Hike

One hike stood head and shoulders above all others when I asked hikers for nominations for this book—the Pictured Rocks circuit known as the Chapel Loop. Take even the briefest of glances at this route's attractions, and the reasons for its reputation are obvious.

This hike begins in a quiet forest and continues to a notable waterfall. Next it arrives on the shores of Earth's largest freshwater lake, but not just in any old spot. For 5 eye-catching miles, the path follows what may well be the U.P.'s most spectacular shoreline. A parade of convoluted cliffs, natural arches, and rushing streams line the trail, which hugs the rim of the escarpment between Chapel Beach and the Mosquito River. Grand Island's sharp northern prow marks the western horizon, while the eastern shore arcs to far-off Au Sable Point.

Begin your loop hike on the north side of the parking area at the Chapel trailhead. Hike north on a broad trail signed for Chapel Falls to that cascade (Mile 1.3). Chapel Falls begins with a 10-foot-high free fall that leads into a long waterslide on a steep rock slab. From the falls continue hiking north, reaching a junction with the

Chapel Loop

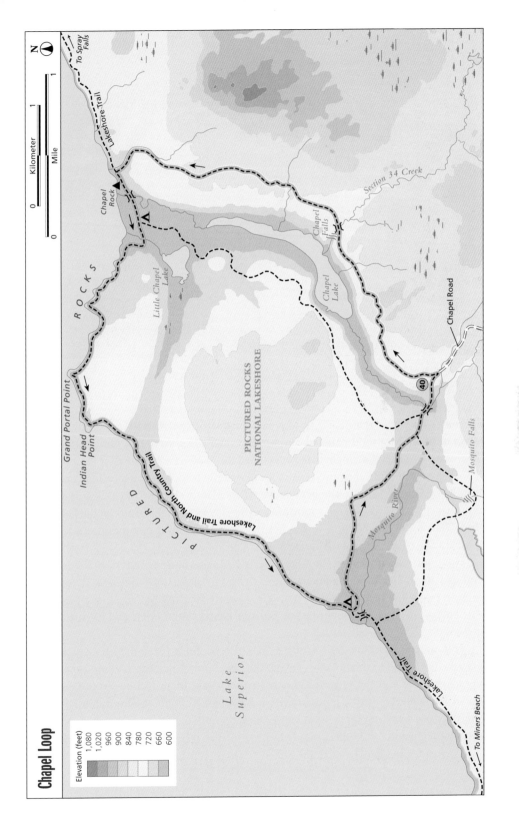

Elevation (feet)

1,080
1,020
960
900
840
780
720
660
600

N

Kilometer
0   1

0   Mile   1

To Spray Falls

Lakeshore Trail

Chapel Rock

Section 34 Creek

Chapel Falls

Little Chapel Lake

Chapel Lake

Chapel Road

Chapel Rock

R   O   C   K   S

Grand Portal Point

Indian Head Point

PICTURED ROCKS NATIONAL LAKESHORE

Lakeshore Trail and North Country Trail

P   I   C   T   U   R   E   D

40

Mosquito Falls

Mosquito River

Lake Superior

Lakeshore Trail

To Miners Beach

A side trip to secluded Mosquito Falls is definitely worth the effort.

Lakeshore Trail (also the NCT), at Mile 3.1. Turn left (west), but before continuing take a moment to view the tunnel-like windows and arches of nearby Chapel Rock. The waves of a previous, higher lake era etched this sandstone landmark.

Hike west on the Lakeshore Trail, crossing a sturdy bridge over the rushing creek that drains Chapel Lake, to the bluff above Chapel Beach. Follow the trail west past the Chapel Beach campsites to a junction at Mile 3.3. Go straight (west) on the Lakeshore Trail at that intersection, as another trail goes left (south) past the west side of Chapel Lake to the Chapel trailhead.

Continue hiking west on the Lakeshore Trail. As that path ascends from the west end of Chapel Beach, it wanders along the rim of several small cliff-bound coves, each a compelling scene. The trail arrives at a significant promontory at about Mile 4.1. This point's west side offers a fine view of Grand Portal Point and its partially collapsed arch, a half-mile farther west.

Follow the Lakeshore Trail west to Grand Portal Point (Mile 4.9). Its wooded, plateau-like top offers memorable views to the east. Savor those eastern views, because the hike's route is about to turn a corner that will leave them behind. From Grand Portal Point hike west to a point known as Indian Head Point at Mile 5.2. A sandy ledge on that headland offers long views along the row of cliffs that lead southwest, the next segment of the hike.

From Indian Head, the cliffs and the Lakeshore Trail ever so slowly descend to meet the Mosquito River at its mouth. Watch for a wooded promontory above a sandstone arch about a half-mile north of Mosquito River. At Mile 7.8 the path arrives at a junction, beside the rushing waters of the Mosquito River. Turn left (east) as the Lakeshore Trail goes right (west) to cross the river on a sturdy bridge. Hike east, following a trail that runs north of the Mosquito River, to the Chapel trailhead.

Go straight (east) at Mile 9.3 as a path from Mosquito Falls enters from the right (south). Then bear right (south) at Mile 9.4, as a path enters from the left (north) from Chapel Beach. Hike south and east, arriving at the Chapel trailhead at Mile 9.7.

Option: A trip to Mosquito Falls is a worthwhile addition to this loop. To add Mosquito Falls, continue on the Lakeshore Trail as it crosses the Mosquito River, rather than turning east at Mile 7.8. Less than 0.2 mile after crossing the river, the Lakeshore Trail meets another trail heading southeast. This trail loops around to Mosquito Falls and then continues on to the Chapel trailhead. This trail will add about 0.75 mile to the length of the loop.

Miles and Directions

0.0 Chapel trailhead.

1.3 Chapel Falls.

3.1 Lakeshore Trail junction (Chapel Rock).

3.3 Junction with trail leading south past west side of Chapel Lake.

4.9 Grand Portal Point.

5.2 Indian Head Point.

7.8 Mosquito River.

9.3 Junction with trail from Mosquito Falls.

9.4 Junction with trail from Chapel Beach.

9.7 Chapel trailhead.

41 Grand Island Loop

Highlights: Pristine Lake Superior shoreline on an offshore island, quiet forest, cliff-top views of Pictured Rocks
Location: 2 miles north of Munising
Type of hike: Loop, with 2 short stems
Distance: 10.9 miles
Difficulty: Difficult due to distance; the hiking is moderate

Fees and permits: There is a daily entrance fee of $2 per person.
Best months: May through October
Camping: Grand Island features remote camping at designated sites only.
Maps: USGS Munising (inc.) quad; Hiawatha National Forest Map
Trail contact: Grand Island National Recreation Area, (906) 387-3700, www.fs.usda.gov

Finding the trailhead: From Munising, drive 2.9 miles north and west on M-28 and turn right (north). Drive 0.3 mile north to the ferry dock. GPS: (ferry dock) 46.443692, -86.663373
Special considerations: A passenger ferry offers service to Grand Island from late May to early October. Call (906) 387-2600 for ferry information. Grand Island's fabled black flies and mosquitoes can be a considerable factor from mid-May through mid-July.

The Hike

Grand Island, aptly named and 8 miles long, is an offshore version of Pictured Rocks. Its quiet north end features miles of scenic sea cliffs, a near mirror image of its mainland sibling. While Grand Island has no shortage of its own attractions, as a Pictured Rocks veteran I found the views of that craggy mainland coast from Trout Bay Overlook remarkable.

This hike features an abundance of junctions; most have directional signs. These intersections do not have names, however, so on the map they have been designated as Junction A, Junction B, and so on, to avoid confusion.

Begin your tour at Williams Landing, walking north on a sandy dirt road to Junction A at Mile 0.1. Turn left (west) on a grassy road that runs a tad inland from the island's shore through a hardwood forest with a sprinkling of hemlocks. About a mile from Junction A, the lane touches the shoreline near a sandy cove and begins a scenic run north. Long sight lines stretch west to little Williams Island and north to the looming cliffs of Grand Island's remote north end.

As the road runs north, the shoreline bluff rises to a cliffy crag, lowering as the lane reaches Junction B at Mile 2.9. Go straight (north); a connector road goes right (east). Walk north, past a campsite to a junction with the Thunder Coves Trail at Mile 3.3. Turn left (west) following the narrow footpath one hundred paces west to the shore, a low cliff. Continue north, past two benches to a point sixty paces north of the second bench, a good turnaround point. Savor the views and retrace your steps to the Thunder Coves Trail junction (Mile 3.9) and Junction B (Mile 4.3).

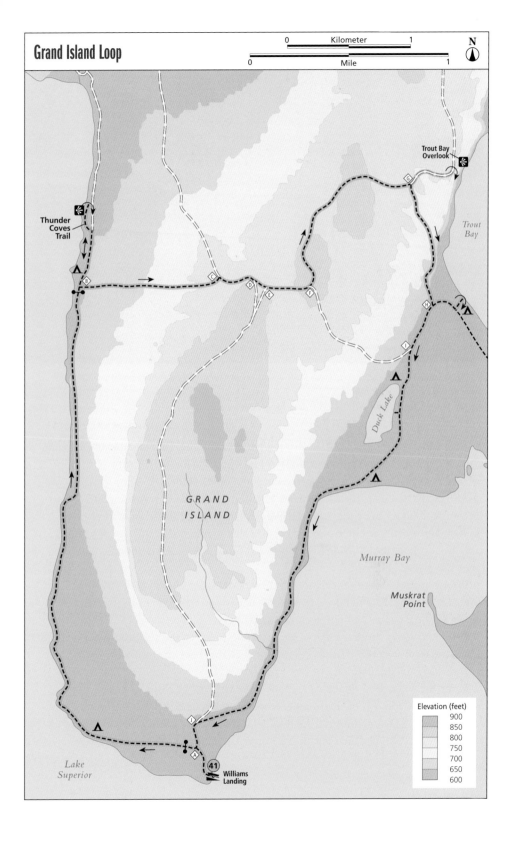

Grand Island Loop

Kilometer
0   1

Mile
0   1

N

Thunder
Coves
Trail

Trout Bay
Overlook

Trout
Bay

GRAND
ISLAND

Duck Lake

Murray Bay

Muskrat
Point

Lake
Superior

Williams
Landing

41

Elevation (feet)
900
850
800
750
700
650
600

Bear claw marks on a beech tree. Beech bark disease is threatening beech trees and their nuts, an important black bear food source.

Turn left (east) and hike along a dirt road that ascends into the island's interior, and begins a compact series of intersections at Junction C (Mile 5.1). Turn right (southeast) on a sandy road that quickly arrives at Junction D (Mile 5.3). Turn left (east) on another sandy woods road that leads to Junction E at Mile 5.4. At Junction E bear left (east) and hike east to Junction F (Mile 5.6), the last of this string of intersections.

Turn left (north) at Junction F and walk a shady mile north and east, following a sandy lane to Junction G (Mile 6.6). Go straight (northeast) as a trail that connects to Trout Bay goes right (south).

Walk a quarter-mile east to Trout Bay Overlook, which may well be the highlight of the day's outing. I visited on a crystalline fall day, and the view from this perch 150 feet above the bay was sublime, even mesmerizing.

Sweeping views stretched across the sparkling water to the Pictured Rocks cliffs, some 5 miles off. Past those last two promontories, the shoreline ran east to the far-off horizon and Au Sable Point.

From the Trout Bay Overlook, retrace your steps to Junction G (Mile 7.0) and turn left (south) on a trail that connects to Trout Bay and follows the route of an overgrown road. Descending off the bluff to the forest floor below, the trail reaches Junction H at Mile 7.7. Turn left (north) onto a sandy lane that quickly arrives at a signboard near Trout Bay at Mile 7.9. At the signboard a boardwalk leads a stone's throw north to benches and Trout Bay's beach, a scenic break spot.

Trout Bay's beach, part of the isthmus that stretches from Grand Island's "mainland" to its "thumb," is an example of the creative power of lake currents and waterborne sand. The isthmus is a tombolo, a land bridge that connects two previously isolated bodies of land.

After visiting Trout Bay return to Junction H (Mile 8.1). Go straight (south) and follow the sandy lane south to Junction I (Mile 8.5). Bear left (south). About a quarter of a mile south of Junction I, the lane enters a long hemlock grove; Duck Lake is visible to the right. A short side-trip is available here—a spur trail leads west eighty paces to a viewing platform on that pond's shore.

After passing Duck Lake the lane continues south, soon running along Murray Bay's western shore and arriving at Junction J at Mile 10.7. Turn left (south) and 0.1 mile later go straight (south) at Junction A. Past that final intersection, the hike arrives at the Williams Landing trailhead at Mile 10.9.

Miles and Directions

0.0 Williams Landing trailhead.

0.1 Junction A.

2.9 Junction B.

3.3 Thunder Coves Trail junction.

3.6 Turnaround point on Thunder Coves Trail.

3.9 Thunder Coves Trail junction.

4.3 Junction B.

5.1 Junction C.

5.3 Junction D.

5.4 Junction E.

5.6 Junction F.

6.6 Junction G.

6.8 Trout Bay Overlook.

7.0 Junction G.

7.7 Junction H.

7.9 Trout Bay Beach (west end).

8.1 Junction H.

8.5 Junction I.

10.7 Junction J.

10.8 Junction A.

10.9 Williams Landing trailhead.

42 Grand Sable Dunes Loop

Highlights: Quiet forest, impressive sand dunes, and Lake Superior shoreline
Location: 2 miles west of Grand Marais
Type of hike: Loop
Distance: 12.2 miles
Difficulty: Difficult
Fees and permits: None for day hikes. There is a fee for backcountry camping permits within Pictured Rocks National Lakeshore (PRNL).

Best months: May through October
Camping: Grand Marais's Woodland Park, 2 miles east of the trailhead, has 125 campsites. Backpacking camping, with a permit, is allowed at designated sites.
Map: USGS Grand Sable Lake (inc.) quad
Trail contact: PRNL, (906) 387-3700 or (906) 494-2660, www.nps.gov/piro

Finding the trailhead: From downtown Grand Marais, drive 1.4 miles west on Alger CR H-58. Turn right (northwest) into the Sable Falls trailhead parking area. GPS: 46.666967, -86.013819
Special considerations: Part of this hike is off-trail, including a descent of the Log Slide, a steep and intimidating dune slope. Below, the route follows Lake Superior's shoreline for miles. In high winds or storms, the shoreline is unpleasant and can be dangerous. Near the end of the hike, the route requires crossing Sable Creek without the benefit of a bridge. I utilized a handy log jam; alternatively it would be an easy wade. Remote shoreline is important wildlife habitat. While you are hiking be sure to give wildlife lots of room, especially during the spring and early summer nesting season.

The Hike

When it comes to sand dunes, the Grand Sable is a knockout. Three hundred feet high and 5 miles long, this massive tan headland towers over the deep blue of Lake Superior. The hike loops around the dunes, first skirting their inland edge where forests meet sand slopes. Then the route plunges from the crest of the dunes to the lakeshore, an adventurous descent that leads to a route along a wild shoreline, beneath the towering dunes. Finally the hike winds along Sable Creek, past Sable Falls.

Begin your hike from the northwest corner of the Sable Falls trailhead parking area, where a broad dirt trail (a segment of the North Country Trail) leads west into the shady woods and a sign reads "Visitor Center 1 Mile." Bear left (south) at Mile 0.2, as the Dunes Trail goes right (north) over a bridge on Sable Creek. Walk south through a fine beech-maple forest; dunes show across the creek now and then. At Mile 1.0 the path arrives at CR H-58, with the PRNL Grand Sable Visitor Center just to the west.

Cross CR H-58 and hike southwest through meadow-like fields and woodlots. At a boat landing the trail comes back to CR H-58 and runs west along its south shoulder to skirt the north end of Grand Sable Lake. As the road continues southwest, the Lakeshore Trail follows the lake's shoreline briefly east and then southwest again before turning west and crossing CR H-58 (Mile 4.1), this time to the northwest.

Grand Sable Dunes Loop

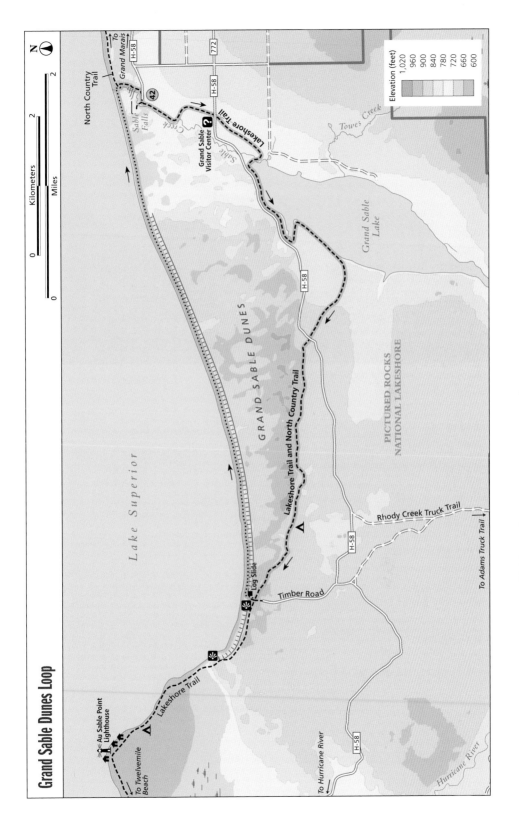

Legend / Labels:

N

Elevation (feet)
1,020
960
900
840
780
720
660
600

Kilometers
Miles

Lake Superior

North Country Trail

To Grand Marais

H-58

772

H-58

Sable Falls

Sable Creek

42

Grand Sable Visitor Center

Lakeshore Trail

Towes Creek

Grand Sable Lake

GRAND SABLE DUNES

H-58

Lakeshore Trail and North Country Trail

PICTURED ROCKS NATIONAL LAKESHORE

Log Slide

Timber Road

H-58

Rhody Creek Truck Trail

To Adams Truck Trail

Lakeshore Trail

Au Sable Point Lighthouse

To Twelvemile Beach

To Hurricane River

H-58

Hurricane River

The immense headland of the Grand Sable Dunes towers above Lake Superior's blue waters.

Now the path runs west through the woods. Dunes sometimes appear to the north and sandy slopes spill past tree trunks. A half-mile or so before you get to the Log Slide, the path ascends a wooded dune northward and emerges onto an open dune with Lake Superior beyond. The Lakeshore Trail then dives back into the woods, arriving at the Log Slide at Mile 6.8. An exhibit here offers historical notes from the logging era, and a broad path leads north one hundred paces to a viewpoint. To the east the shoreline is an appealing crescent below the immense mass of the Grand Sable Dunes.

While savoring the view, take time for a reality and weather check. Scan the beach below that leads east past the dunes. Typically, waves don't wash completely across the narrow beach, but this is a good time to verify the conditions. Then consider the descent route itself. Just east of this viewpoint is the steep sandy slope where a logging era chute dropped logs to the lake below. Eyeball the Log Slide and see how you feel about it. Note a park service sign that cautions that the base of the route is not pure sand; buried rocks may also be present.

When you are ready descend the Log Slide, step after sliding step. As I dropped down I found myself fascinated with the aquamarine color and changing hues of Lake Superior's water.

Once on the beach, when your "land legs" return, walk east along the shoreline. To your right (south) is the immense slope of the dunes. You'll hear their soundtrack—a pitter-patter of pebbles and small rocks bouncing down to the beach. Several green swaths—vegetated alcoves with gushing springs—also run to the shore. As I walked the beach, an eagle flushed out of one of these lush ravines and a deer retreated into another one. Merganser families cruised along the shoreline.

Five miles east of the Log Slide, the dunes' wall lowers as Sable Creek cuts through and runs to the lake (Mile 11.8). Sable Creek is not large, but it is usually more than a hop to cross. I found a log jam to use as a bridge to the east side. There, at the base of the ravine's slope, turn right (south) on a maintained trail leading to Sable Falls, a multi-tiered drop of about 20 feet (Mile 12.0). From the falls continue hiking south to the Sable Falls trailhead at Mile 12.2.

Options: West of the Log Slide, the Lakeshore Trail leads to two appealing options. One would be to walk about a mile northwest, where the trail curls north along the edge of the wooded bluff, offering striking views to the east. I believe this may well be the optimum view of the Grand Sable Dunes and shoreline, a graceful arc stretching east.

Alternatively, hike northwest to Au Sable Point. The point and its lighthouse are 2 miles from the Log Slide. Lighthouse history and nearby shipwreck remnants are the point's attractions; the Lakeshore Trail that winds its way there has considerable charm.

Miles and Directions

0.0 Sable Falls trailhead.

1.0 CR H-58 (first crossing).

4.1 CR H-58 (second crossing).

6.8 Log Slide.

11.8 Sable Creek mouth.

12.0 Sable Falls.

12.2 Sable Falls trailhead.

43 Miners Falls

Highlights: A notable waterfall and fine maple-beech forest
Location: 7 miles northeast of Munising
Type of hike: Out-and-back
Distance: 1.2 miles
Difficulty: Easy
Fees and permits: None

Best months: May through October
Camping: Pictured Rocks National Lakeshore's (PRNL) Little Beaver Lake Campground, 20 miles east of the trailhead, has 8 campsites.
Map: USGS Indian Town quad
Trail contact: PRNL, (906) 387-3700 or (906) 387-2607, www.nps.gov/piro

Finding the trailhead: From Munising, drive 5.3 miles east on Alger CR H-58. Turn left (north) onto Miners Castle Road, drive 3.6 miles north, and turn right (east) on the road signed for Miners Falls. Drive 0.6 mile east to the Miners Falls Trailhead parking area. GPS: 46.473882, -86.542766

The Hike

Miners Falls, a 50-foot free fall tumbling into a mossy nook, is a big payoff for a short walk. The visual beauty of the falling water is only part of the story here. A shady alcove behind the falls, and potholes carved into the bedrock below, offer a kind of etch-mark history of this place. Access is by way of a smooth constructed trail that winds through a fine maple-beech forest. This is an apt prelude for the show to come.

The 50-foot drop of Miners Falls at dusk.

Miners Falls

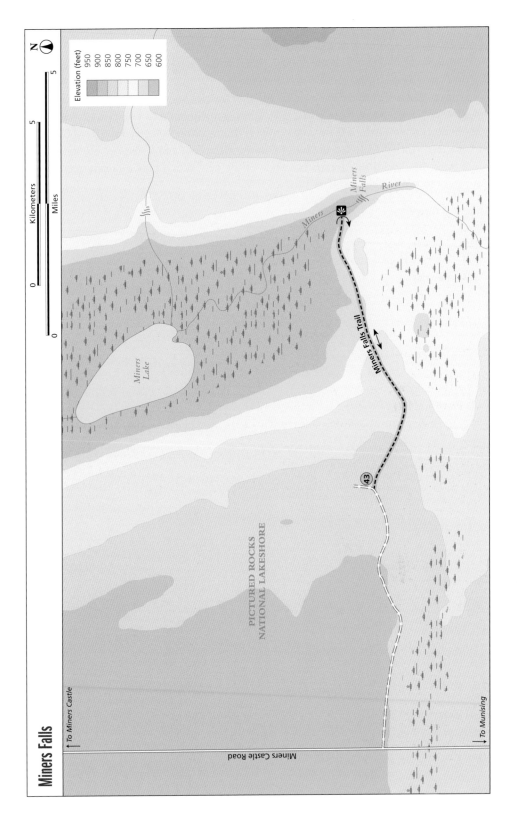

Elevation (feet)
950
900
850
800
750
700
650
600

Kilometers

Miles

N

Miners Lake

PICTURED ROCKS NATIONAL LAKESHORE

Miners Falls Trail

Miners

Miners Falls

River

43

Miners Castle Road

To Miners Castle

To Munising

Begin at the southeast area of the trailhead parking area. The broad Miners Falls Trail heads south and immediately curves around to the east. Hike east, through pleasing open woodland, as the trail slowly descends.

Halfway to the falls the slope eases as the trail travels along an east-west–oriented ridge. Steep slopes fall away on either side, offering a glimpse into treetops, as well as peek-a-boo views north of the forest-swathed Miners River Valley and the deep blue of Lake Superior. At Mile 0.6 the trail reaches a viewpoint and a stairway of eighty-some steps that lead down to another view of the falls. When you are ready, retrace your steps to the trailhead.

Miles and Directions

0.0 Trailhead.

0.6 Miners Falls; turnaround point.

1.2 Trailhead.

44 Twin Waterfalls

Highlights: Two beautiful waterfalls set in memorable sandstone glens
Location: Munising
Type of hike: Out-and-back
Distance: 0.8 mile, in 2 segments
Difficulty: Moderate
Fees and permits: None, but consider a donation to Michigan Nature Association, www.michigannature.org

Best months: May through October
Camping: Bay Furnace, a Forest Service campground 5 miles west of Munising on M-28, has 50 campsites.
Map: USGS Munising quad (inc.)
Trail contact: Michigan Nature Association, (866) 223-2231, www.michigannature.org

Finding the trailhead: From Munising drive 1.3 miles east and north on Alger CR H-58, then turn left (north) on Washington Street, drive 0.1 mile, and park. There are a couple of pullout spots on your right next to a cement utility building just after you turn onto Washington. Do not park on the shoulder of CR H-58. GPS: Segment 1: 46.417149, -86.629677; Segment 2: 46.417588, -86.626279

Special considerations: This hike travels through the Twin Waterfalls Plant Preserve, a property of the Michigan Nature Association. Treat it well. A loose, erosion-prone slope lies between the two trails described. Let your karma add to the future charm of this lovely place, and don't walk on that slope or other fragile spots.

The Hike

I had driven by the wooden steps that lead to Olson Falls for years. When I finally stopped to investigate, I was stunned. Olson Falls is a gem, and falling water is only part of the story; the sandstone cove setting is hauntingly picturesque. Better yet, Olson Falls' attractive twin, Memorial Falls, is nearby.

Begin segment one of your hike by crossing CR H-58 eastward and ascending the wooden stairs. Take a few moments to read the blue Michigan Nature Association signboard, and pay your respects to those who were here before us—those who protected this place.

Continue hiking eastward on the trail, entering a striking hemlock- and fern-lined sandstone canyon. The trail runs along the base of a cliff, then dips to cross the creek on a bridge. Here is a scene that seems transported from southern Utah. An arc of overhanging rock leads to Olson Falls, a sparkling bridal veil that begins in cascading steps and then free-falls 40 feet.

The path, now much narrower and less constructed, swings around to the north side of the canyon, ascending to just below the rock band, and follows it west. As the cliff band ends, the trail climbs the spur ridge's shoulder, drops into the next drainage, and turns west to CR H-58.

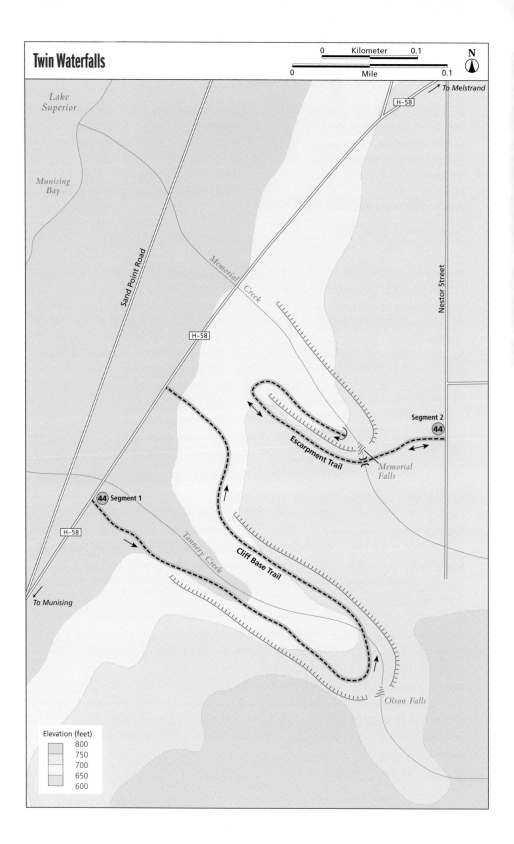

Narrow trail along overhanging sand-stone cliff on the way to Olson Falls

Return to your vehicle and drive 0.3 mile northeast on CR H-58 and turn right (south) on Nestor Street. Drive almost 0.2 mile south and park on the right (west) side of the street. This is the start of segment two.

A sign here reads "to MNA Memorial Falls, Overlook T." From that sign walk west on a graveled footpath. One hundred thirty paces later, the trail is directly above Memorial Falls: not a good spot to stumble. Crossing the creek on a bridge, the path swings southwest along the lip of the gorge and 145 paces later swings sharply east and descends into the canyon. Now the trail runs east to Memorial Falls, along the base of the cliff.

Memorial Falls, a narrower plume but roughly the same height as Olson Falls, plunges off a deeply undercut sandstone shelf. That broad overhang rivals the falls as an attraction; the two together have an effect that is both subtle and powerful. I found myself fascinated with the different perspectives that came from moving just a few feet, as one would in composing a landscape photograph. When you're ready, retrace your steps to Nestor Street to complete the hike.

Miles and Directions

Segment 1

0.0 Cliff Base Trailhead on CR H-58.

0.2 Olson Falls.

0.4 Cliff Base Trail returns to CR H-58; end of first segment of hike.

Segment 2

0.0 Escarpment Trailhead on Nestor Street.

0.2 Memorial Falls; turnaround point for second segment of hike.

0.4 Escarpment Trailhead.

45 Pictured Rocks

Highlights: A spectacular walk along the lip of the Pictured Rocks cliffs, broad Lake Superior views, and a parade of sandstone rock formations
Location: 10 miles northeast of Munising
Type of hike: One-way shuttle
Distance: 13.3 miles
Difficulty: Difficult
Fees and permits: None for day hikes. There is a fee for backcountry camping permits within Pictured Rocks National Lakeshore (PRNL).

Best months: May through October
Camping: Backpack camping is allowed at designated backcountry campsites with a permit from PRNL. Its Little Beaver Lake Campground, 24 miles east of the trailhead, has 8 campsites.
Maps: USGS Indian Town, Wood Island SE, Grand Portal Point, Trappers Lake quads; PRNL trail map
Trail contact: PRNL, (906) 387-3700 or (906) 387-2607, www.nps.gov/piro

Finding the trailhead: From Munising, drive 5.3 miles east on Alger CR H-58, and turn left (north) onto Miners Castle Road. Drive 5.5 miles north and bear right (east) on Miners Beach Road (H-13). Drive east and north 1.0 mile and turn right (east). Drive 0.3 mile east to the trailhead parking. GPS: 46.497854, -86.531868

Special considerations: This hike follows the Lakeshore Trail, part of the North Country Trail (NCT), along the Pictured Rocks shoreline. As a shoreline route it can be glorious in fine weather, but windy and exposed in poor conditions. Sometimes the Lakeshore Trail runs right along the top of the cliffs, other times it is a stone's throw inland. Along the latter stretches, unofficial spur paths often lead to the cliff tops and worthwhile views. Use caution near the edges of the cliffs. The Pictured Rocks cliffs consist of undercut and honeycombed sandstone, and often if you stand close to the cliff edge, you may not be on solid rock. Within PRNL, many trails, with the exception of the Lakeshore Trail, have no official names. Trail junctions, however, tend to be well marked with directional arrows and mileage to landmarks, other trail junctions, and so on.

The Hike

I believe the spectacular route from Miners Beach to Beaver Lake is the best choice for a single day hike at Pictured Rocks. If it's not possible to leave a vehicle at the endpoint, Alger County Transit does provide shuttle service within Pictured Rocks National Park. Visit their website to make an advance reservation for pickup or drop off. Even the briefest glance at what the hike offers reveals compelling reasons to see it for yourself.

For 12 spectacular miles this route traces the rim of the Pictured Rocks escarpment, one of the truly iconic landscapes of the U.P. Mile after mile of sandstone landscape art passes by, a rich collection of arches, sea caves, and overhangs. Spray Falls cascades off the craggy cliff, clear-running streams rush to Lake Superior, and the view down, into the aquamarine water, is not too shabby either.

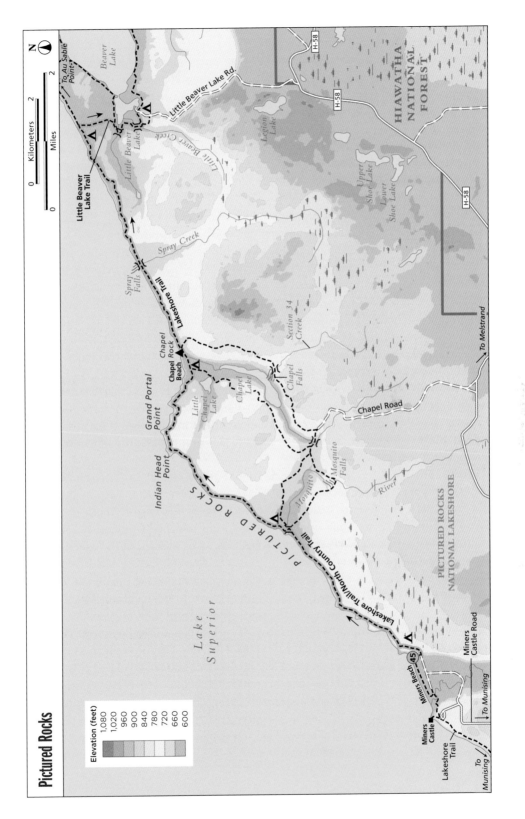

Pictured Rocks

Elevation (feet)
1,080
1,020
960
900
840
780
720
660
600

0   Kilometers   2

0   Miles   2

N

To Au Sable Point

Beaver Lake

Little Beaver Lake Rd.

H-58

HIAWATHA NATIONAL FOREST

Little Beaver Lake Trail

Little Beaver Lake

Little Beaver Creek

Legion Lake

Spray Creek

Spray Falls

Lakeshore Trail

Upper Shoe Lake

Lower Shoe Lake

H-58

Section 34 Creek

Chapel Rock Beach

Grand Portal Point

Chapel Rock

Little Chapel Lake

Chapel Lake

Chapel Falls

Indian Head Point

Chapel Road

To Melstrand

Mosquito Falls

Mosquito River

PICTURED ROCKS

Lakeshore Trail/North Country Trail

PICTURED ROCKS NATIONAL LAKESHORE

Lake Superior

Miners Beach 45

Lakeshore Trail

Miners Castle

Miners Castle Road

To Munising

To Munising

H-58

The thing is, the sum total of walking this wild and craggy coast is considerably more than a mere list of its components. The long views from the points and promontories offer a strong sense of place, a feeling of traveling along a timeless landscape.

Begin your tour at the Miners Beach trailhead, walking east into the woods on the Lakeshore Trail (also a segment of the NCT). Quickly the trail ascends a short, steep pitch, aiming for a break in a sandstone cliff line. Pause as the trail nears a rock band to your left and notice a faint path descending to your left (northwest), along the sandstone wall, and the pleasant sound of water falling. Follow that path along the base of the stone wall 30 yards to a mossy sandstone cove and a small waterfall free-falling 25 feet off an overhang.

Return to the Lakeshore Trail and ascend the short distance to the plateau above and walk north and east, following the trail through a fine maple forest. Short spur trails lead to the cliff tops. About a mile into the hike, an overlook on a point offers a classic sample of the many long views to come. More high views follow before the trail descends steep manufactured steps and skirts beautiful shoreline ledges. Go straight (northeast) at Mile 3.1, continuing on the Lakeshore Trail as a trail leading to Mosquito Falls goes right (southeast). Follow the Lakeshore Trail on the footbridge over the Mosquito River. Then turn left (north) at a junction at Mile 3.2, again following the Lakeshore Trail as another trail goes right (east) to the Chapel trailhead. Hike north on the Lakeshore Trail.

North of Mosquito River's gap in the escarpment, the cliffs and the trail steadily regain their height. Watch for a wooded promontory above a sandstone arch as the Lakeshore Trail winds its way along the coast, arriving at Indian Head Point at Mile 6.2. A sandy ledge there is the perfect veranda for looking back on the long row of cliffs leading southwest.

Indian Head's famous neighbor, Grand Portal Point, a mere 0.3 mile east, marks the escarpment's turn east. Its wooded, plateau-like top offers long views east along the shoreline to Twelvemile Beach and beyond. The best views of Grand Portal Point itself, however, are from another promontory, a half-mile farther east. Large chunks of the roof of Grand Portal Point's namesake arch collapsed in the winter of 1999, and the debris is clearly visible.

Continue hiking east. The shoreline is full of scenic nooks and crannies as the plateau slowly descends to Chapel Beach. Go straight (east) at a junction at Mile 7.7, where a trail goes right (south), passing the west side of Chapel Lake. Then follow the Lakeshore Trail farther east, crossing the Chapel Creek Bridge and arriving at another intersection at Mile 7.9. Go straight (east) on the Lakeshore Trail, as a trail goes right (south) to Chapel Falls. Chapel Rock, a Pictured Rocks landmark, is nearby. Waves of a previous, higher, lake era carved arches and window-like tunnels into the rock. These days Chapel Rock appears fragile, as if its long-term tenure on the coast may be nearing an end.

East of Chapel Rock, the Lakeshore Trail and shoreline cliffs slowly rise, and the path reaches the bridge over Spray Creek at Mile 9.5. You can follow a creek-side path to Spray Falls, but the view is poor and the viewpoint severely undercut. Four hundred paces east of the bridge, a promontory offers a spectacular view of the falls as they cascade off the cliff.

Resume hiking east on the Lakeshore Trail. A half-mile east of Spray Creek, the cliffs crest and begin a gradual descent to the east. You may want to linger on one of the viewpoints, savoring the fortification-like profile of Grand Portal Point before the trail loses elevation. A set of steps drops the trail to a shelf close to lake level. After a brief ascent over and around a shoreline headland, the trail settles down into the sandy soil of the low bluff that lines aptly named Twelvemile Beach. At Mile 11.9 turn right (south) on a cutoff trail that leads to Little Beaver Lake as the Lakeshore Trail goes straight (east). Walk south 0.5 mile to a junction and turn right (west) on the Little Beaver Lake Trail.

Follow the path first west then south on a boardwalk over marshy Arsenault Creek. Next the trail curls east, passing sandstone cliffs and the sea caves of a bygone era. Immediately after Little Beaver Creek's bridge, one last intersection appears. Bear left (east) on the White Pine Trail, as a spur trail goes right (south). Hike east a half-mile to the Little Beaver Lake Campground, the end of the hike.

Miles and Directions

0.0 Miners Beach trailhead.

3.1 Junction with trail to Mosquito Falls.

3.2 Junction with trail to the Chapel trailhead.

6.2 Indian Head.

6.5 Grand Portal Point.

7.7 Junction with trail from Chapel Beach.

7.9 Junction with trail to Chapel Falls.

9.5 Spray Creek.

11.9 Little Beaver Lake Trail junction.

12.4 Junction (north shore of Little Beaver Lake).

12.8 Little Beaver Creek junction.

13.3 Little Beaver Lake Campground trailhead.

46 Rock River Falls

Highlights: A delightful waterfall in a quiet wilderness setting
Location: 5 miles northwest of Chatham
Type of hike: Out-and-back
Distance: 1.8 miles
Difficulty: Moderate*
Fees and permits: None
Best months: May through October

Camping: Backpack camping is allowed along the trail within zero-impact guidelines. The Hiawatha National Forest's Au Train Lake Campground, 11 miles east of the trailhead, has 37 campsites.
Map: USGS Rock River quad (inc.)
Trail contact: Hiawatha National Forest, Munising Ranger District, (906) 387-3700, www.fs.usda.gov/hiawatha

Finding the trailhead: From Chatham drive 3.3 miles north on Rock River Road (H-01). Turn left (west) on FR 2276 (437/Johnson Lake Tower Rd.). Drive 3.6 miles northwest on FR 2276 and turn left (south) on FR 2293 (408). Drive 0.7 mile south on FR 2293 to the trailhead for the Rock River Falls Trail. The trailhead isn't signed, but there is a small parking area, and the trail heading west directly in front of the parking area is easy to spot. GPS: 46.423265, -86.974229

Special considerations: The forest roads here are generally good-condition packed dirt, and should be navigable by most vehicles, but keep in mind that during wet periods, these back roads can be impassable without a sturdy four-wheel drive. Waterproof boots and trekking poles help at a few damp spots near the falls. Rock River Falls is within the Rock River Canyon Wilderness. Treat it well.

The Hike

Having a waterfall to yourself is a mighty fine thing. The setting of Rock River Falls in an obscure wilderness valley adds to the ambience of the experience.

Rock River Falls is enchanting, and the hike to reach it is only a mile. Somewhat overlooked, it is a vivid reminder of the rich rewards awaiting those who explore the U.P.'s hidden nooks and crannies.

Begin your hike by walking west from the trailhead on an old two-track road, gently descending through a pleasing hardwood forest. A wilderness boundary sign marks entry into the Rock River Canyon Wilderness, a 4,640-acre preserve.

Quickly swinging southwest, then south, the two-track runs along the rim of a ravine that branches off the Rock River and then descends south into the shady river valley. Watch for a path branching off to the east when the old road reaches the valley floor (Mile 0.8). Turn left (east) on that path, finesse one challenging wet spot, and follow the trail as it swings around to the south and arrives at the base of Rock River Falls at Mile 0.9.

Rock River Falls, perched on a wide and multitiered ledge, drops some 20 feet into a dark pool, a cove lined with ferny, mossy walls. At moderate flows the left side free-falls, while the center and right side tend to step down, bouncing off a terrace or two during their descent and creating a series of sparkling horsetails.

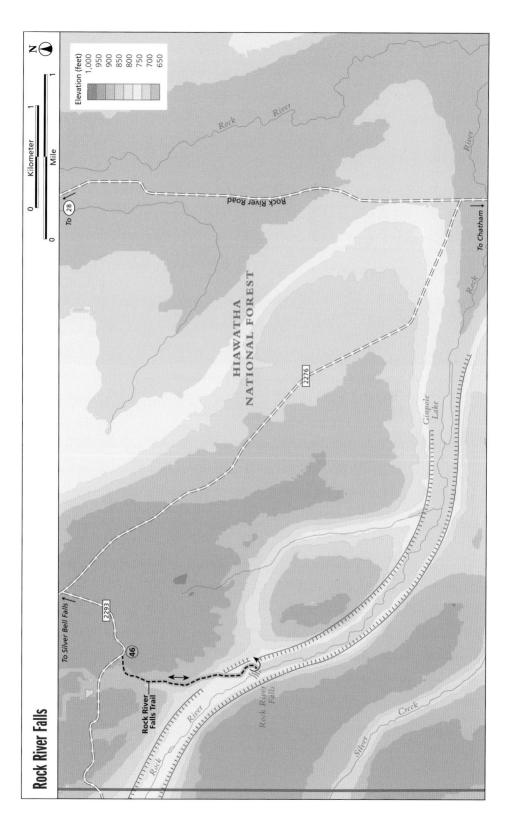

Rock River Falls

Elevation (feet)
1,000
950
900
850
800
750
700
650

0   Kilometer   1
0   Mile   1

N

To 28

Rock River Road

To Chatham

HIAWATHA
NATIONAL FOREST

2276

Ginpole
Lake

Rock River

Rock River

River

Rock River

To Silver Bell Falls

2293

46

Rock River
Falls Trail

Rock River Falls

Silver Creek

Rock River Falls, a hidden gem in the Rock River Canyon Wilderness

Miles and Directions

0.0 Rock River Falls Trailhead (on FR 2293).

0.8 Path leaves two-track.

0.9 Rock River Falls; turnaround point.

1.8 Rock River Falls Trailhead.

Manistique Area Hikes

The hikes in this section range out in three directions from Manistique. To the east, Birch Point and Point Patterson take you either east or west from the Gould City Park along lonely stretches of Lake Michigan shoreline. Likewise, Portage Bay to the west gives hikers another opportunity to explore some unique Great Lakes ecosystems, including a rare dune and swale complex (formed by changing water levels) between Buck Fever Lake and Lake Michigan. To the north of Manistique, Seney National Wildlife Refuge provides an entirely different experience. This preserve is a sprawling complex of lakes and wetlands, ideal habitat for a variety of species. On a short summer visit, even at midday, I spotted coyote, loons, an eagle, sandhill cranes, and a muskrat. On previous evening trips, I have also observed beaver, otter, and white-tailed deer in Seney.

Manistique is a typical Great Lakes port town, built where the Manistique River meets Lake Michigan. There are some lovely historic lighthouses along the shore in this area, and although it doesn't require hiking, Kitch-iti-kipi, a 40-foot deep spring, is a unique and awe-inspiring sight. Visitors can propel themselves to the center of the pond-sized spring on a pontoon-style raft and look straight down through the clear water to watch thousands of gallons of water bubbling up through the sandy bottom. Huge brown trout also frequent the spring. A Michigan DNR Recreation Passport is required for entry to Kitch-iti-kipi (roughly translates as "Big Spring").

For gear and supplies in Manistique, try Top O' Lake Sport Shop. This local business has been around since 1951. If you're heading to Seney National Wildlife Refuge, stop in at Northland Outfitters in Germfask.

Manistique Tourism Council
1119 E. Lakeshore Dr.
Manistique, MI 49854
(906) 341-6656
www.visitmanistique.com

Northland Outfitters
8174 Hwy. M-77
Germfask, MI 49836

Top O' Lake Sport Shop
206 S. Cedar St.
Manistique, MI 49854

47 Birch Point

Highlights: Secluded Lake Michigan shoreline, beaches, dune and swale topography, wildlife, and solitude
Location: 26 miles east of Manistique, 10 miles south of Gould City
Type of hike: Out-and-back
Distance: 5.2 miles
Difficulty: Moderate
Fees and permits: None
Best months: May through October

Camping: Backpack camping is allowed on state forest land, within zero-impact guidelines, with a Michigan Department of Natural Resources (DNR) permit. Gould City Township Park features a rustic camping area 100 yards northwest of the parking area.
Map: USGS Point Patterson quad
Trail contact: Michigan DNR, (906) 477-6048, www.michigan.gov/dnr

Finding the trailhead: From Gould City, drive 9.6 miles south on Gould City Road. Turn left (northeast) into the parking area of Gould City Township Park. GPS: 45.964049, -85.688392
Special considerations: This hike is an off-trail shoreline route. While most of this coast is pleasant hiking, occasional rock gardens and cobble may be challenging. Be aware that shoreline routes are glorious in good conditions but merciless in their exposure to high winds when the weather gets rowdy. Changes in lake water levels may have vast influence on the ease of travel on a shoreline route. In recent years, water levels on Lake Michigan have been increasing, and areas that had deep beaches and dry cobble can be boggy and slippery, making early- and late-season hikes especially unpredictable. Further, evidence of the zebra mussel infestation is particularly apparent in this area, and some beaches are piled with shells rather than sand. The phenomenon is both fascinating and somewhat disturbing.

Remote shorelines are important wildlife habitat. As you are hiking, be sure to give wildlife lots of room, especially during the spring and early summer nesting season.

The Hike

This coast, arguably some of the most remote mainland shoreline on Lake Michigan, has a way of growing on you. A feeling of spaciousness pervades this place—a sense that you could wander these shores for days, and there would always be another wave-washed point and soul-satisfying solitude ahead.

An immense swath of nearly 20 miles of public shoreline brackets Gould City Township Park. Except for a small private section just west of Birch Point, the stretch from Hughes Point in the west to several miles north of the mouth of the Crow River is state forest. Thanks to a strategic move by The Nature Conservancy (TNC) in the 1990s, this chunk of prime habitat, home to wolves and loons, is intact. TNC bought some 10,000 acres near the mouths of the Cataract and Crow Rivers, then transferred title to the state of Michigan. Two locations, near Seiner's Point and the Crow River, have protected status as state natural areas.

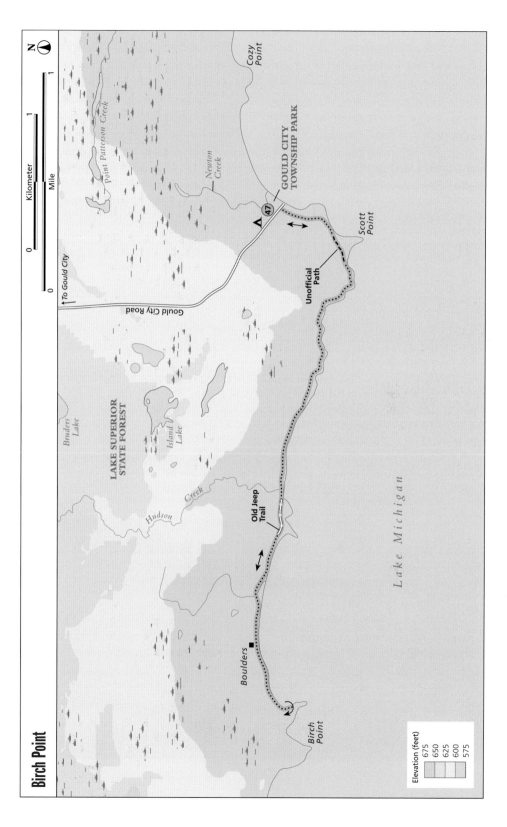

Any visit to these shores will be memorable, but one stretch draws me back time and again. That is the ramble west toward Birch Point from Gould City Township Park, a simple, rustic facility blessed with location. This is a scalloped shoreline, a series of shallow indentations in the coast. Passing the points that separate those bays reminds me of turning the page in a magazine that features both striking landscape photographs and text. Immediately your eye is drawn to the new broad view of the bay (the photograph) and then to the text (the detail noticed as you walk). During my visits to this coast, bald eagles and osprey seemed to fly by on an almost hourly basis. Eagles often flushed from roosts on snags located on the points.

Begin your hike by walking southwest, along the shore, from Gould City Township Park. A quick 0.2 mile later, round a broad point and notice the low sand dunes north of Scott Point at Mile 0.4 ahead. Walk west, scanning for a worn path that ascends into the dunes in a southwesterly direction. Follow that path west and south to the sandy beach west of Scott Point.

Halfway around this bay, a stretch of cobble and rock begins, at about Mile 0.6. Persevere. The footing improves, and what is ahead is well worth the effort.

Continue hiking the shoreline west, swinging around another bay, to another large point at about Mile 1.0. Beyond this point, a long stretch of sand beach stretches

Boulders along the shoreline route to Birch Point

to Hudson Creek, an easy jump. Wide expanses of dolomite bedrock slabs are on the shore here.

Two points punctuate the shoreline a quarter-mile west of Hudson Creek. I would suggest choosing the old jeep track that runs west through the woods, a viable shortcut, rather than rounding them on the shore. Look for the old jeep track at the edge of the woods, west of Hudson Creek.

West of these two points, a 1-mile-long bay begins. The shore is a sandy beach dotted with occasional rocks. At Mile 2.1, about halfway around the bay, these rocks become notable. Several dolomite boulders, the size of Volkswagen Beetles, feature vegetated tops.

Resume hiking west, and the sand beach of the bay ends in the rocky cobble of the eastern lobe of Birch Point. Footing is a tad tedious, but it is a short walk out to the point. From here most of the route you have just hiked is visible to the east. Scan the south-southeast horizon. On a good day you can see the dark smudges of the Beaver Island archipelago, 15 miles off. Retrace your steps to return to the trailhead.

Miles and Directions

0.0 Gould City Township Park.

0.4 Scott Point.

1.5 Hudson Creek.

2.1 Limestone boulders.

2.6 Birch Point (eastern prong); turnaround point.

5.2 Gould City Township Park.

48 Point Patterson/Cataract River

Highlights: Remote Lake Michigan shoreline, beaches, dune and swale topography, wildlife, and solitude
Location: 26 miles east of Manistique, 10 miles south of Gould City
Type of hike: Out-and-back
Distance: 7.2 miles
Difficulty: Moderate
Fees and permits: None
Best months: May through October

Camping: Backpack camping is allowed on state forest land, within zero-impact guidelines, with a Michigan Department of Natural Resources (DNR) permit. Gould City Township Park features a rustic camping area 100 yards northwest of the parking area.
Map: USGS Point Patterson quad
Trail contact: Michigan DNR, (906) 477-6048, www.michigan.gov/dnr

Finding the trailhead: From Gould City, drive 9.6 miles south on Gould City Road. Turn left (northeast) into the parking area of Gould City Township Park. GPS: 45.964049, -85.688392
Special considerations: This hike is an off-trail shoreline route. While most of this coast is pleasant hiking, occasional rock gardens and cobble may be challenging. Be aware that shoreline routes are glorious in good conditions, but they can be merciless in their exposure to high winds when the weather is rowdy. Changes in lake water levels may have a vast influence on the ease of travel on a shoreline route. In recent years, water levels on Lake Michigan have been increasing, and areas that had deep beaches and dry cobble can be boggy and slippery, making early- and late-season hikes especially unpredictable.

Remote shorelines are important wildlife habitat. As you are hiking be sure to give wildlife lots of room, especially during the spring and early summer nesting season.

The Hike

If you like shoreline hikes, and I do, it is pretty hard to go wrong when your outing starts at the rustic parking area known as Gould City Township Park. Walk east or west from there, along the Lake Michigan coast, and peace and quiet are as commonplace as the broad lake vistas, waves, and eagles.

Begin by walking east from the parking area at Gould City Township Park. Hop little Newton Creek, find firm sand near the water's edge, and follow the beach east. Just before Cozy Point (Mile 0.9), the shoreline changes from sand beach to a mixture of sand and rock cobble.

As I approached Cozy Point, a bald eagle flushed. A few moments later, as I rounded a small cove east of the point, a second eagle took wing. Past that sandy cove the beach becomes rocky with a few boulders the size of compact cars accenting the cobble.

Continue hiking east, following the shoreline to Point Patterson Creek (Mile 1.8). I was able to rock hop it, but trekking poles came in handy. Yet another eagle flew around

Point Patterson/Cataract River

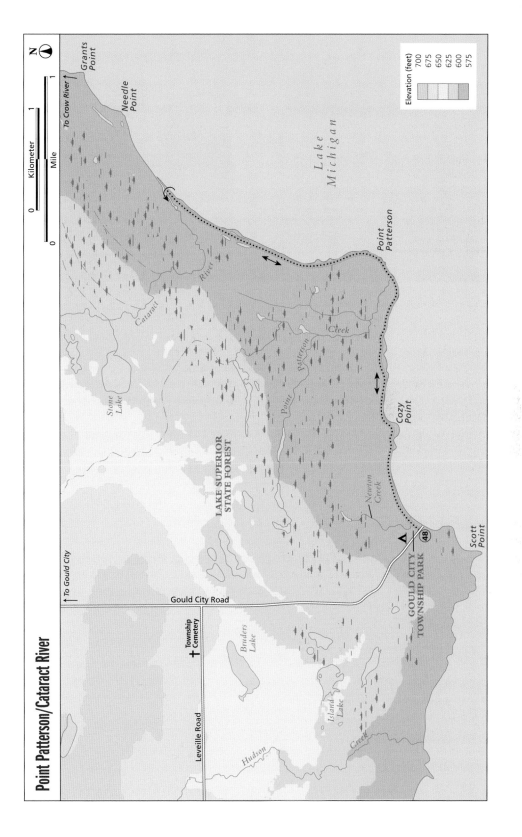

Grants Point

Needle Point

To Crow River

Lake Michigan

Point Patterson

Cataract River

Patterson Creek

Point Patterson

STONE Lake

Stone Lake

LAKE SUPERIOR STATE FOREST

Cozy Point

Newton Creek

Scott Point

GOULD CITY TOWNSHIP PARK

48

To Gould City

Gould City Road

Township Cemetery

Leveille Road

Bruders Lake

Island Lake

Hudson Creek

N

0   1   Kilometer
0   Mile   1

Elevation (feet)
700
675
650
625
600
575

Shore birds resting on scattered boulders the size of small cars

the point; a great blue heron stood sentinel at the creek's mouth. Once past the creek make your way east and north, rounding Point Patterson's broad round perimeter.

North of Point Patterson I found broad flats that were part sand and part puddles and a sprinkling of rock. Travel was pleasant, with occasional route finding required around the larger puddles.

About a mile north of the point, the flats slowly became a classic sand beach; marshy ponds were just inland. Sandhill cranes bugled from the marsh. The Cataract River, not much more than a creek at its sandy mouth, bisects the beach at Mile 3.6, a natural turnaround point for the hike.

Options: You don't have to walk long distances to enjoy this tranquil coast. The 2-mile round-trip hike to the sandy cove east of Cozy Point is a convincing sample.

Energetic hikers may want to consider venturing beyond the Cataract River. Crossing that stream may require a short shin-deep wade or an energetic leap. Beyond, miles of state-owned shoreline stretch to the mouth of the Crow River and beyond. The mouth of the Crow River is 7.3 miles from Gould City Township Park.

Miles and Directions

0.0 Gould City Township Park.

0.9 Cozy Point.

1.8 Point Patterson Creek.

2.0 Point Patterson.

3.6 Mouth of the Cataract River.

7.2 Gould City Township Park.

49 Portage Bay

Highlights: Remote Lake Michigan shoreline and solitude
Location: 5 miles south of Garden
Type of hike: Out-and-back
Distance: 12.2 miles
Difficulty: Difficult
Fees and permits: Michigan DNR Recreation Passport
Best months: May through October

Camping: Backpack camping is allowed on state forest land, within zero-impact guidelines, with a DNR permit. The Portage Bay State Forest Campground at the trailhead has 23 campsites.
Maps: USGS Devil's Corner, Garden, Hiram Point quads
Trail contact: Michigan DNR, (906) 452-6236, www.michigan.gov/dnr

Finding the trailhead: From Garden, drive 5.3 miles south and west on M-183 (LI Road). Turn left (south) and drive 1.2 miles south on "08 Road" (LI Road, gravel). Then turn left (east) on Portage Bay Road (12.75 Lane) and drive 4.6 miles to the Portage Bay boat landing. GPS: 45.723158, -86.534207

Special considerations: This hike is an off-trail shoreline route. While most of this coast is pleasant hiking, occasional rock gardens, cobble, and puddles may be challenging. Be aware that shoreline routes are glorious in good conditions but merciless in their exposure to high winds when the weather is rowdy. Changes in lake water levels may have a vast influence on the ease of travel on a shoreline route.

Remote shorelines are important wildlife habitat. While you are hiking be sure to give wildlife plenty of room, especially during the spring and early summer nesting season.

The Hike

Portage Bay is literally the end of the road—a quiet shoreline at the terminus of a miles-long dusty gravel road. Every time I visit this inlet's state forest campground, one thought comes to mind: This is the way it is supposed to be.

On a fine June evening here, I settled in on the low dunes beyond the beach to watch the evening light. Off to the east the watery horizon had just begun to turn mauve when I realized that I was not alone. A huge snapping turtle was lumbering up the sandy slope in front of me. About 20 feet out she stopped and began a time-less ritual: She scooped out a tunnel-like hole in the sand with a rear leg, laid an egg, pushed the egg into the hole, covered the egg with some sand, and repeated this again and again.

Things only get quieter as you walk the beach north from the campground. Known to few beside locals, 7 miles of state forest land lines the Lake Michigan shore here.

Begin your hike at the boat landing just south of the Portage Bay State Forest Campground. Walk the open beach north to a broad protrusion (Mile 1.3) I call

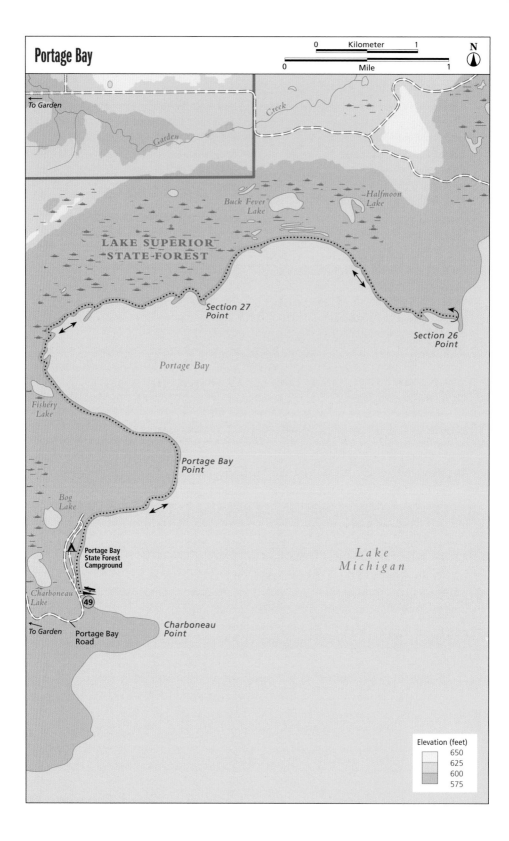

0   Kilometer   1

0   Mile   1

N

To Garden

Creek

Garden

Buck Fever
Lake

Halfmoon
Lake

LAKE SUPERIOR
STATE FOREST

Section 27
Point

Section 26
Point

Portage Bay

Fishery
Lake

Portage Bay
Point

Bog
Lake

Portage Bay
State Forest
Campground

Lake
Michigan

Charboneau
Lake

49

To Garden

Portage Bay
Road

Charboneau
Point

Elevation (feet)

650
625
600
575

Shoreline wildflowers at sunset are attractive to bees and photographers alike.

Portage Bay Point. I found pleasant travel here; the shore is a combination of sand and a sprinkling of rock cobble.

Continue hiking along the Lake Michigan shoreline, following the waterline as it swings west, the beginning of a bay. I found vast damp flats—part firm wet sand, part puddles—as I rounded this inlet to its north side. There the shoreline returned to the familiar mix of dry sand and rock cobble, and I walked eastward to Section 27 Point (Mile 3.8).

East of Section 27 Point, I followed low dunes, just off the beach, eastward toward the hike's turnaround spot, Section 26 Point.

Miles and Directions

0.0 Trailhead.

1.3 Portage Bay Point.

3.8 Section 27 Point.

6.1 Section 26 Point; turnaround point.

12.2 Trailhead.

50 Seney National Wildlife Refuge

Highlights: Wildlife, including trumpeter swans, moose, and many others
Location: 1 mile southwest of Germfask, 40 miles northeast of Manistique
Type of hike: Out-and-back
Distance: 6.0 miles
Difficulty: Easy
Fees and permits: None
Best months: May through October

Camping: Mead Creek State Forest Campground, 5 miles southwest of the trailhead, has 10 campsites.
Maps: USGS Seney, Germfask (inc.) quads; Northern Hardwoods Ski Trails Map (available at Seney National Wildlife Refuge headquarters)
Trail contact: Seney National Wildlife Refuge, (906) 586-9851, www.fws.gov/refuge/seney

Finding the trailhead: From Germfask, drive south 0.5 mile on M-77 and turn right (west) onto Robinson Road. Drive 0.6 mile west on Robinson Road to the trailhead parking for the Northern Hardwoods Ski Trails. GPS: 46.241312, -85.938884

The Hike

This is easy hiking on wide, flat, gravel and dirt paths. Few and far between are the places where you have a good chance of seeing trumpeter swans. Odds are stacked in your favor, though, if you visit Seney National Wildlife Refuge in the open water months of April through November.

Aptly named, trumpeter swans have a deep, sonorous call. Their long, graceful necks, snow-white bodies, 7-foot wingspan, and status as North America's largest native waterfowl add to their aura.

This hike offers long sight lines, framed by white pines, across the quiet flowages known by the names A Pool and B Pool. There, trumpeter swans, sometimes a dozen at a time, were a common sight during my visit. I also saw a coyote retreating through the trees, a muskrat swimming for an embankment den, loons, sandhill cranes, and various other waterfowl. Though the odds of seeing a moose on a day hike are slim, the population here is denser than many other places, and they are spotted on occasion.

Begin your hike at the Northern Hardwoods Ski Trailhead and walk west, past a gate, on a broad gravel road, crossing over marshy Grays Creek on a bridge, to an intersection at Mile 0.8.

Turn right (north) onto a two-track dirt road. This lane follows the top of A Pool's dike, wandering north along that flowage's eastern shore. For this stretch it is also called the Otter Run Ski Trail. Broad views open to the west, over A Pool's watery expanse. I saw and heard both trumpeter swans and sandhill cranes here.

Near A Pool's northeastern corner, the lane swings northwest, the Otter Run Ski Trail signs end, and the White Pine Natural Area begins. Now the lane follows

Seney National Wildlife Refuge

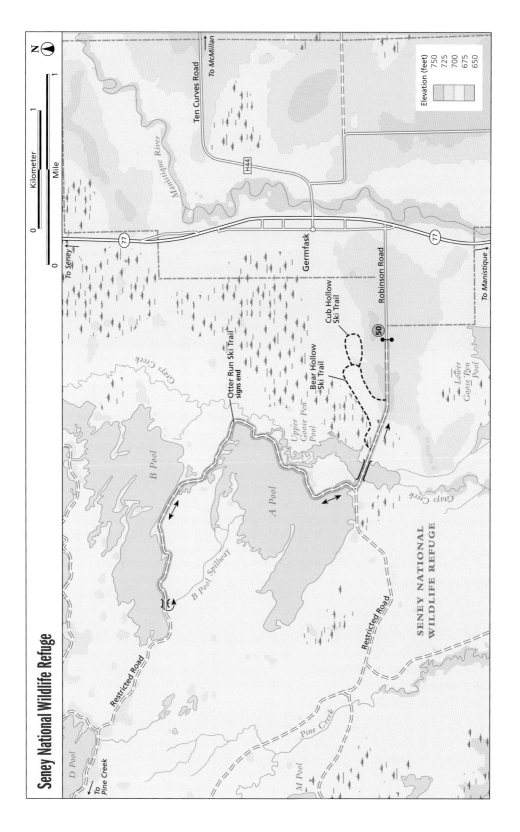

Rare and graceful trumpeter swans, stars of the Seney National Wildlife Refuge wildlife show

low ridges sprinkled with white pines. Harriers patrolled the marshes on either side during my visit. About a half-mile after that decisive turn northwest, B Pool's island-studded waters appear to the right (north).

B Pool sported an abundance of trumpeter swans during my visit, and it seemed that any time spent here was a gift. The open vistas, wildlife, white pines, and abundant peace and quiet lent a special feeling to this place. B Pool's outlet, at the southwest corner of that flowage, is at Mile 3.0 of the hike, a suitable turnaround point. Retrace your steps south and east on the dirt and gravel roads that lead back to the trailhead at Mile 6.0.

Miles and Directions

0.0   Northern Hardwoods Ski Trailhead.

0.8   Junction, begin Otter Run Ski Trail.

1.7   End Otter Run Ski Trail.

3.0   B Pool spillway; turnaround point.

5.2   Junction.

6.0   Northern Hardwoods Ski Trailhead.

Newberry/Paradise Area Hikes

This is an area of the Upper Peninsula that has been celebrated in literature and song for both its beauty and the danger inherent in such a wild place. Newberry and Paradise are both gateway towns to the Tahquamenon Falls area. Newberry, to the southwest, is the larger of the two, with a population of about 1,500. From here, you can explore the Two Hearted River of Ernest Hemingway fame. Although, locals know that it was really the Fox River that Hemingway mostly fished—he just liked the name of the Two Hearted better. A variety of hiking options in Tahquamenon Falls State Park range from viewing the second-largest waterfalls east of the Mississippi to exploring the quieter stretches of river all the way to the river mouth where it reaches Whitefish Bay. There is also a restaurant and microbrewery on site, if you need a break from the backwoods.

From Paradise, a village of only about 471 people, you can drive the winding road along the western shore of Whitefish Bay up to Whitefish Point, a windswept area of driftwood beaches and shipwrecks. It is just 15 miles from here that the famous *Edmund Fitzgerald* rests at the bottom of Lake Superior. There's a fine shipwreck museum at the Point, as well as a light station and the Whitefish Point Bird Observatory. If you pass through in spring, you may be lucky enough to witness the migrations in progress. Flocks of birds gather here before winging off across the narrow strip of Lake Superior to Canada. In a few short hours, I counted over twenty hawks and eagles. On another visit, the trees were weighed down with hundreds of blue jays.

Newberry Area Tourism Council
PO Box 308
Newberry, MI 49868
(906) 293-5562
www.newberrytourism.com

Paradise Area Tourism Council
PO Box 64
Paradise, MI 49768
(906) 492-3927
www.michigansparadise.com

North Store and Follow Me Outfitters
18383 CR 407
Newberry, MI 49868
(906) 658-3450

51 Giant Pines Loop

Highlights: Tahquamenon Falls, virgin forest, and giant white pine trees
Location: 16 miles west of Paradise
Type of hike: Loop, with 2 short stems
Distance: 4.1 miles
Difficulty: Moderate
Fees and permits: Michigan DNR Recreation Passport

Best months: May through October
Camping: Tahquamenon Falls State Park's (TFSP) Lower Falls Campground, 4.5 miles east of the trailhead, has 188 campsites. TFSP does not allow backpack camping along the trail.
Maps: USGS Betsy Lake South (inc.) quad; Tahquamenon Falls State Park trail map
Trail contact: TFSP, (906) 492-3415

Finding the trailhead: From Paradise, drive 15 miles west on M-123 and turn right (west) into the trailhead parking at the Stables Picnic Area. GPS: 46.591309, -85.252452

The Hike

This short loop hike on Tahquamenon Falls State Park's west end offers a compelling sample of the park's attractions. The circuit stops at two vistas to view the Upper Falls, perhaps the preeminent shrine for nature lovers in the eastern U.P. In addition the loop passes a subtle but powerful parade of old-growth forest, an unusual chance to take a journey back in time. To top it all off, the route passes a rare grove of ancient white pine trees.

Begin your hike at the Stables Picnic Area, crossing M-123 and walking southeast on the Giant Pines Trail. Wide as a jeep road, the trail begins a mile-long run south, through a beech-maple forest to the northeast corner of the Upper Falls parking lot (Mile 1.0).

Walk south, following the eastern edge of the parking lot to its southeast corner. There hike south for about 0.3 mile, on the Nature Trail, to an intersection with a broad paved trail that runs along the river canyon's rim. Turn left (south) and walk one hundred paces to an intersection (Mile 1.3), designated Junction A on the map. Turn right (west), descending stairs, as the River Trail goes left (east). Descend a little more than one hundred steps and walk north 200 yards to a viewpoint (Mile 1.4). This location offers a frontal view of the Upper Falls' spectacular, almost 50-foot free fall.

When you are ready return to the top of the stairs (Mile 1.5) and turn left (northwest), following the paved path along the rim of the gorge. Now and then the falls peek through the trees along this stretch. Walk a total of 450 paces from Junction A to Junction B (Mile 1.8), where another set of stairs descends left (southwest), as the Giant Pines Trail goes right (northwest). Walk down those stairs to a viewpoint on a ledge beside the top of the Upper Falls at Mile 1.9. Sight lines here, along the lip of the falls' drop, are spectacular.

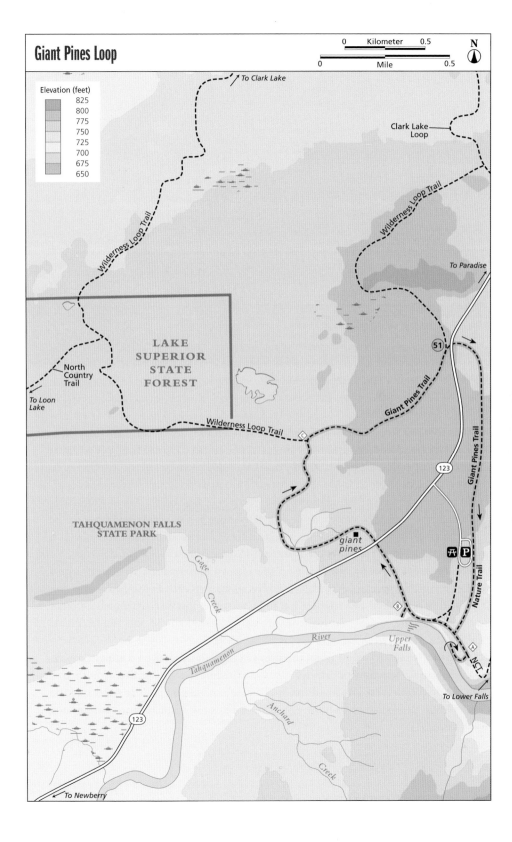

Giant Pines Loop

Elevation (feet)
825
800
775
750
725
700
675
650

To Clark Lake

Clark Lake Loop

Wilderness Loop Trail

To Paradise

Wilderness Loop Trail

LAKE
SUPERIOR
STATE
FOREST

North Country Trail

To Loon Lake

51

Giant Pines Trail

Giant Pines Trail

Wilderness Loop Trail

C

123

TAHQUAMENON FALLS
STATE PARK

Gage Creek

giant pines

Nature Trail

8

4

Upper Falls

To Lower Falls

Tahquamenon River

123

Anchard Creek

To Newberry

Kilometer
0   0.5

Mile
0   0.5

N

Wildflowers along the verge of Tahquamenon Fall

Retrace your steps up to Junction B and turn left (northwest) on the Giant Pines Trail, a broad jeep road that is also a segment of the North Country Trail (NCT). Bear left (north) 0.1 mile later, as the trail becomes a graded service road and continues on to cross M-123 at Mile 2.3.

On the north side of the highway, hike north and west on the Giant Pines Trail, arriving at the namesake trees at Mile 2.5. This grove is a haunting reminder of the vast pine stands of the U.P., now long gone. One elder here is estimated to be 175 years old and is almost 5 feet in diameter and 120 feet high.

Continue hiking west and north on the Giant Pines Trail, arriving at an intersection designated Junction C (Mile 3.3). Go straight (north) as the NCT goes left (west). Hike north and east another 0.8 mile, passing impressive specimens of older beech, white pine, and hemlock before arriving at the trailhead, the Stables Picnic Area, at Mile 4.1.

Option: A side-trip west from Junction C is quietly addictive—a route I would gladly repeat. At Junction C turn left (west), following a footpath that is both part of the park's Wilderness Loop and the NCT. That path begins among hemlocks and then follows sand ridges to an intersection 1.3 miles west, a suitable turnaround spot.

Miles and Directions

0.0 Trailhead.

1.0 Upper Falls parking lot.

1.3 Junction A (top of stairs).

1.4 River viewpoint.

1.5 Junction A.

1.8 Junction B (top of stairs).

1.9 Upper Falls.

2.0 Junction B.

2.3 Giant Pines Trail crosses M-123.

2.5 Giant Pines Grove.

3.3 Junction C (Wilderness Loop Trail).

4.1 Trailhead.

52 Mouth of the Blind Sucker River

Highlights: Lake Superior shoreline and mouth of the Blind Sucker River
Location: 12 miles east of Grand Marais
Type of hike: Out-and-back
Distance: 9.0 miles
Difficulty: Moderate*
Fees and permits: None
Best months: May through October
Camping: Backpack camping is allowed on state forest land along the trail with a permit from the Michigan Department of Natural Resources (DNR). The Lake Superior State Forest Campground, 1 mile west of the trailhead, has 18 campsites.
Maps: USGS Muskallonge Lake West quad (inc.); North Country Trail Map TMI09, Curley Lewis Road to Grand Marais
Trail contact: Michigan DNR, (906) 293-5024, www.michigan.gov/dnr; the North Country Trail Association website, www.northcountrytrail.org

Finding the trailhead: From Grand Marais, drive 5.9 miles east on Alger CR H-58. At that point H-58 becomes Luce CR 407 (also the Grand Marais Truck Trail) as it crosses the county line. Continue driving east on CR 407 for 6.3 miles. At that point CR 407 makes a ninety degree turn south, away from the Lake Superior shoreline it has been paralleling. Park in the pullouts adjacent to this turn. GPS: 46.676694, -85.743814

Special considerations: I found the trail's paint blazes older and less distinct, and the trail itself fainter and brushier, as I neared the mouth of the Blind Sucker River. During a September trip, the Blind Sucker River was a knee-deep, 12-foot-wide wade. High-water episodes could make this ford dangerous. This hike's route is along, or just inland from, the Lake Superior shore. While glorious in good conditions, bad weather or high winds could make this route unpleasant.

Remote shorelines are important wildlife habitat. As you are hiking be sure to give wildlife lots of room, especially during the spring and early summer nesting season.

The Hike

West of the Blind Sucker River, the Lake Superior shoreline forms the gentlest of radiuses, a broad crescent of a bay. Seen from the low bluff above the beach, that coast, ever so slightly curving, is an eye-pleasing line as it stretches to a peninsula some 5 miles off. I happened to be there at the tail end of a hurricane, on a day when the surf was rowdy. The offshore breakers highlighted the symmetry of the long beach.

Shore-side the visuals aren't too shabby either. Winding its way through an open white birch forest, the trail offers peek-a-boo views of the lake from a bluff 20 feet above the beach. Between the forest, the shore, and the lake, it is an eye-pleasing route and one I would gladly repeat.

Walk east from the trailhead on the North Country Trail (NCT), and the ambience begins immediately as the path winds its way along the lip of the low bluff behind the beach. At Mile 1.6 an opening without any screening tree or brush appears on the edge of the bluff, offering broad views of the lake and shore.

Mouth of the Blind Sucker River

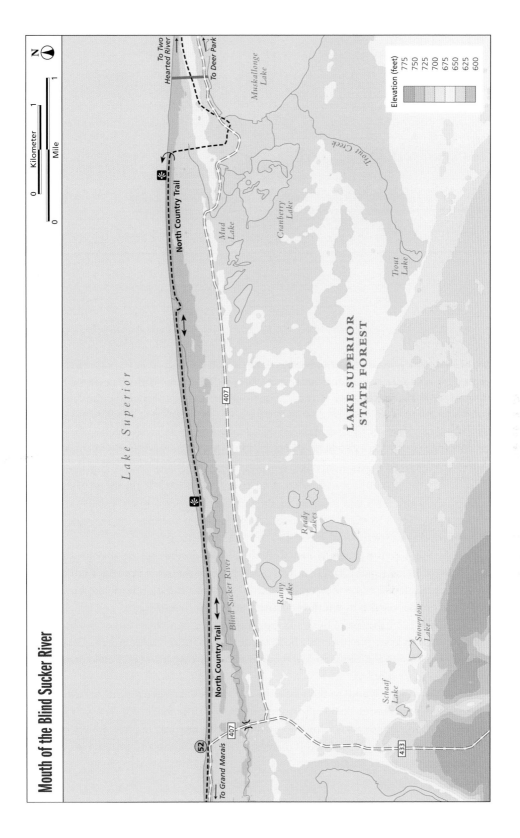

A classic shoreline hike, the North Country Trail follows the Lake Superior shoreline west of the mouth of the Blind Sucker River.

As I walked east from this point, the trail grew fainter and brushier and the markings less distinct. Navigationwise this is hardly a problem. The trail's route here is along a very elongated peninsula, with the lake to the north and the Blind Sucker River to the south. That said, if following the trail becomes problematic, I would suggest dropping down to the beach, a stone's throw north, while marking the spot for your return trip westward.

A little more than a half-mile east of the first viewpoint, the peninsula's plateau-like top narrows to a mere 30 feet in width as a bend of the river swings toward the lake. That topography makes it tempting to think the river mouth is near, but it turns out the peninsula regains its width and there is still a good mile to go.

Eventually I lost the last of the trail's remnants, but by then there was only a short stretch of woods left—the peninsula became a gravel bar at the river mouth. A short wade brought me to the Blind Sucker River's south bank, where a NCT marker post signaled the trail's route.

Ducking into the woods to the south, the trail quickly swings eastward, following an old woods road. About a half-mile east of the crossing, the trail becomes a path just off the beach, running through low wooded dunes. An opening at Mile 4.1 offers a spacious view, and at Mile 4.5 the NCT swings decisively south and inland. This is a good turnaround point for the hike.

Options: Walking to the mouth of the Blind Sucker River only, and skipping the ford and mile of trail east of the river, is an attractive option. It would be a 6.8-mile round-trip hike. One other tactic is appealing: Walk eastward on the trail, returning on the shoreline. The water's edge and the trail are seldom 50 yards apart.

Miles and Directions

0.0 Trailhead on CR 407.

1.6 First viewpoint.

3.4 Mouth of the Blind Sucker River.

4.1 Second viewpoint.

4.5 North Country Trail turns inland; turnaround point.

9.0 Trailhead.

53 Naomikong Point

Highlights: A Lake Superior shoreline ramble, wildlife, and views of the Canadian highlands 40 miles across Whitefish Bay
Location: 20 miles west of Bay Mills
Type of hike: Out-and-back
Distance: 7.0 miles
Difficulty: Moderate
Fees and permits: None
Best months: May through October

Camping: Hiawatha National Forest regulations allow dispersed camping south of the Curley Lewis Highway only, not on the shoreline. The Forest Service Bay View Campground, 11 miles east of the trailhead, has 24 campsites.
Map: USGS McNearney Lake quad
Trail contact: Hiawatha National Forest, (906) 635-5311, www.fs.usda.gov/hiawatha

Finding the trailhead: From Paradise, drive 11 miles south on M-123 and turn left onto Lake Shore Drive (Forest Highway 42). After 6 miles, turn left (north) into the trailhead parking area. GPS: 46.477114, -84.983102

Special considerations: This hike's route is along a shoreline. While shoreline hikes may be glorious in good conditions, bad weather or high winds can make this route unpleasant. Changes in lake water levels may have vast influence on the ease of travel on a shoreline route.

Remote shorelines are important wildlife habitat. As you are hiking be sure to give wildlife lots of room, especially during the spring and early summer nesting season.

The Hike

Time spent along the Lake Superior shore is rarely a loss, and it seems to hold an almost uncanny potential to be a real treat. That was the case the day I hiked the shoreline to Naomikong Point. The lake was in a mirage-like calm—a giant reflecting pool dotted with mergansers. Far off on the horizon, some 40 miles distant, the highlands of the Canadian shore loomed above the flat water. Walking along the shore in these conditions was an optical delight, and it seemed that every step offered a wonderful choice. I could scan the nearby shore, enjoying sandbars, white pines, and herons. Or I could practice the fine art of Lake Superior gazing, trying to pick out far-off landmarks or savoring the sheer pleasure of its vast open space. The texture of the shore made foot travel a pleasure. Three-quarters of it was sand beach; the only obstacle was one or two sandbar-and-puddle route puzzles to decipher. The points featured some rock cobble. In those spots, there was a touch of tedious footwork—a reasonable price for the reward.

Begin your hike by walking north from the trailhead through a narrow strip of trees, to the Lake Superior shoreline, a mere stone's throw north. Extensive shallows stretch offshore here, and rocks and boulders pierce the surface far out into the lake. Hike east along the shore until you near the mouth of Naomikong Creek at Mile 0.7. Walk south through low dunes to the North Country Trail, utilizing its sturdy suspension bridge to cross to the creek's east side.

Naomikong Point

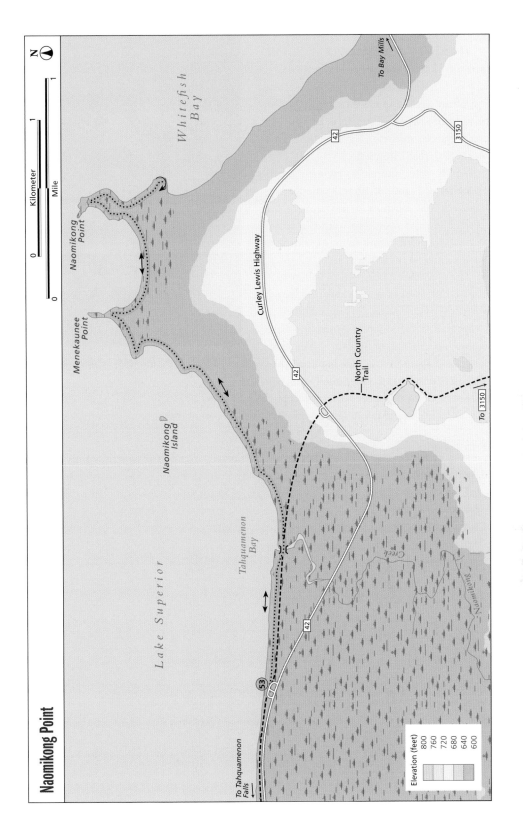

Once on the east side of the creek, turn north to the shore as soon as a dry route is visible. I ended up walking the waterline east of the creek mouth on a long sandbar. Inland from the sandbar a long lagoon-like pond drained into the big lake through a small creek that I hopped.

Slowly the shoreline swings north. Naomikong Island, small and wooded, sits a quarter-mile offshore, a mile east of the creek. Then the lakeshore rounds a broad west-facing point before swinging north to Menekaunee Point (Mile 2.3).

East of Menekaunee Point, a half moon–shaped bay features a pleasant sand beach backed by white pines. An eagle flushed as I approached Naomikong Point, the bay's eastern tip. Naomikong Point offers fresh views, and the Mission Hill highlands line the coast 10 miles east. Continue hiking east and south along the shore to a small inlet a quarter-mile past the point. The inlet is the hike's turnaround spot.

Colorful surprises often hide in the undergrowth.

Miles and Directions

- **0.0** Trailhead.
- **0.7** Naomikong Creek.
- **2.3** Menekaunee Point.
- **3.3** Naomikong Point.
- **3.5** Inlet south of Naomikong Point; turnaround point.
- **7.0** Trailhead.

54 Tahquamenon Falls

Highlights: Famous waterfalls and cascades of the Tahquamenon River, virgin forest, and wildlife
Location: 16 miles west of Paradise
Type of hike: One-way shuttle
Distance: 6.4 miles
Difficulty: Moderate
Fees and permits: Michigan DNR Recreation Passport

Best months: May through October
Camping: Tahquamenon Falls State Park's (TFSP) Lower Falls Campground, 0.2 mile east of the trailhead, has 188 campsites. TFSP does not allow backpack camping along the trail.
Maps: USGS Timberlost (inc.); Betsy Lake South (inc.) quads; TFSP trail map
Trail contact: TFSP, (906) 492-3415

Finding the trailhead: From Paradise, drive 11.1 miles west on M-123 and turn left (south) onto the road to the Lower Falls. Drive 0.7 mile south to the Lower Falls trailhead parking area. GPS: 46.605075, -85.201805

The Hike

Mention Tahquamenon Falls State Park, and most Michigan nature lovers think of the famous waterfalls. The Upper Falls, nearly 50 feet high and 200 feet across, is a well-known icon. Its sibling, the roaring series of drops known as the Lower Falls, is a beauty in its own right.

The Upper Falls may well be Michigan's most famous, but it is not the only superlative in these parts. Between the falls, beside the river, is the largest old-growth hardwood forest remnant in the eastern U.P. This virgin forest features 2,300 acres of sugar maple, American beech, eastern hemlock, and yellow birch. Few and far between are the remaining significant chunks of Michigan's old-growth forest. The last large stands are here, along the Tahquamenon River and in the Porcupine Mountains and Sylvania Wildernesses. Add this all together and you have the makings of an outstanding hike. The route begins at the Lower Falls and threads its way through the ancient forest beside the river for 5 miles to the Upper Falls. Better yet, it continues another half-mile to visit two giant white pine trees, one of them 175 years old and almost 5 feet in diameter.

Begin your tour by walking west on a broad paved trail from the Lower Falls trailhead. Just 125 paces from the parking area, a broad view of the Lower Falls appears. This is a complex and beautiful series of drops bracketing an island in the river. I visited in early May, and an eagle and osprey were squabbling over fishing rights for the falls.

Walk northwest on a boardwalk that bridges a damp stretch of seeps and springs that is rich with marsh marigolds in May. This is the beginning of the route to the Upper Falls. Known as the Tahquamenon River Trail, or simply the River Trail, this

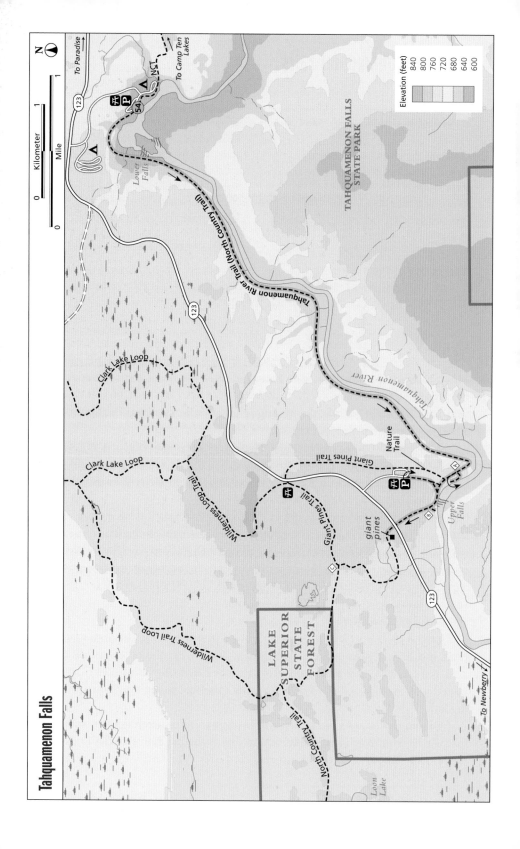

Tahquamenon Falls

The northern branch of Tahquamenon's Lower Falls, though not as immediately impressive as the 50-foot drop of the Upper Falls, is majestic in its own right, surrounded by fall colors.

route is also part of the North Country Trail (NCT). It circles a broad pool and arrives beside the Lower Falls, a spectacular whitewater show, at Mile 0.3. Three thumping, booming drops line the river's north channel here for a descent of about 20 feet.

Continue hiking on the River Trail, now heading south and climbing above the river's rapids. The path stays high for a bit, passing beautiful hemlocks and a cascading brook before descending to a ledge some 10 feet above the river. Below, a steep dropoff leads to the stream. I found a dramatic, almost lyrical sense of place in this stretch of trail, and I couldn't help wondering who else, perhaps centuries before me, paused to soak in the ambience here. The sights and sounds of the rapids, forest, and brook have an aura of agelessness about them.

About a mile after the beginning of the hike, the river current, as well as the slope beside it, mellow. As the valley widens, the River Trail descends to a floodplain and soon arrives at a bench next to the 2-mile marker.

Continue hiking west on the River Trail, passing huge hemlocks before the trail again bends to the rhythm of the river valley terrain, ascends a bluff, and crosses a floodplain. At about Mile 4 of the hike, the trail makes a final ascent onto a headland that holds broad swaths of purple and white spring beauty in May.

Sounds of the Upper Falls drift through the woods as you approach a paved trail junction at Mile 4.5, designated Junction A. The River Trail ends at this junction.

Turn left (west), descending stairs to a viewpoint as the NCT goes straight (north) along the rim of the gorge. Descend around a hundred steps, then walk 200 yards north on a boardwalk. At that point (Mile 4.6), there is a frontal view of the Upper Falls, a near 50-foot free fall, almost 200 feet wide.

Retrace your steps, ascending to Junction A (Mile 4.7), and turn left (north), following the NCT, a broad paved path along the rim of the river gorge. Follow the railing along the rim of the canyon northward, the falls playing peek-a-boo through the trees, for 450 paces to Junction B (Mile 5.0). Turn left (southwest) and descend steps to the falls, as the Giant Pines Trail goes straight (northwest). At the bottom of the steps (Mile 5.1) is an oft-photographed view of the falls, a stunning view along the lip of its drop.

When you are ready retrace your steps, ascending to Junction B (Mile 5.2). Turn left (northwest) onto the Giant Pines Trail, a broad jeep road that is also the NCT. Bear left (north) 0.1 mile later as the trail becomes a graded service road and continues on to cross M-123 at Mile 5.5.

On the north side of the highway, hike north and west on the Giant Pines Trail, arriving at the namesake trees at Mile 5.7, a haunting reminder of the vast pine stands of the U.P., now long gone. A sign states that the largest tree is 120 feet high.

From the Giant Pines Trail, retrace your steps to Junction B (Mile 6.2). From that intersection walk southeast about 100 yards on the wide paved trail and turn left (north) on a broad paved trail that leads to the Upper Falls trailhead (Mile 6.4), the end of the hike.

Miles and Directions

0.0 Lower Falls trailhead.

0.3 Lower Falls.

2.0 Bench.

4.5 Junction A, spur trail.

4.6 End of spur trail.

4.7 Junction A.

5.0 Junction B, spur trail.

5.1 Upper Falls.

5.2 Junction B.

5.5 M-123.

5.7 Giant pines.

5.9 M-123.

6.2 Junction B.

6.4 Upper Falls trailhead.

55 Tahquamenon West/North Country Trail

Highlights: Solitude, remote sand ridges and marsh, giant white pines, and Tahquamenon Falls

Location: 15 miles west of Paradise

Type of hike: One-way shuttle

Distance: 7.3 miles

Difficulty: Difficult*

Fees and permits: None, but consider a donation to The North Country Trail Association, www.northcountrytrail.org

Best months: July through October

Camping: Backpack camping is allowed along the trail on state forest land with a permit from the Michigan Department of Natural Resources (DNR). Pike Lake State Forest Campground, 7 miles west of the trailhead, has 23 campsites.

Maps: USGS Betsy Lake South (inc.) quad; North Country Trail Map TMI09

Trail contact: Michigan DNR, (906) 293-5024, www.michigan.gov/dnr; The North Country Trail Association, (866) 445-3628, www.north countrytrail.org

Finding the trailhead: From the town of Paradise, drive 18.9 miles west on M-123. Then turn right (north) on Luce CR 500 and drive 2.8 miles north to the North Country Trail (NCT) crossing. GPS: 46.601002, -85.334314

Special considerations: Several short boggy stretches can make for a watery adventure when hiking in May or June. Waterproof boots and trekking poles come in handy. Parts of the NCT here have faint or nonexistent wear marks. Trail blazes, though, were adequate, making navigation reasonable but occasionally demanding concentration when searching for the next blaze.

The Hike

Walk a little west and north of Tahquamenon Falls, and the landscape reverts to a pattern that is representative of vast swaths of the eastern U.P. Low sand ridges, arranged in long arcs, overlook flat bogs; the water level in those bogs rises with the snowmelt and falls steadily in summer. That seasonal water level bedeviled me when I first saw this hike in May. Long stretches of the route intrigued me, but a few short wet areas were almost technical. I hopped from squishy clump to clump for 100 feet. I returned in September and found those short boggy segments reasonable. It all boils down to this. This is a neat hike in quiet, remote country. Skilled hikers, who aren't fazed by following faint trails or having to search for the next blaze, should consider it. In the spring and perhaps early summer, count on water levels that may come over the tops of your boots at the boggy spots.

Still interested? Then begin your hike by walking east, following the NCT, on a dirt lane. About a half-mile east of CR 500, the NCT swings north on a lesser two-track and quickly becomes a trail running northeast through a moist bottomland of ferns, moss, and hemlocks. Then the NCT crosses a north-running creek on bundled logs and ascends to a low ridge running eastward.

Hike east on the NCT as it passes impressive old hemlocks on that ridge for about half a mile. When the ridge ends, the trail crosses a short damp stretch and picks up

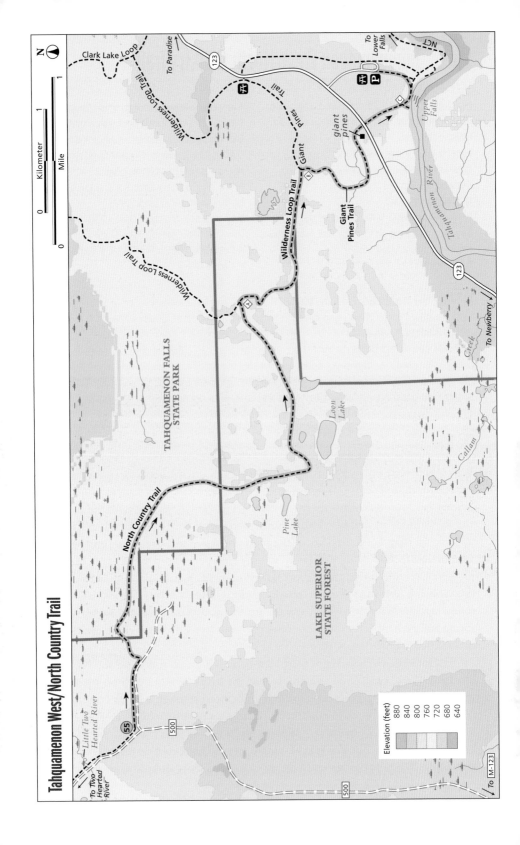

Tahquamenon West/North Country Trail

Clark Lake Loop

To Paradise

123

To Lower Falls

NCT

Wilderness Loop Trail

Giant Pines Trail

Giant Pines Trail

giant pines

Upper Falls

N

Kilometer

Mile

0   1

0   1

Wilderness Loop Trail

Tahquamenon River

Loon Lake

To Newberry

Creek

Callam

TAHQUAMENON FALLS
STATE PARK

North Country Trail

Pine Lake

123

LAKE SUPERIOR
STATE FOREST

Little Two
Hearted River

55

500

To Two
Hearted River

500

To M-123

Elevation (feet)

880
840
800
760
720
680
640

another low ridge. This ridge is drier and sandier than the previous one and features a scattering of lichen-covered meadows. Roughly a mile later two boggy stretches, each about 150 feet long, can be challenging early in the season.

The NCT then swings east, offering a view of Loon Lake south of the trail. Continue hiking east on the NCT. The trail is sometimes faint to nonexistent, with blazes a bit of a hunt at times. About a mile and a half east of Loon Lake, a final boggy stretch tests your mettle. A quarter-mile east of that damp spot, the NCT arrives at an intersection designated Junction A on the map to avoid confusion.

Turn right (south) onto the Wilderness Loop Trail of Tahquamenon Falls State Park (also the NCT). The path runs south, then east. The scenery is reminiscent of earlier segments of the hike—broad views from sandy ridges sprinkled with stately red and white pines—but now the trail shows more signs of use. Next the NCT arrives at another intersection at Mile 5.4, designated Junction B. Turn right (south) on a lane that is the Giant Pines Loop Trail as well as the NCT. This lane runs south, then east, arriving at its namesake trees at Mile 6.2. One of these magnificent specimens is an estimated 175 years old, almost 5 feet in diameter, and 120 feet high.

Continue hiking east on the Giant Pines Loop Trail (also the NCT) to M-123 (Mile 6.4). Cross the highway and walk south on a gravel road, then follow the NCT

A highlight of this hike, the verge of the impressive Upper Tahquamenon Falls

markings onto another woodsy lane that runs south to an intersection designated Junction C (Mile 6.7). Turn right (southwest) and descend steps to a viewpoint (Mile 6.8) that offers a classic view of the Upper Falls of the Tahquamenon River. Sight lines here, along the 50-foot free fall at the lip of the falls, are spectacular.

Retrace your steps to Junction C (Mile 6.9) and turn right (southeast), walking along a broad paved path that follows the rim of the river gorge. Hike about 100 yards southeast and turn left (north) on a broad constructed path. Walk that broad path north to the Upper Falls trailhead, the hike's end (Mile 7.3).

Miles and Directions

0.0 CR 500 trailhead.

0.6 Creek (unnamed, flowing north).

2.2 Loon Lake.

4.1 Junction A.

5.4 Junction B.

6.2 Giant pines.

6.4 M-123.

6.7 Junction C.

6.8 Upper Falls.

6.9 Junction C.

7.3 Upper Falls trailhead.

56 Two Hearted River

Highlights: Lake Superior shoreline and the fabled mouth of the Two Hearted River
Location: 33 miles north of Newberry
Type of hike: Out-and-back
Distance: 5.8 miles
Difficulty: Moderate
Fees and permits: None
Best months: May through October
Camping: Backpack camping is allowed on state forest land along the trail with a permit
from the Michigan Department of Natural Resources (DNR). The Mouth of Two Hearted River State Forest Campground at the trailhead has 39 campsites.
Maps: USGS Betsy Lake NW quad (inc.); North Country Trail Map TMI09, Curley Lewis Road to Grand Marais
Trail contact: Michigan DNR, (906) 293-5024, www.michigan.gov/dnr; The North Country Trail Association website, www.northcountrytrail.org

Finding the trailhead: From Newberry, drive 18.2 miles north and east on M-123 and turn left (north) on Luce CR 500. Drive 6.2 miles north on CR 500 and turn left (west) on Luce CR 414. Drive 4.8 miles west on CR 414 and turn right (north) on Luce CR 423. Drive 4.3 miles north to the trailhead at the mouth of the Two Hearted River. GPS: 46.698535, -85.421728

Special considerations: This hike's route is on, or just inland from, the Lake Superior shore. While glorious in good conditions, bad weather or high winds can make this route unpleasant. Remote shorelines are important wildlife habitat. As you are hiking be sure to give wildlife lots of room, especially during the spring and early summer nesting season. This area sustained significant damage from the 2012 Duck Lake forest fire. While the Superior Shorelines chapter of the North Country Trail Association has been working diligently to keep this section of trail clear, fire damage and rising lake levels are causing more downed trees and erosion, as well as significant growth of groundcover on the trail. Still, the trail is newly marked, open, and navigable, but keep this in mind as you begin your hike in this area.

The Hike

The name Two Hearted River is full of mystery and romance. Ernest Hemingway's short story "Big Two Hearted River" gave the river icon status—a back-of-beyond stream of the north where the trout were large and life was good. There is abundant evidence that Hemingway was fibbing to camouflage his favorite fishing hole, the Fox River; but the mythology took root and grew.

Today the mouth of the Two Hearted River is a remote outpost. Graded dirt roads lead there, but it is a good 15 miles to the pavement in any direction. Due to the 2012 Duck Lake forest fire, the small outpost here was destroyed. However, the State Forest Campground has been reopened, and the owners of the Rainbow Lodge are in the process of rebuilding the chapel, cabins, and the store that has been servicing the Two-Hearted area since the 1960s.

This area was where the Duck Lake fire burned the hottest, and it is obvious. Forest fire, although it can be tragic for us, actually serves an important purpose in

Two Hearted River

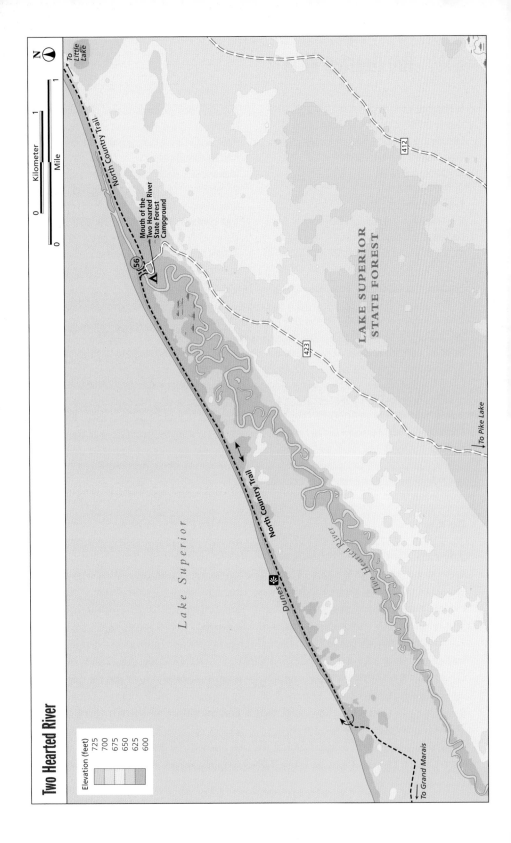

Elevation (feet)
725
700
675
650
625
600

N

To Little Lake

North Country Trail

Mouth of the Two Hearted River State Forest Campground

56

Kilometer

Mile

412

LAKE SUPERIOR STATE FOREST

423

To Pike Lake

Lake Superior

North Country Trail

Dunes

Two Hearted River

To Grand Marais

The North Country Trail hugs the Lake Superior shore west of the Two Hearted River.

forest ecology. Fire allows a new cycle of growth to begin, and the beauty here is in the awe-inspiring ability of both humans and nature to start over from ashes. The landscape is scarred, but the new growth is thick and vibrant, and worth exploring.

The North Country Trail (NCT) runs along the coast on either side of the mouth of the Two Hearted River and bisects the campground. A suspension bridge in the campground carries the trail across the river, leading to a hike along the shoreline to the west.

Begin your hike at the river mouth's parking area and walk west to the nearby suspension bridge, crossing that bouncy span to the river's north bank. There Lake Superior fills the horizon, and the trail makes a sharp left, running west along the top of low dunes. The dunes end quickly, and after a momentary flirtation with the river-bank, the NCT settles into the course that will characterize this hike: a route parallel to and just inland from the beach.

Continue hiking west on the NCT. The trail occasionally ascends a low bluff or dips to touch the beach. At Mile 1.8 the path ascends a series of steep, vegetated dunes before returning to the beach. A short jaunt off-trail at the crest of these wooded dunes brings you to the highest viewpoints of the outing.

After another mile beside the wave-washed shore of Lake Superior, the trail turns inland at the base of a large, forested dune (Mile 2.9). This turn marks the first of several miles where the trail spends more time inland than on the shore. It's a good turnaround point for the hike.

Miles and Directions

0.0 Trailhead, mouth of Two Hearted River.

1.8 Steep dunes.

2.9 Large forested dune; turnaround point.

5.8 Trailhead.

57 Whitefish Point

Highlights: Raptor, owl, waterbird, and song-bird migrations, wind- and water-scoured Lake Superior shoreline
Location: 11 miles north of Paradise
Type of hike: Out-and-back
Distance: 2.4 miles
Difficulty: Easy
Fees and permits: None, but consider a donation to the Whitefish Point Bird Observatory
Best months: April, May, September, October

Camping: Tahquamenon Falls State Park's Lower Falls Campground, 21 miles southwest of the trailhead, has 188 campsites.
Maps: USGS Whitefish Point quad (inc.); Seney National Wildlife Refuge's Whitefish Point map.
Trail contact: Seney National Wildlife Refuge, (906) 586-9851, www.fws.gov/refuge/seney; Whitefish Point Bird Observatory, (906) 492-3596, www.wpbo.org

Finding the trailhead: From the flashing light in Paradise, drive north 11 miles on Whitefish Point Road to the sand pullout for the John Helstrom Addition on the right side of the road, less than a quarter-mile before the main parking area. GPS: 46.767668, -84.960903
Special considerations: If you're here in June, July, or August, large portions of the beach will be closed for piping plover nesting. Please respect closed areas; trails are available to detour around beach sections. Whitefish Point, even more than many other sections of Lake Superior shoreline, often experiences high wind and wave action along the north shore (as evidenced by the piles of driftwood that accumulate here). Keep in mind that weather conditions can adversely affect hiking on shoreline routes.

The Hike

On a trip to the Upper Peninsula, you're likely to see a hawk or an eagle, and maybe even several if you're here for a few days. However, only at Whitefish Point can you hope to see twenty raptors in just an hour or two. Of course, you have to be there at the right time, and that's tricky to calculate. Your best bet is to go from mid-March to mid-May, when there is still ice on the lake and snow on the ground. On one trip, I found myself surrounded by flocks of bluejays. On another, Vs of sandhill cranes flew over one after another. Neither of these were wasted trips, but we expect to see these birds in flocks. On the other hand, to witness a gathering of raptors is so unexpected as to be almost surreal. Add to that the strange atmosphere of shoreline that is almost constantly scoured by wind and waves, and Whitefish Point begins to feel other-worldly. But don't expect to be alone here. The point draws birdwatchers, shipwreck enthusiasts, photographers, and rock hounds, and access to the beach is easy. Still, this is a unique place, and well worth a visit.

Begin your hike from the trailhead in John Helstrom Addition, a tract of land added to the Whitefish Point area in 2012. Head southeast on the trail in a nearly direct line to the beach, just 0.2 mile away. This is a calm section of shoreline on Whitefish Bay, sheltered by the point from the worst of the Lake Superior winds. It

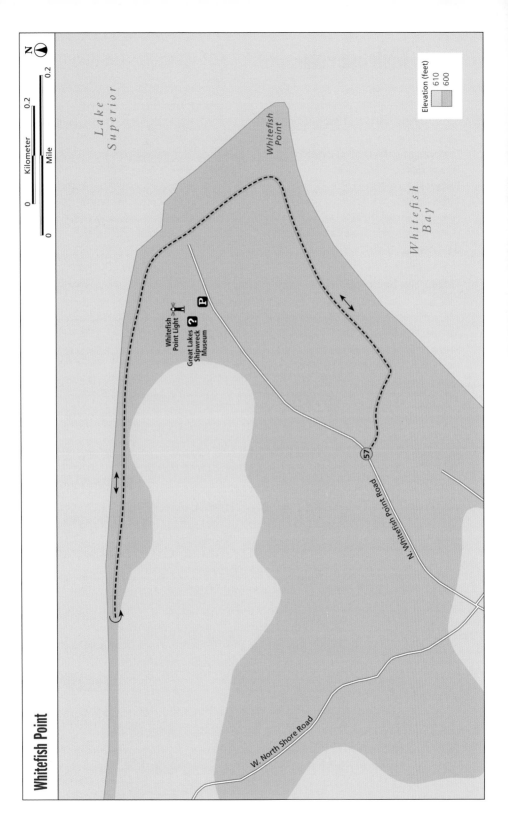

Whitefish Point

Lake Superior

Whitefish Point

Whitefish Bay

Whitefish Point Light
Great Lakes Shipwreck Museum

N. Whitefish Point Road

W. North Shore Road

57

N

Kilometer
0   0.2

Mile
0   0.2

Elevation (feet)
610
600

Freighters are a regular sight here, passing into the sheltered waters of Whitefish Bay on their way to the Locks at Sault Ste. Marie and from there on to the lower Great Lakes.

is along this stretch that piping plover lay their eggs each summer. Pay attention to signs for closed areas. Detouring around nesting sites is easy and can help save these endangered birds.

Walk along the beach to your left (northeast), heading toward the point. The land to the southwest is private property, so be sure to stay within Forest Service areas. At about 0.5 mile, you'll reach the point, and on most days, begin to feel the strong gusts of wind from the northwest. The lake often seems like two different bodies of water—one quiet and peaceful, the other raging with waves. Also on the point is a small shelter, usually brimming with eager photographers armed with binoculars. It's the perfect point from which to view birds as they head out over the lake (or return in fall). Continue around the point, now heading north and west (left). The beach is sand mixed with cobbled rocks, creating a mosaic of color. Scattered along the north beach are the bleached trunks of driftwood that are continually deposited here by currents and waves. Make your way through the driftwood graveyard and past the trails to the Shipwreck Museum Complex at about Mile 0.8. You'll also pass the remains of four wooden docks poking up out of the shoreline. The shore turns due west at Mile 0.9 and you can continue down the beach for about another 0.3 mile before reaching the boundary of State land at Mile 1.2. Turn around here and retrace your steps back to the trailhead. Alternately, take the path to the Shipwreck Museum and light station to learn about the famous *Edmund Fitzgerald* shipwreck, resting just 17 miles from Whitefish Bay. At the southwest corner of the museum complex, a boardwalk leads up into the dunes for a nice viewpoint and another migration lookout point. You can also stop in at the small Whitefish Point Bird Observatory. During migrations, whiteboards display daily bird counts and a small nature center offers more information on migration research.

Miles and Directions

0.0 John Helstrom Addition Trailhead.

0.2 Beach on Whitefish Bay.

0.5 Whitefish Point; Bird Observation Shelter.

0.8 Stairs to Great Lakes Shipwreck Museum Complex.

1.2 Turnaround point; boundary of Michigan DNR land.

2.4 Trailhead.

St. Ignace Area Hikes

C oming over the mighty Mackinac Bridge from Michigan's Lower Peninsula, if you roll down your windows you'll notice, perhaps, a difference in the air here, and you'll begin to realize that you're in a place where the air is tinted with fresh water and earth and trees. St. Ignace is truly a gateway town, as the Mackinac Bridge is the major point of entry into the eastern Upper Peninsula. St. Ignace features a delightful waterfront and downtown area, and is also one of two towns offering ferry service to Mackinaw Island, a historic tourist attraction and home of the opulent Grand Hotel. Hiking around the island is a worthwhile activity, though you'll certainly be sharing space with others.

The three hikes in this area offer classic U.P. charm and beauty, from high rock ridges and inland lakes to secluded stretches of shoreline. This is the only place that the Upper Peninsula meets its third Great Lake, Huron, almost as if dipping in the tip of a finger. Lake Huron is separated from Lake Michigan by the Straits of Mackinac, the narrow neck of water under the Bridge, while water from Lake Superior flows through the locks at Sault Ste. Marie to help fill Huron's basin. From another perspective, the U.P., only 40 miles wide in places, is the only thing keeping these three lakes from being one massive body of water.

Ace Hardware & Sporting Goods
7 State St.
Saint Ignace, MI. 49781
(906) 643-7721

Mackinac Outfitter
7448 Main St.
Mackinac Island, MI 49757
(906) 847-6100

St. Ignace Visitors Bureau
6 Spring St., Ste. 100
Saint Ignace, MI 49781
(906) 643-6950
www.stignace.com

58 Horseshoe Bay

Highlights: A pristine Lake Huron beach and wildlife viewing
Location: 6 miles north of St. Ignace
Type of hike: Out-and-back
Distance: 7.4 miles
Difficulty: Moderate
Fees and permits: None
Best months: May through October

Camping: Backpack camping is allowed along the trail and shore within zero-impact guidelines. Straits State Park, 6 miles south of the trailhead, has 270 campsites.
Maps: USGS Evergreen Shores quad (inc.); USDA Forest Service Horseshoe Bay Hiking Trail
Trail contact: Hiawatha National Forest, (906) 643-7900, www.fs.usda.gov/hiawatha

Finding the trailhead: From St. Ignace, drive 3.8 miles north on I-75. Take exit 348, turning right (east) on business I-75. Drive 0.2 mile southeast and turn left (north) on Mackinac CR H-63 (also known as the Mackinac Trail). Drive north 2.4 miles and turn right (east) into a gravel parking area just past the defunct Foley Creek Campground entrance. Just east of the parking area is the paved campground road that leads north (left) to the official trailhead. GPS: 45.938075, -84.751162

Special considerations: This trail is in the Horseshoe Bay Wilderness, a special place. Treat it well. Also, this outing's route is along a shoreline. While shoreline hikes may be glorious in good conditions, bad weather or high winds can make this route unpleasant. Changes in lake water levels may have a vast influence on the ease of travel. I was initially suspicious of the potential impact of the nearby interstate on this outing's soundtrack. That said, I am describing what I found on two separate visits: onshore, easterly breezes and a hike I would gladly repeat. On both occasions, traffic noise faded a half-mile down the trail and soon disappeared.

Remote shorelines are important wildlife habitat. As you are hiking be sure to give wildlife lots of room, especially during the spring and early summer nesting season.

The Hike

Just around the corner from St. Ignace's hustle and bustle, the Lake Huron shoreline seems like a trip back in time. Eagles roost in white pine trees, otters dot the shore with their splay-footed tracks, and the rattling bark of sandhill cranes carries over the marsh grass inland. Waves gather and rush to the shore, just as they have for thousands of years.

Seven miles of this coast is within the Horseshoe Bay Wilderness, and the southern third is a sandy beach, which makes for a natural hiking route. Better yet, a maintained trail eases the hiker through the only obstacle in sight—a damp cedar area along the way to the coast.

Begin your hike by walking north from the parking area through the defunct Foley Creek Campground. At the far end of the campground, about 0.5 mile north, the trailhead for the Horseshoe Bay Hiking Trail appears as a wide sandy path continuing north. After passing a wilderness boundary sign, the trail winds its way northeast

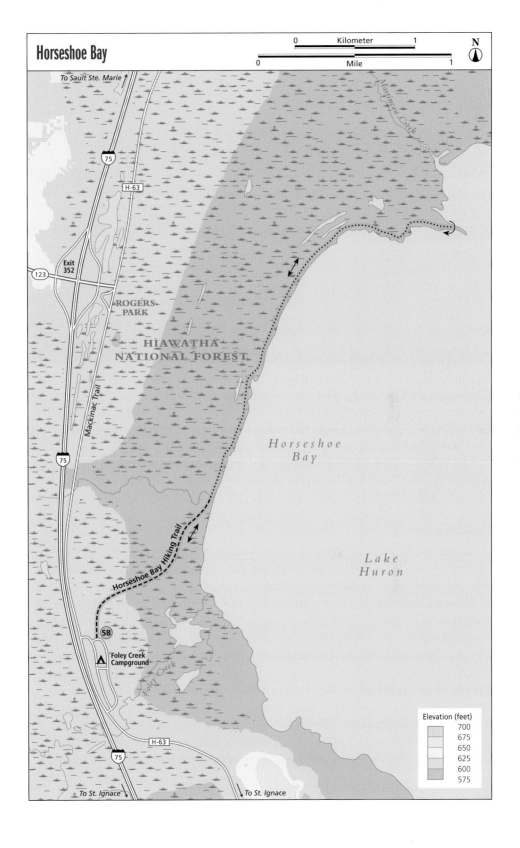

Horseshoe Bay, a timeless beach hike a stone's throw from busy St. Ignace

through the woods to the shore. As the trail nears the beach, the light brightens as the forest canopy thins, and the rhythmic sounds of surf drift inland.

The trail blends into open sandy areas here. This is a good time to take a moment to memorize the setting for the return trip before walking east to the wave-washed Lake Huron shore. There, a broad beach, thirty paces wide, stretches north to a miles-off point—the hike's destination. Behind the beach low vegetated dunes lead to taller, forested dunes.

A small creek bisects the beach and enters Lake Huron just north of the trail's end. I eyeballed it and considered a running jump, but opted for a bridge of driftwood. Alternatively it would be the easiest of wades.

Cross the creek and hike north along the shore. On a topographic map this shore-line appears forbidding: a marshy mess. I found fine hiking on a beach sometimes damp, but a route that works. I noticed a similar phenomenon on many hikes along the Lake Michigan and Lake Huron shores: Lower lake levels create hiking routes, which may not have been viable for a generation. However, keep in mind that lake levels are in a constant state of flux. During high-water spells, hiking here can become less pleasant.

Continue walking north along the shore. A strong onshore breeze blew during my visits, and white swans, just far enough off that I couldn't make out the fine iden-tifying details of their heads, rode the swells beyond the breakers. At the northern end of the crescent-shaped beach, at about Mile 3.0, a broadly braided, shallow creek ran across the beach to the shore. Having waterproof boots, I found a particularly shallow spot and walked through inch-deep water to cross it. Next, I glanced south, puzzled by the sight of a graceful tower on the horizon. It was a few moments before I realized I was looking at the northern tower of the Mackinac Bridge.

Resume hiking along the shore, now turning east to the first of two points, where cedar groves are handy shelter from the wind (Mile 3.4). Continue hiking eastward to a second, more prominent point at Mile 3.7.

Just north of the second point is a secluded bay. It was full of waterfowl on my September visit. Beyond, the shoreline appears intriguing. Martineau Creek empties into the bay, though, and its mouth appears to be a considerable, watery obstacle to further hiking. This second point is the turnaround spot for the hike.

Miles and Directions

0.0 Trailhead at Foley Creek Campground.

1.6 Lake Huron shore (trail ends).

3.4 First point.

3.7 Second point; turnaround point.

7.4 Trailhead.

59 Maple Hill

Highlights: A dolomite reef, quiet woods, trillium, a beaver dam, and a boardwalk through a cedar swamp
Location: 10 miles north of Moran
Type of hike: Out-and-back
Distance: 10.6 miles
Difficulty: Difficult* due to distance; the hiking is moderate
Fees and permits: None
Best months: May through October

Camping: Backpack camping is allowed along the trail, on Hiawatha National Forest land, within zero-impact guidelines. The Hiawatha National Forest's Carp River Campground, 10 miles southeast of the trailhead, has 20 campsites.
Map: USGS Ozark NE quad (inc.)
Trail contact: Hiawatha National Forest, (906) 643-7900, www.fs.usda.gov/hiawatha; The North Country Trail Association website, www .northcountrytrail.org

Finding the trailhead: From St. Ignace, drive about 7 miles north on I-75 to exit 352. From the exit, turn left (west) onto M-123 and drive about 8 miles to Moran. From Moran, drive 0.2 mile north on M-123 and turn right (east) onto Mackinac CR 424 (also known as Charles Moran Road). Drive 0.2 mile and turn left (north) on Mackinac CR 434 (also known as FR 3119 and East Lake Road). Drive 9.6 miles north and park on the wide grassy shoulder where FR 3114 enters from the right (east). GPS: 46.124288, -84.784281
Special considerations: Rare plants and snails inhabit the Maple Hill dolomite reef. Think of them and consider staying off the rocks unless you are a researcher.

The Hike

This stretch of trail is quietly persuasive. An older, open maple forest that is a pleasure to the eye lines the first few miles. The forest leads to a convoluted cliff band rising from a trailside slope, reminiscent of some long ago fortification. A cedar swamp, conveniently crossed on a boardwalk, follows the rock wall. Better yet, a classic Northwoods attraction—an impressive 150-foot-long beaver dam—rounds out the day.

Begin your hike by walking 135 paces south on East Lake Road to the signed NCT crossing. Walk east on the NCT, and Guard Lake appears to your right (east) at Mile 0.2. For the next quarter-mile, the trail rounds that pond's west side before heading north into a beautiful, open maple forest and reaching FR 3114 at Mile 1.1.

Cross FR 3114 and continue hiking north on the NCT. I saw this stretch in May, and the forest floor was a vast, rolling carpet of white trillium blossoms and bright green leaves. From time to time the profusion of ground cover, trillium, and ferns obscured any trace of the trail below. Trail markings on trees were adequate, though, and hardly gave me a moment's pause.

The first hint of the Maple Hill escarpment is a scattering of boulders on the slope rising west of the trail, followed by a garage-size rock by the trail, complete with a shrubby "garden" top. Upslope, rock outcrops morph into a continual cliff band at

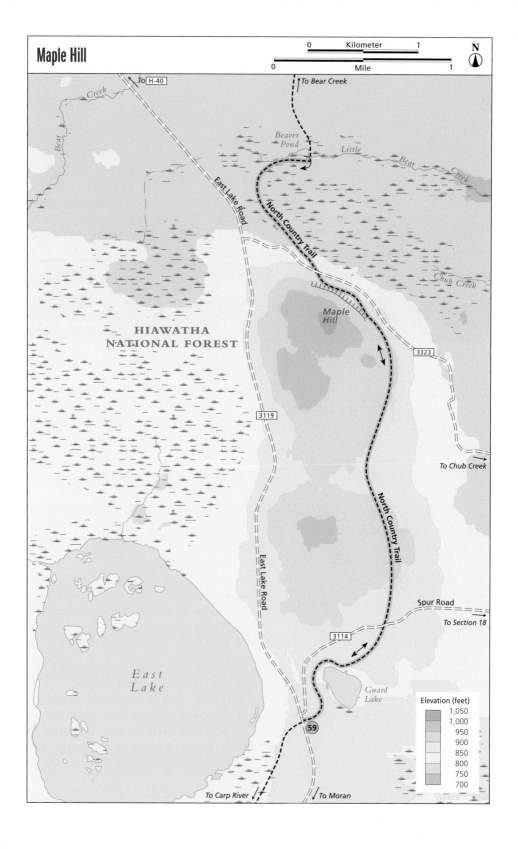

A whitetail doe "hiding" behind a fallen tree

Mile 4.0. Here and there the wall may reach an honest 50 feet in height; much of it is less. Low and long, the outcrop is part of a dolomite reef that arcs from New York's Niagara Falls (the multistate rock formation is called the Niagara Escarpment) to Wisconsin's Door County peninsula.

Leaving the gray cliff, the NCT drops to FR 3323 at Mile 4.3 and runs north. A well-constructed boardwalk segment carries the path through a damp cedar swamp section before the trail swings east to parallel a marshy pond along Little Bear Creek. Continue hiking east on the NCT, and an extensive beaver dam appears. This is a good break spot and the turnaround point for the hike.

Miles and Directions

- **0.0** North Country Trail at East Lake Road.
- **0.2** Guard Lake.
- **1.1** FR 3114.
- **4.0** Maple Hill escarpment.
- **4.3** FR 3323.
- **5.3** Beaver Pond on Little Bear Creek; turnaround point.
- **10.6** North Country Trail at East Lake Road.

60 Marble Head

Highlights: Marble Head, a headland that is arguably the first place in the U.P. to be touched by the rising sun. This viewpoint is on a remote Lake Huron shoreline far from the busy shipping lanes to Drummond Island's west.
Location: Drummond Island
Type of hike: Out-and-back
Distance: 8.6 miles
Difficulty: Difficult
Fees and permits: None

Best months: May through October
Camping: Backpack camping is allowed along the trail on state forest land with a Michigan DNR Recreation Passport. Drummond Township Park, 16 miles west of the trailhead, has 46 campsites.
Maps: USGS Marble Head (inc.); Drummond SE quads
Trail contact: Michigan DNR, (906) 635-5281, www.michigan.gov/dnr

Finding the trailhead: From the Drummond Island ferry terminal, drive east 7.8 miles on M-134 (East Channel Road) to a four-way intersection known as Four Corners. Drive straight (east) on Johnswood Road for 7 miles. At that point turn left (east) onto gravel Kreaton Road(a sign there designates this Sheep Ranch Road). Drive east and north 0.8 mile and turn right (east) at an unmarked four-way intersection. Now on Glen Cove Road, drive east and northeast 5.5 miles to a point where the road surface becomes cobble in a clearing. Pull off here and park. GPS: 45.999624, -83.536064
Special considerations: Driving to Drummond Island requires a short ferry ride. For schedules and fares visit www.drummondislandchamber.com or call (906) 493-5245.

Timing may be the key ingredient to enjoying a Marble Head hike. I visited in early May and camped at the viewpoint. The trail was wet, with major puddle obstacles, but I would gladly repeat the trip. The view is exceptional, and I had the trail and Marble Head to myself. This hike, however, follows a designated off-road vehicle trail that shows signs of abundant use. I don't think I'd care to do this hike on Memorial Day.

Remote shoreline is important wildlife habitat. As you are hiking be sure to give wildlife lots of room, especially during the spring and early summer nesting season.

The Hike

Drummond Island, a 20-mile-long chunk of land at the far eastern end of the U.P., has a remote east end that looks intriguing on a map. Vast swaths of state land, including long miles of Lake Huron shoreline, and a lack of good roads drew my interest. As I studied the maps, Marble Head, a headland on the island's easternmost point, moved onto my short list of must-do trips. It was a blank spot on the map that I had to fill in. When I went there I found a view that was everything I hoped it would be.

I suggest beginning your hike at the clearing where Glen Cove Road turns to cobble. It is possible to drive farther—in fact you can drive all the way to Marble Head—but that driving becomes a technical, high-clearance, four-wheel-drive expedition.

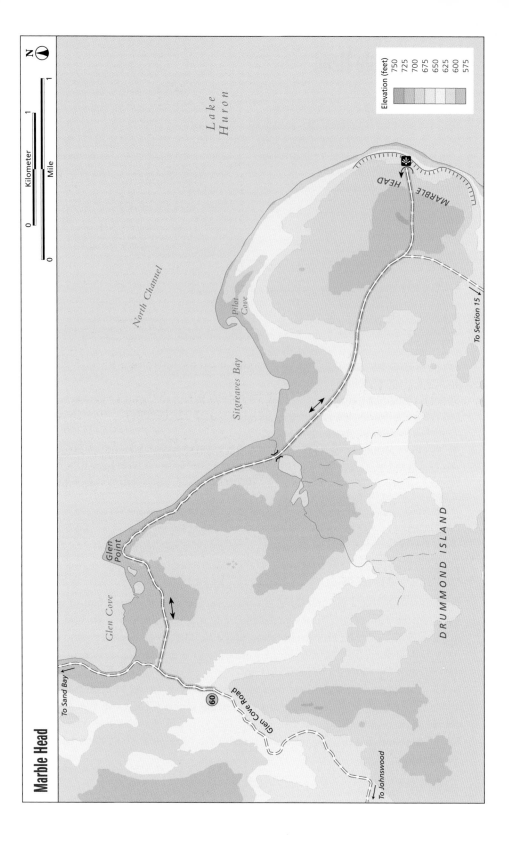

Marble Head

Elevation (feet)

750
725
700
675
650
625
600
575

N

Kilometer
0   1
Mile
0   1

L a k e
H u r o n

North Channel

Pilot
Cove

Sitgreaves Bay

Glen Cove

Glen
Point

MARBLE HEAD

DRUMMOND ISLAND

To Sand Bay

60
Glen Cove Road

To Johnswood

To Section 15

From the edge of the clearing, hike northeast on Glen Cove Road. It descends through woods to a junction at Mile 0.3. Turn right (east) on a woods road as Glen Cove Road goes left (north). Follow the rough woods road, a designated off-road vehicle route, as it runs east to Glen Point and then southeast, paralleling the Lake Huron shoreline. The jeep trail nears the shore, and a path runs 75 feet northeast to meet it. Loons swam offshore here during my hike.

At Mile 2.2 this rough road reaches an open area, crossing a bridge over a creek that runs into nearby Sitgreaves Bay. Loons and mergansers were offshore here, a harrier worked the grassy meadow upstream, and the primeval bark of sandhill cranes echoed across the marsh. Leaving the shore the jeep trail runs east and south, ascending a low plateau—an area that is half open and half scrubby 30-foot-tall aspens. Grouse broke cover ahead of me; several deer spotted me and ambled off, although I could see them for hundreds of yards. Turn left (east) at a junction at Mile 3.7, where a sign points east to viewpoint. Follow the spur jeep trail 0.6 mile east, descending slightly over ledges, to Marble Head at Mile 4.3.

Marble Head is a low headland 100 feet above Lake Huron. While the elevation may not be impressive, the location is. Sweeping views stretch 40 miles and more, taking in much of Lake Huron's North Channel while Canada's Cockburn Island looms large to the southeast. A series of highlands rise on the Canadian mainland, the north shore of the North Channel.

I was fortunate the day I visited, with crystal visibility and a calm lake. Loons dallied in the lake below me, their calls carrying on the evening air. Both sunset and sunrise were memorable.

Marble Head has a sense of place about it—a feeling of perching on the rim of a vast sound, the North Channel. During my May visit, the view was sweeping, pristine, and mesmerizing. Only a far-off glint hinted at a powerboat. There was a feeling of visiting a timeless panorama. I was reluctant to leave.

Miles and Directions

0.0 Trailhead on Glen Cove Road.

0.3 Off-road vehicle track.

2.2 Bridge over creek at Sitgreaves Bay.

3.7 Spur trail to Marble Head.

4.3 Marble Head; turnaround point.

8.6 Trailhead.

Appendix A: Hike Finder

Hike Number	Hike Name	Waterfalls	Quiet Inland Lakes	Great Lakes Shoreline	Rivers and Streams	Memorable Forest	Views from High Places	Moderate Hikes	Loops/Lollipops	Long Day Hikes	Overnight Backpacking	Solitude	Wildlife Viewing
1	Black River Waterfalls	•			•	•							
2	Escarpment						•	•			•		
3	Lake Superior Shoreline			•		•	•			•	•	•	•
4	Lake Superior/Big Carp River Loop	•		•	•	•	•		•	•	•		•
5	Little Carp River Cascades	•		•	•	•		•		•	•		
6	Mirror Lake Loop		•		•	•	•		•	•	•		
7	Norwich Bluff						•				•	•	•
8	Norwich Bluff to Victoria	•				•	•				•	•	•
9	Presque Isle River Waterfalls Loop	•			•	•			•	•			
10	Shining Cloud Falls	•		•	•	•					•	•	
11	Trap Hills Loop					•	•		•	•	•	•	•
12	Trap Hills Traverse	•				•	•			•	•	•	•
13	Union River Cascades Loop	•			•				•	•			
14	Bond Falls	•	•										
15	Clark Lake Loop		•			•			•	•		•	•
16	Deer Island Lake		•			•				•	•	•	•
17	O-Kun-de-Kun Falls	•										•	•
18	Bare Bluff			•			•	•				•	

Hike Number	Hike Name	Waterfalls	Quiet Inland Lakes	Great Lakes Shoreline	Rivers and Streams	Memorable Forest	Views from High Places	Moderate Hikes	Loops/Lollipops	Long Day Hikes	Overnight Backpacking	Solitude	Wildlife Viewing
19	Canyon Falls	•			•			•					
20	Craig Lake		•		•	•		•	•		•	•	•
21	Estivant Pines Loop							•	•				
22	Horseshoe Harbor			•				•					•
23	Isle Royale			•		•			•		•		•
24	Tibbets Falls/ Oren Krumm Shelter	•			•			•			•	•	
25	White Deer Lake		•		•	•		•		•	•	•	•
26	Blueberry Ridge							•	•				
27	Echo Lake		•			•	•	•					•
28	Falls of the Yellow Dog	•			•	•					•	•	
29	Hogback Mountain						•	•					
30	Laughing White-fish Falls	•			•	•		•					
31	Little Garlic River	•			•	•		•				•	
32	Morgan Creek/ Carp River Falls	•											
33	Whitefish Lake Preserve		•			•		•	•			•	•
34	Cedar River Loop				•	•		•	•			•	•
35	Bay de Noc– Grand Island National Recreation Trail				•	•				•		•	
36	Piers Gorge	•			•			•					

Hike Number	Hike Name	Waterfalls	Quiet Inland Lakes	Great Lakes Shoreline	Rivers and Streams	Memorable Forest	Views from High Places	Moderate Hikes	Loops/Lollipops	Long Day Hikes	Overnight Backpacking	Solitude	Wildlife Viewing
37	Au Sable Point/ Log Slide			•			•	•			•		•
38	Beaver Lake Loop		•	•	•	•			•	•	•	•	•
39	Bruno's Run Loop		•		•	•		•	•		•	•	•
40	Chapel Loop	•		•	•	•	•	•	•		•		•
41	Grand Island Loop			•			•		•	•	•		
42	Grand Sable Dunes Loop	•	•	•	•	•	•		•	•	•	•	•
43	Miners Falls	•				•							
44	Twin Waterfalls	•						•					
45	Pictured Rocks	•		•	•	•	•			•	•		•
46	Rock River Falls	•			•	•		•			•	•	
47	Birch Point			•				•			•	•	•
48	Point Patterson/ Cataract River			•	•			•			•	•	•
49	Portage Bay			•						•	•	•	•
50	Seney National Wildlife Refuge		•		•	•		•				•	•
51	Giant Pines Loop	•			•	•		•	•				
52	Mouth of the Blind Sucker River			•	•	•		•			•	•	•
53	Naomikong Point			•	•			•				•	•
54	Tahquamenon Falls	•			•	•		•					•
55	Tahquamenon West/NCT	•	•		•	•				•	•	•	•
56	Two Hearted River			•	•			•			•	•	

Hike Number	Hike Name	Waterfalls	Quiet Inland Lakes	Great Lakes Shoreline	Rivers and Streams	Memorable Forest	Views from High Places	Moderate Hikes	Loops/Lollipops	Long Day Hikes	Overnight Backpacking	Solitude	Wildlife Viewing
57	Whitefish Point			•									•
58	Horseshoe Bay			•				•			•	•	•
59	Maple Hill					•				•	•	•	
60	Marble Head			•			•			•	•		•

Appendix B: Contact Information and Additional Resources

Crystal Falls Field Office
1420 US 2 West
Crystal Falls, MI 49920
(906) 875-6622

Cusino/Shingleton Field Office
M-28 West
PO Box 67
Shingleton, MI 49884
(906) 452-6236

Dickinson County Area Partnership
600 South Stephenson Ave.
Iron Mountain, MI 49801
(906) 774-2002
www.dickinsonchamber.com

Escanaba Field Office
6833 Highway 2, 41, and M-35
Gladstone, MI 49837
(906) 786-2351

Grand Island National Recreation Area
Hiawatha National Forest
Munising Ranger District
400 East Munising Ave.
Munising, MI 49862
(906) 387-3700
www.grandislandmi.com

Gwinn Management Unit
410 West M-35
Gwinn, MI 49841
(906) 346-9201

Hiawatha National Forest
Forest Headquarters
2727 North Lincoln Rd.
Escanaba, MI 49829

(906) 786-4062
www.fs.usda.gov/hiawatha

Isle Royale National Park
800 East Lakeshore Dr.
Houghton, MI 49931-1896
(906) 482-0984

Kenton Ranger District
4810 East M-28
Kenton, MI 49967
(906) 852-3500

Michigan Department of Natural
Resources
www.michigan.gov/dnr
Baraga Operations Service Center
427 US 41 N.
Baraga, MI 49908
(906) 353-6651

Michigan Nature Association
2310 Science Pkwy., Ste. 100
Okemos, MI 48864
(866) 223-2231
www.michigannature.org

Munising Ranger District
400 East Munising Ave.
Munising, MI 49862
(906) 387-3700

The Nature Conservancy
Upper Peninsula Office
101 South Front St., Ste. 105
Marquette, MI 49855
(906) 225-0399
www.nature.org

Naubinway Field Office
W11569 US-2
Naubinway, MI 49762
(906) 477-6048

Newberry Field Office
PO Box 428
5666 State Hwy M-123
Newberry, MI 49868
(906) 293-5024

North Country Trail Association
229 East Main St.
Lowell, MI 49331
(866) HIKENCT (445-3628)
www.northcountrytrail.org

Ontonagon Ranger District
1209 Rockland Rd.
Ontonagon, MI 49953
(906) 884-2085

Ottawa National Forest
Supervisor's Office/Bessemer Ranger
District
E6248 US 2
Ironwood, MI 49938
(906) 932-1330
www.fs.usda.gov/ottawa

Ottawa Visitor Center
US 2 and Highway 45
PO Box 276
Watersmeet, MI 49969
(906) 358-4724

Pictured Rocks National Lakeshore/
Hiawatha National Forest
Interagency Visitor Center
400 East Munising Ave.
Munising, MI 49862-0040

National Park Headquarters: (906)
387-2607
Interagency Visitor Center information:
(906) 387-3700
www.nps.gov/piro

Pictured Rocks National Lakeshore
Grand Sable Visitor Center
E21090 CR H-58
(906) 494-2660

Porcupine Mountains Wilderness State
Park
33303 Headquarters Rd.
Ontonagon, MI 49953
(906) 885-5275
www.mi.gov/porkies

St. Ignace/Sault Ste. Marie Ranger District—St. Ignace Office
W1900 US 2, St. Ignace, MI 49781
(906) 643-7900

Sault Ste. Marie Field Office
PO Box 798
2001 Ashmun
Sault Ste. Marie, MI 49783
(906) 635-5281

Sault Ste. Marie USDA Service Center
2847 Ashmun St.
Sault Ste. Marie, MI 47983
(906) 635-5311

Save the Wild UP
413 N. 3rd St.
Marquette, MI 49855
(906) 228-4444
www.savethewildup.org

Seney National Wildlife Refuge
1674 Refuge Entrance Rd.
Seney, MI 49883
(906) 586-9851
www.fws.gov/refuge/seney

Sierra Club
Michigan Chapter
109 East Grand River Ave.
Lansing, MI 48906-4348
(517) 484-2372
www.michigan.sierraclub.org

Superior Watershed Partnership and Land Trust
2 Peter White Dr., Presque Isle Park
Marquette, MI 49855
(906) 228-6095
www.superiorwatersheds.org

Sylvania Wilderness
Ottawa National Forest
Watersmeet Ranger Station
E23979 US 2 East
Watersmeet, MI 49969
Sylvania Wilderness Entrance: (906) 358-4404

Tahquamenon Falls State Park
41382 West M-123
Paradise, MI 49768
(906) 492-3415
www.michigandnr.com

Trap Hills Conservation Alliance
PO Box 223
Marquette, MI 49855

Upper Peninsula Environmental Coalition (UPEC)
PO Box 673
Houghton, MI 49931
www.upenvironment.org

Van Riper State Park
851 CR Ake,
Michigamme Township, MI 49814
(906) 339-4461

Watersmeet & Iron River Ranger Districts
E23979 US 2 East
Watersmeet, MI 49969
(906) 358-4551

Whitefish Point Bird Observatory
16914 N Whitefish Point Rd.
Paradise, MI 49768
(906) 492-3596

About the Author

Eric Hansen has hiked and backpacked extensively and now divides his time between the mountains and canyons of the West and the woods and waters of the northern Great Lakes. He has climbed most of the high peaks in Montana's Glacier National Park and completed twenty-one treks to the bottom of the Grand Canyon. After 20 years of exploring Michigan's Upper Peninsula, he hiked nearly 900 miles to research this guidebook. Eight hundred miles of hiking went into his earlier guidebook, *Hiking Wisconsin*.

He has written extensively for *Backpacker* magazine. His regional outdoor writing has appeared in *Milwaukee Magazine*, the *Milwaukee Journal-Sentinel*, *Shepherd Express*, *Silent Sports* magazine, and *Wisconsin Trails* magazine.

About the Reviser

Rebecca Pelky has spent half of her life in the Upper Peninsula and the other half being a zookeeper. During her 20 years in the U.P., she's hiked extensively, and though she couldn't say how many miles it's been, hopefully every one of them has added something to this revision. She has degrees in zoology and English, and an MFA in writing. To this book she hopes to contribute the combination of science, research, and creative writing skills that she's acquired over many years.